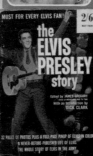

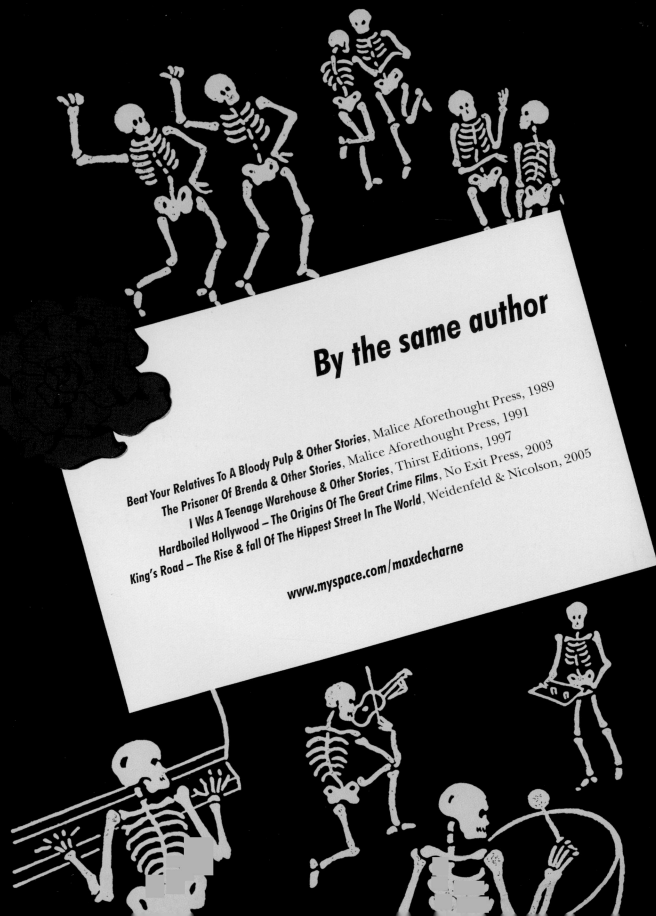

By the same author

Beat Your Relatives To A Bloody Pulp & Other Stories, Malice Aforethought Press, 1989

The Prisoner Of Brenda & Other Stories, Malice Aforethought Press, 1991

I Was A Teenage Warehouse & Other Stories, Thirst Editions, 1997

Hardboiled Hollywood – The Origins Of The Great Crime Films, No Exit Press, 2003

King's Road – The Rise & fall Of The Hippest Street In The World, Weidenfeld & Nicolson, 2005

www.myspace.com/maxdecharne

STRAIGHT FROM THE FRIDGE, DAD

STRAIGHT FROM THE FRIDGE, DAD

A DICTIONARY OF HIPSTER SLANG

MAX DÉCHARNÉ

NO EXIT PRESS

This revised and updated third edition published in 2009
by No Exit Press, P.O.Box 394, Harpenden, Herts, AL5 1XJ

www.noexit.co.uk

Previously published by
No Exit Press in 2000 and 2004

A CIP catalogue record for this book is available from the British Library.

ISBN 978-1-84243-288-4

2 4 6 8 10 9 7 5 3 1

Typeset by Elsa Mathern
Printed and bound in China

Für Katja
direkt aus dem Kühlschrank

ACKNOWLEDGEMENTS

To Ion Mills for saying yes to the book proposal in the first place, and to Claire, Floss and everyone at No Exit. To Derek Duerden, Margaret Duerden, Geoffrey Openshaw, Ann Scanlon and Cathi Unsworth for help and inspiration, and to Ant Hanlon and Stewart Pannaman for all the solid sounds down through the years.

Thanks also to John Whitfield, Claire Munro and Sophie Braham for letting me clutter up their office at a time of no sleep and not enough beer.

A very special thank you to Mark Rubenstein of New York (a prime source of the hep, the gone and the downright wig-tightening) and to Nicole Hofmann, Joe Gardiner, Zoe and Mr. Wax who passed the good word along.

A swingin' 2009 thank you to my agent, Caroline Montgomery at Rupert Crew Ltd, for making the Third Edition of this here tome a reality, and to her and Doreen Montgomery for rolling out the welcome mat in 2007.

Many thanks also to Claire Watts at No Exit Press and Elsa Mathern for their sterling work in preparing the new edition for press.

Most of all, thanks to Katja Klier, for photography, living space, food and encouragement, without whom this book just couldn't have been written.

The 3rd, man...

Well then there now, as Jimmy the D used to mumble, what have we got here? Just when you thought it was safe to go back and listen to Ethel Waters, here comes the third edition.

This here slab o'wax first hit the main stem back in 2000, then in 2004 it got a re-bore, some boss new fins and tailpipes, not to mention a whole heap of extra chrome and a three-tone paint job that'd cool all the studs and gators down on the strip. In short, it was bigger, with more entries, and a side-order of illustrations.

Ok, so what's all the panic about this time? Fur trimmings? Reet pleats? Ol' Dippermouth himself guesting on horn? Well, I ain't sayin' you're right an' I ain't sayin' you're wrong, neither. Let's just rest the weight for a while and we can discuss this.

First off, there's a stack of new entries, from bug spray to goof syrup, from lupara sickness to a juice jolt. If you're drowning under a whole heap of meadow mayonnaise, thinking of nosing a Tommy, lamping some ski jumps, harvesting a crop of lettuce, cattin' around or heading straight down to hell in a low-top car, this edition might just melt the gold fillings in your mouth. Back seat bunnies, zip-gun angels, pucker-paint merchants and wolf-trap blondes – not to mention the strange return of the chinchilla killer diller – all these and more have been added, alongside box workers, main brains, dome docs, bears from the fair, lifelong gong kickers and three-dollar bills. What comes in when they leave the doors open? Why buy a cow when you can get milk through a fence? Is this stuff old enough to vote? How about that mess, and what are you going to do for friends when your brain gives out? The answers to these and many other pressing questions which have tormented philosophers down through the ages can now be found within.

Last time out of the gate, this here book also contained a handful of the pictures I'd been wanting to use, but this time, we've gone right overboard and doubled the size of the pages, while pretty much upping the number of images by a factor of ten. And brother, what pictures... Daddy-O, to employ the wise words of the late Erskine Caldwell, they're the kind that really make you want to get down on the floor and start to lickin' somethin'. Gasp in astonishment at the frankly asymmetrical moustache of pulp author McCall Horgan, the jiving skeletons adorning the dust jacket of Jonathan Latimer's masterly *Red Gardenias*, or the ton-up boys on the cover of *Gently Go Man*, a novel which prompted none other than the Sunday Telegraph to declare 'You'll make with this book like crazy'. How right they were. See burleycue sensation Gypsy Rose Lee pretending to write her novel *The G-String Murders*, "Beatnik favourite Louis 'Satchmo' Armstrong playing his famed trumpet in a 'beatnik' hangout", Gene Krupa worn out after a strenuous bout of drumistics, what the well-dressed female sax player was wearing in 1911, and documentary evidence that young people were driven wild by the thought of a Shag back in 1937.

I'm scoring straight for you – this one'll knock you bow-legged.

Fetch me my liquid ham and eggs,

MAX DÉCHARNÉ
London, 2009

INTRODUCTION
to the All-New, Drape-Shape, Low-Slung, Solid-Sent, Stripped-Down, Hopped-Up & Swingin' Like a Gate Edition

So anyway, there I was at home getting into executive session with a bottle of redeye and a stack of Frankie "Half-Pint" Jaxon's most righteous contributions to the art of wax when the good people from No Exit called up asking for a new expanded edition of this here hipster dictionary. Why not, I thought? After all, it's the fortieth anniversary of *She Said* by Hasil Adkins, the fiftieth anniversary of *One Bad Stud* by the Honey Bears, the sixtieth anniversary of *We The Cats Shall Hep Ya* by Cab Calloway, the seventieth anniversary of *She Done Sold It Out* by the Memphis Jug Band and the eightieth anniversary of *Anybody Here Want To Try My Cabbage* by Maggie Jones — hell, I'd imagine the whole country feels like celebratin' a little. Who knows, maybe this will be the year that the Post Office will finally get around to issuing a set of Kip Tyler & The Flips commemorative stamps.

What you've got here in your biscuit-snatchers is everything that was in the last edition, plus a whole load more entries drawn from similar sources, just in case you've run out of fresh things to say to people during the intervening four years. On top of all that there's a selection of pictures, so you can check out the wig formations of solid cats like Babs Gonzales and Lavada Durst, and cop a squint at Harry 'The Hipster' Gibson climbing sideways up the north face of a piano back in 1947. It may also help to convince a few doubting souls who weren't sure that books such as the immortal *Two Timing Tart* by John Davidson actually exist. Here's a chance to gaze in awe at the cover artwork of the original paperback and give thanks for the existence of such treasures in our godless age.

The purpose of this dictionary, as I attempted to explain last time, is to give solid examples of hep as it was spoken during roughly the first sixty-five years of the 20th century, quoting where possible from the Joes in the know, or the scribblers and dribblers who were setting it down or making it up. By listing the titles of jazz or blues songs which might have been using words like 'funky' or 'jelly roll' back in the twenties, the aim is to show that these were terms which were certainly in circulation among a section of the community by that time. Frequently, half the fun of this was that the straight world hadn't a clue what the songs were about, and so an outfit like Harlan Lattimore & His Connie's Inn Orchestra could get on the radio in 1932 with a double-sided disc called *Reefer Man / Chant Of The Weed*, safe in the knowledge that the hip fraternity would dig it and those of a cubistic persuasion would be completely oblivious. If that sounds pretty far-fetched in these more enlightened times, don't forget that as recently as 1972, even though BBC Radio One would regularly ban other records on the grounds of obscenity, they happily played Lou Reed's *A Walk On The Wild Side* to death, because no-one in the relevant department had a clue what the phrase 'giving head' meant. As far as salacious subject-matter goes, amateur music historians whose record collections start in 1962 often claim that the Beatles were really pushing the boundaries with their line about a girl being a 'big teaser' in the song *Day Tripper*, assuming that all popular songs from previous decades were 100% 'moon-June' sappy sentimentality. However, a cursory listen to items like Jimmie Logsdon's *I Got A Rocket In My Pocket* (1958) or Margaret Carter's *I Want Plenty Grease In My Frying Pan* (1926) would seem to suggest that this view is mistaken, Jack.

If you're looking for the origins of many of these words and phrases, you'd frequently wind up back in the sleazy back-alleys of London two hundred years ago, in the area around Covent Garden, which is now an upmarket joint for fleecing the tourists, but in those days was so riddled with gin-joints and whorehouses that one of the slang names for a streetwalker was a Covent Garden Nun. Check back to the Daddy-O of slang dictionaries – Captain Francis Grose's *Dictionary of the Vulgar Tongue* (1785) – and you can find numerous words and phrases then current among London's criminal fraternity with which 20th century US mobsters were familiar. For instance, Grose defines 'Fly' as: 'Knowing. Aquainted with another's meaning or proceeding. The rattling cove is fly; the coachman knows what we are about.' As for gangster's molls, a moll in those days was defined simply as a 'whore'. Similarly, a 'square' was always a square: 'honest, not roguish. A square cove, ie: a man who does not steal.' Oh yeah, and one of the slang names for a policeman back in 18th century London was a 'pig'. How times change. Call someone a punk, even in Shakespeare's day, and you'd be insulting them.

With a lot of the words and phrases in this book, we could play a game of chasing their origins most of the way back to the Norman Conquest, and you could all check in at the orthopaedic ward of your local germsville after having fractured your spine attempting to carry home the 3,000-page volume this here item would have turned into. Then, if times were hard, maybe you could hollow the thing out, live inside it and raise a family. To recap, the examples given - of songs, books and films which use the phrases concerned – are there to pinpoint the fact that these words were in some sort of usage at the time stated, and also to maybe hip you to some fine stuff along the way. Your life may or may not be enhanced by the knowledge that an outfit by the name of Doctor Sausage & His Five Pork Chops were treading the boards back in the 1940s, but they may just realign your wig if you give them the chance.

It's also worth remembering that there aren't necessarily any perfect explanations as to how all of these phrases came into being. Take the word 'hip' for example. The most commonly-accepted theory is that it comes from the language of 19th century opium dens. You'd lay there stoned out of your gourd for days on end, propped up on one hip, smoking away at your pipe, until after enough years of this healthy lifestyle your hip-joint would start to decay, and your fellow enthusiasts could tell you a mile off from the messed-up way you walked. 'He's on the hip, he's a hip guy.' ie: he smokes the stuff, he's one of us. Sounds reasonable, but there are also other conflicting explanations. Mostly, I've tried to steer clear of speculation, and just nail the words down to what they were supposed to mean in various contexts. Of course, it was all mostly a game, designed to exclude the squares, and the meanings could change by the week. The hip people knew what they meant by 'hip', and if you didn't dig it, Dad, how unhip was that?

So here's a revised and illustrated attempt at setting down some of the things you might have heard out of the mouths of wise guys, hoods, dime-a-dance frails, short-con artists, B-girls, snowbirds, hack-jockeys, finger men, hot-rodders, jazz babies, ivory-whippers, flat-top cats, grifters and two-bit porch-climbers. If you're thinking of taking up any of these professions yourself, or even if you've just been wondering what Tom Waits has been going on about all these years with his talk of 'walking Spanish down the hall' or going 'up north for a nickel's worth', this might just be the E-Flat Dillinger you've been waiting for.

Stay cool, hang loose, admit nothing,

MAX DÉCHARNÉ
Berlin, April 2004

Introduction to the First Edition

"Where in English we are concerned with communicating *exactly* what we want to convey and nothing else, the hipster is satisfied if what he says manages to *include* what he means. Imagine the difference between shooting at a dime from twenty paces with a .22 rifle, and with a 40-gauge shotgun, and you will have a rough approximation of the difference between English and Hip."

FROM THE ALBUM *HOW TO SPEAK HIP*, DEL CLOSE AND JOHN BRENT, 1959

Back in the old days before the dawn of colour TV, genuine hep-cats like Cab Calloway and Lavada Durst published dictionaries of hipster slang that took a narrower definition than the present volume and, not surprisingly, wound up with booklets that ran for about twelve pages, although the prize in this department must go to Babs Gonzales, whose *Boptionary* contains a whole fifty-three phrases spread out over two small, but immaculately cool pages.

What you have here is something more inclusive, drawing on phrases and words from pulp novels, classic noir and exploitation films, blues, country and rock'n'roll lyrics and other related sources. Millions of people down through the years have happily read Raymond Chandler's novels without necessarily knowing what a roscoe might be, and generations of Louis Armstrong fans have enjoyed listening to *Struttin' With Some Barbecue*, only occasionally wondering why the great man felt the need to walk around apparently clutching an item of alfresco cooking equipment. If you attempt to use more than a few of these phrases in normal conversation, you'll most likely be shunned by ordinary, decent people or taken away for special tests at a secure establishment in the country somewhere. Nevertheless, even though many of the words in this dictionary may be the product of sick-minded individuals inventing hip phrases to fill out the dialogue in numerous low-budget teen films and crime stories, they have a life of their own and most of them refuse to lie down and play dead.

Half the people trying to write the 'Great American Novel' fifty years ago seemed to think that the best way to do that was to employ an over-educated style which would have made Marcel Proust look like someone with a limited vocabulary, whereas no-nonsense pulp products like *Hot Dames On Cold Slabs* by Michael Storme or *Two Timing Tart* by John Davidson had an entirely different audience in mind. Although the works of great writers like Chandler and Hammett are rich in authentic slang, it's also true that some of the tackiest or most obscure pulp hacks provide the best and most individual examples of hip as it should be spoken. The blues and rockabilly performers of the 1950s were often making records for small labels with only a very limited, local audience, so they could get away with using phrases which might mean something to a farming community in Texas but be completely incomprehensible in New York, such as Hank Stanford's version of *She's A Hum Dum Dinger* (*From Dingersville*) which contains the immortal line "She's long, she's tall, she's a handsome queen / She's got ways like a mowing machine".

Many of the books and much of the music quoted here which are now hailed as classics were sneered at or marginalised as throwaway entertainment for the lower orders, and were often produced by people who didn't know if their career was going to last out the week. The general law that seems to have applied in such cases appears to be that if you worked for peanuts, starved most of the time and died in almost total obscurity, you are then free to be hailed as a genius. When the great Jim Thompson died in 1977 none of his books were in print in the USA. Nelson Algren, Chicago's finest, was in a pretty much similar position a few years later at the time of his own death, and, by pulp standards, they were two of the howling great success stories. Hell, even Hollywood came calling on relatively regular intervals. Both writers have now been the subject of extensive reissue programmes, but, on balance, they probably don't care much one way or the other these days.

In general, the language contained here originated either with jazz musicians or gangsters in the early part of the 20th century. There's an enormous amount of crossover between these basic reference points, which isn't surprising, since musicians frequently played in venues run by mobsters, and the tough guys with the machine guns were often fans of the music. The well-known tale of Frank Sinatra arriving in Cuba to visit Lucky Luciano and the heads of all the US mafia families, allegedly carrying a suitcase containing a million green pictures of George Washington, is just one example. Both of these two sections of the community enjoyed going to the movies, so once Hollywood started putting out crime films featuring people like Cagney and Bogart, the language was passed around even more, with many real-life hoods trying to dress and behave like George Raft.

It probably won't escape the notice of the more attentive reader that many of these slang phrases concern drink, drugs, sex and violent crime. Jazz music emerged from the Storyville district of New Orleans, a red light area so wide open that the government sent in the troops in 1917 to close the whole place down, and a life spent hanging around in whorehouses and bargain-basement gambling joints is hardly likely to produce a group of people given to speaking like characters from a Jane Austen novel. Attitudes to women, in particular, sometimes make the average caveman look like a bleeding-heart liberal, but, on the other hand, some of the female characters who show up in film noir and hardboiled crime fiction are as sharp as a razor and nobody's fool. Veronica Lake, Gene Tierney, Lauren Bacall and any number of Jim Thompson characters could talk back with the best of them and eat most men for breakfast. Sure, attitudes have changed a lot since those days, but that's true across all sections of society and popular culture – the casual racism of children's comics back in the 1940s is breathtaking to modern sensibilities.

The overall tone of hipster slang is a kind of deadpan cynicism – not entirely unexpected from a section of society that often spent much of its time trying to avoid the law and scrape the rent money together. The dark tone and worldview of film noir is all the more understandable when one considers that a great many of the people responsible for the genre had escaped from Europe one step ahead of Uncle Adolf and his playmates. Flouting some aspects of the law didn't seem particularly strange back in the twenties, once the stern moralists with the big sticks had succeeded in having booze outlawed – a particularly smart move which drove nearly the whole adult population into some sort of contact with organised crime in their search for dishonest refreshment.

The earliest examples of slang given here are from around the turn of the last century, and the most recent are taken from the middle years of the 1960s, which was roughly the time when the people who thought they were cool stopped wearing suits, gave up holding onto each other when dancing, and both sexes started a competition to see who could have the longest hair. All cut-off points are pretty arbitrary, but as a handy frame of reference, you could say that Sinatra's Rat Pack in Las Vegas in the early sixties represents the end of the hipster era as defined by this book. By 1968, four lovable moptops from Liverpool had decided that what rock'n'roll really, really needed was a serious injection of brass band music and string quartets, and a hippie fan of theirs named Charles Manson out in California was turning on his family to the White Album: 'Are you hep to what the Beatles are saying? Helter Skelter is coming down. The Beatles are telling it like it is.' Cab Calloway would have understood the use of the word 'hep' in that last sentence, but he sure wouldn't have been likely to have gone up to any stray flower children on the street in Haight-Ashbury and asked them for the address of their tailor.

For the most part, though, it really doesn't matter very much whether you think *Ocean's Eleven* is the name of a football team, or that The Grifters were the vocal group who recorded *Save The Last Dance For Me*. While it's probably true that the language used in films such as *High School Confidential* bears only a slight relation to that way that drug-crazed gang members actually spoke, it still has something of the authentic flavour of those times. Mostly, though, it's just there to be enjoyed, and it's worth it just to imagine hordes of impressionable teenage filmgoers back in 1958 attempting to impress their dates with lines like "Give me an introduction to this snake and I'll hitch up the reindeers for you."

Anyhow, I'd better hop in my kemp and take off for the casbah.

Plant ya now, dig ya later,

MAX DÉCHARNÉ
Berlin, May 2000

A-1

The best, top of the heap

"'That's my baby,' I said. 'We'll have our good times. Just you and me and thirty grand; maybe five or ten more if it's an A-1 job.'" **FROM THE NOVEL** *SAVAGE NIGHT*, JIM THOMPSON, 1953

A-Bomb juice

Moonshine liquor

A-ok

Fine, all in order, just right

A double this time, waiter. Your singles keep leaking

The correct way to order drinks

From *Ocean's Eleven*, the novel of the film screenplay, George Clayton Johnson and Jack Golden Russell, 1960

A shape in a drape

Someone who looks good in clothes, is sharply dressed

Abbreviations

Underwear

"I grinned at Holly Hill, who had paused behind a folded screen in the middle of wriggling out of her abbreviations." **FROM THE NOVEL** *THE CRAZY MIXED-UP CORPSE*, MIKE AVALLONE, 1957

Abyssinia

See you later (I'll be seein' ya)

Ace

1. Something superlative, the top
2. One dollar
3. A marijuana cigarette
4. A policeman

"'Who's chasin' you, Frankie?' 'The aces. They're goin' to pin the sluggin' on me.'" **FROM THE NOVEL** *THE MAN WITH THE GOLDEN ARM*, NELSON ALGREN, 1949

5. "An outstanding, regular fellow" From the booklet *The Jives Of Doctor Hepcat*, Lavada Durst, 1953

Ace high

The best, number one, top of the heap

"...to belong to the Night Hawks is just about the most there is. Guys are always trying to get in – but Rand holds it down to just six. He says too many guys and someone'll be talking. And it don't matter where we go, we're ace-high and nobody tangles with us." **FROM THE NOVEL** *THE BLACK LEATHER BARBARIANS*, PAT STADLEY, 1960

There was a short-lived pulp crime magazine in 1936 called *Ace-High Detective*

Ace in the hole

Something in reserve, an advantage, secret weapon deriving from card players having an ace up their sleeve

See the jazz recording *Ace in the Hole*, The Black Diamond Seranaders, 1926

See also the novel *Ace-in-the-Hole Haggarty*, R M Hankins, 1945

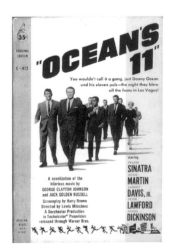

A double this time waiter, your singles keep leaking – sound refreshment advice from the only version of Ocean's 11 worth a damn.

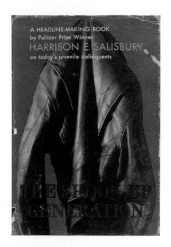

This 1958 study of teenage crime came complete with a short glossary of 'street gang argot' which hipped the squares to words like *pad*, *rumble* and *dig*.

Harrison E Salisbury, the *New York Times* reporter who got down among the J.D.'s with his 1958 book *The Shook-Up Generation*.

Ace out

Cheat, defraud

Aces up

Something mighty fine, excellent

Action

What's happening

eg: "Where's the action pops?"

1957 troubled-teen film *The Delinquents* – directed by a young Robert Altman – was advertised as "The hard-hitting motion picture that takes off the kid gloves and puts on the brass knuckles in a smashing exposé of today's children of violence – who just 'gotta have action'"

Adobe dollar

Mexican peso

Age of pain

Prohibition, the time of the 18th Amendment, which lasted from January 1920 until December 1933

Agitate the gravel

Leave, depart, vamoose

Ain't no sin to take off your skin, and dance around in your bones

1. Enjoy yourself, get with it, relax
2. Let's get naked

"Sure, he's been after me. He made a heavy pass at the New Year's party, right in his own house. He suggested we ought to take off our clothes and dance around in our bones." FROM THE NOVEL *THE WYCHERLY WOMAN*, ROSS MAC-DONALD, 1961

Ain't nothin' you can tell me I don't already know

I'm right, you're wrong, shut up

Alabama lie detector

Police baton

All broke out with the blues

Depressed, low down

All creeped up

Scared, apprehensive, frightened

All-electric

Far better looking than the average

"Ordinarily, too, I am not a guy who goes ga-ga on lamping a babe, even though, like this one, she makes it appear that other gals run on gas and she's an all-electric." FROM THE NOVEL *SLAB HAPPY*, RICHARD S.PRATHER, 1958

All gone

Drunk, intoxicated

All over them like a cheap suit

Sticking really close to someone

eg: "That guy at the dance was all over my sister like a cheap suit."

All sharped up

Well dressed, suavely turned out

All shook up

Disturbed, hopped up, excited, real gone

"Cool down Eve, you look all shook up." FROM THE NOVEL *SCANDAL HIGH*, HERBERT O. PRUETT, 1960

see also the novel *All Shook Up*, Peyson Antholz, 1958

New York Times journalist Harrison E. Salisbury published a book-length study of juvenile delinquent gang culture in 1958 called *The Shook-Up Generation*, which came complete with a short glossary of "street gang argot"

All steamed up like a pants presser

Sexually excited

All the front burners are on

Things are hotting up

"My corpsucles were kicking around so much, steam should have been pouring out of my nostrils... All the front burners were on, man, and I was percolating." FROM THE NOVEL *NAUGHTY, BUT DEAD*, G.G. FICKLING, 1962

All the way from go to stop

From head to toe, and everywhere in between

"She was wearing a gown cut Chinese style, high-necked and form-fitting all the way from go to stop, with a slit up the side so she could walk." FROM THE NOVEL *BLONDE, BAD AND BEAUTIFUL*, CARTER BROWN, 1957

All wet

Disappointing, worthless

Alligator

1. *Down Beat's Yearbook of Swing*, 1939, lists this as, "A swing fan who plays no instrument, or musician who frequents places where orchestras are playing."
2. Hipster term of address, often shortened to *Gator*. Similar in meaning to *Cat* or *Hepcat*. However, in his 1956 rockabilly recording *Alligator Come Across*, Arlie Duff gives his own explanation: "Alligator is a gal that lives in my hometown, / We call her Alligator 'cause she creeps around."

Already slated for crashville

Out of control, doomed

eg: "We could see that the car was already slated for crashville."

Alreet

In order, fine, very good

Alroot

See Alreet

Big Joe Turner and his band give a masterclass in the use of these words towards the end of his 1954 song *Well All Right*, recorded the same day he cut *Shake, Rattle & Roll*, including the rarely-heard alrote:

"Well alright then... / Well alreet then... / Well alroot then... / Well alrote then..."

Alvin

A rube, a sucker, an easy mark

Amscray

Scram, run away (backslang)

Ankle

To walk

Ants in my pants

Sexually excited

"I'm gonna hug you / Baby good and tight, / Now love me baby / Like you done last night, / Cause I got ants / In my pants, / Baby for you..." FROM THE BLUES RECORDING *ANTS IN MY PANTS*, BO CARTER, 1931

Anything you stick up, he'll wipe it right off

He's a natural-born jazz blower, he can play the phonebook and swing it like a gate

Anywhere

Possessing drugs

eg: "Is you anywhere?" ie: Do you have any? From the autobiography *Really The Blues*, Mezz Mezzrow with Bernard Wolfe, 1946

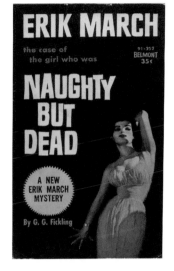

My corpsucles were kicking around so much, steam should have been pouring out of my nostrils... All the front burners were on, man, and I was percolating.

She was wearing a gown cut Chinese style, high-necked and form-fitting all the way from go to stop, with a slit up the side so she could walk.

Jazz clarinet players being encouraged to get that real-gone mellow tone by sticking their axe down an imitation fire hydrant, 1931.

Ape

A big guy, musclebound, especially in the top storey

For a refined, sensitive treatment of this theme in the style of Jane Austen, see the novel *The Lustful Ape*, Russel Gray (a.k.a. Bruno Fischer), 1950

"Sometimes it was MURDER... Sometimes it was EVEN WORSE!"

Applesauce

Flattery, insincere praise, a load of old flannel

eg:"Don't hand me that applesauce, Pops."

Ark

"Dance hall, coliseum, any building for dances, meetings and etc." FROM THE BOOKLET *THE JIVES OF DOCTOR HEPCAT*, LAVADA DURST, 1953

Artillery

Guns

As bare as hell's back yard

Completely empty

As busy as a one-legged tapdancer

Extremely busy

As dead as five cent beer

Dead and buried

As drunk as two sailors

Soused, plastered, three sheets to the wind

As full as a pair of goats

Totally drunk

"Before long we were as full as a pair of goats." FROM THE SHORT STORY *THE GOLDEN HORSESHOE*, DASHIELL HAMMETT, 1924

As homely as a mud fence

A hick from the sticks

As hot as the last bump in a stripper's grind

Hotter than hell, too hot to handle

"Your boss paid off fifty gees to some snatchers. I never knew you to be in on a swindle before, but the only way I can figure it, you're in on a swindle now. The money's hot as the last bump in a stripper's grind. The serial numbers are printed in all the rags." FROM THE NOVEL *SHOOT A SITTING DUCK*, DAVID ALEXANDER, 1955

Ashes

Having sex

eg: "Getting your ashes hauled"

"She said I could haul her ashes / Better than any other man, / She said I could sow my seed / Anytime in her ash can." FROM *ASH CAN BLUES*, BOB CLIFFORD C.1930

"I worked all winter / And I worked all fall, / I've gotta wait until spring / To get my ashes hauled." FROM THE BLUES RECORDING *TIRED AS I CAN BE*, BESSIE JACKSON (LUCILLE BOGAN), 1934

See also *Alleyman (Haul My Ashes)* Sadie Green, 1926 and *Looking For My Ash Hauler*, Washboard Sam, 1937

Awash

Drunk

Axe

Musical instrument

Bb

B-girl

Bar girl, usually working in a clip joint, whose job is to encourage the customers to buy more alcohol

"Settling down in Baltimore, she found lucrative and undemanding work as a B-Girl. Or, more accurately, it was undemanding as far as she was concerned. Lilly Dillon wasn't putting out for anyone; not, at least, for a few bucks or drinks." **FROM THE NOVEL** *THE GRIFTERS*, JIM THOMPSON, 1963

See also the short story *Bullet For a B-Girl* by Edwin Truett in the January 10 1942 edition of *Detective Fiction* magazine, and the novel *Confessions Of A B-Girl*, Sim Albert, 1953 ("She was a Honkey-tonk Stripper who tricked men")

Baby blues

Eyes

Back door man

Lover, someone who sneaks in through the back door when the husband is away

See *I'm A Front Door Woman With A Back Door Man*, a blues recording by Lillian Glinn, 1929

Back seat bunny

Dame who's spent so much time in parked cars they've started marking her on maps

See the novel *Back Seat Bunny*, Greg Hamilton, 1966

"All the boys kept calling for a date because of her reputation as a Back Seat Bunny."

Bad

1. Good
2. Evil

Bad face

"A no-good cat who'd beat his mother for beer money." **FROM THE ARTICLE** *THE ARGOT OF JAZZ* BY ELLIOTT HORNE, *NEW YORK SUNDAY TIMES*, 1957

Bag

Your interests, your preferences or habitual doings

Bag man

Go-between, drug dealer, person to whom protection money is paid

Ball the jack

1. To move fast

"Suppose you were riding that manifest out of Denton, the fast meat train that balls the jack all the way into El Reno." **FROM THE NOVEL** *SAVAGE NIGHT*, JIM THOMPSON, 1953

2. Having sex

"'I was pretty obnoxious myself,' Deedee giggled. 'I mean, I don't really think you and Moms were balling the jack together. You know that, Brad.'" **FROM THE NOVEL** *RUN TOUGH, RUN HARD*, CARSON BINGHAM, 1961

3. Have a wild time, get real gone

See *Ballin' The Jack*, The Victor Military Band, 1914 (The following year they recorded a title called *Blame It On The Blues*)

See also *Ballin' The Jack*, recorded by The Louisiana Rhythm Kings, 1929

Bam

Girlfriend, steady date, parking pet

Bandrats

Groupies

Bar-polisher

Habitual drinker, frequenter of gin-joints

Barbecue

Girlfriend, good looking woman

"She faced him now, her eyes blazing, her face flushed. 'I don't think I particularly enjoyed your role the night of the party either, if you want the honest truth about it, Brad Dixon! Strutting off with that blonde barbecue the minute you set foot in the house!'" **FROM THE NOVEL RUN TOUGH, RUN HARD, CARSON BINGHAM, 1961**

Louis Armstrong & His Hot Five released a record called *Struttin' With Some Barbecue* in 1927, ie: Dancing with a pretty girl

Barbecue stool

The electric chair

Barfly

Regular drinker, ginmill cowboy, serious lush-head

See *Bill the Bar Fly*, a country record by Tex Ritter, 1935

See also the novel *Bar-Fly Wives*, Wright Williams, 1944

Barrel fever

Drunkenness, a raging thirst

Barrelhouse

1. Gin-joint, taproom, speakeasy, brothel, always with music

"That was the Crescent City in them days, full of bars, honky-tonks and barrel houses. A barrel house was just a piano in a hall. There was always a piano player working. When I was a kid, I'd go into a barrel house and play 'long with them piano players 'til early in the mornin' We used to play nuthin' but the blues." **BUNK JOHNSON, QUOTED IN THE ORAL HISTORY *HEAR ME TALKIN' TO YA – THE STORY OF JAZZ BY THE MEN WHO MADE IT*, NAT SHAPIRO AND NAT HENTOFF, EDS., 1955**

See the jazz recordings *Barrel House Man*, Elzadie Robinson, 1926 and *Barrel House Man*, Will Ezell, 1927

2. Style of boogie piano playing. *Down Beat's Yearbook of Swing*, 1939 calls it "Swing music played in a 'dirty and lowdown' style"

Batter the drag

Beg on the street

Battle axe

Musician's slang for a trumpet

Beanery

No-nonsense food joint

Beastly

Very good

Beat

1. Exhausted, worn out

"Art sounded more than tired, he sounded beat." **FROM THE NOVEL *THE GOLDEN KEY*, WILLIAM O'FARRELL, 1962**

See also the novel *Why I Am So Beat*, Nolan Miller, 1954

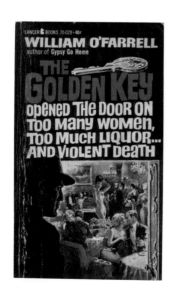

Art sounded more than tired, he sounded beat.

2. Broke, out of cash, tapsville

3. Hipster of the late 1940s and 1950s defined by the literary group around Kerouac, Ginsberg, Corso etc

"The night was getting more and more frantic. I wished Dean and Carlo were there - then realized they'd be out of place and unhappy. They were like the man with the dungeon stone and the gloom, rising from the underground, the sordid hipsters of America, a new beat generation that I was slowly joining." FROM THE NOVEL ON *THE ROAD*, JACK KEROUAC, 1957

Kerouac recorded an album in 1959, *Poetry For The Beat Generation*, on which he read out compositions of his such as *Charlie Parker* and *Deadbelly*, accompanied by pianist Steve Allen. It was turned down by Dot Records on the grounds that some of the words spoken were "off colour" and in "bad taste", and was then released uncut by another company

"In a recent edition of Esquire, *Clellon Holmes defines Beat as being 'at the bottom of your personality, looking up'."* FROM THE INTRODUCTION TO THE COLLECTION *PROTEST: THE BEAT GENERATION AND THE ANGRY YOUNG MEN*, GENE FELDMAN & MAX GARTENBERG, EDS., 1959

The 1958 short story collection *Bad Girls* ('They prowl the fringe of the underworld for kicks'), edited by Leo Margulies, was billed on the cover as 'Eleven Masterpieces of today's Beat Generation.'

See also the wildly inaccurate 1959 exploitation film *The Beat Generation* – "Sullen rebels, defiant chicks... searching for a life of their own!" – and the novel *Beat Nymph*, Peggy Swenson (Richard E Geis), c. 1961: "Lana was a swinging chick, reckless and uninhibited in the ways of love – but she was unprepared for the overwhelming torrent of depravity

and strange passions which engulfed her in the beatnik colony." Richard E Geis later gave the world novels such as *Girlsville, Whistle Them Willing, Discotheque Doll, Orality '69* and the sci-fi classic *Star Whores*

4. To steal

Beat it out

Play it hot, emphasize the rhythm

Beat me Daddy, eight-to-the-bar

Play some boogie-woogie for me

The left hand basslines in typical boogie-woogie piano feature a driving, eight-to-the-bar rhythm

"In a little honky-tonky village in Texas / There's a guy who plays the best piano by far, / He can play piano any way you like it, / But the kind he likes the best is eight-to-the-bar, / When he jams it's a ball, / He's the Daddy of 'em all." FROM THE BOOGIE-WOOGIE RECORDING *BEAT ME DADDY, EIGHT TO THE BAR*, THE WILL BRADLEY TRIO, 1942

Beat someone for their bread

Swindle or rob someone

"I knew the cab driver had beat me for my bread, but there was no use crying, it was gone." FROM THE AUTOBIOGRAPHY *I, PAID MY DUES, GOOD TIMES... NO BREAD, A STORY OF JAZZ*, BABS GONZALES, 1967

Beat the boards

Tapdance

Beat the gong

Smoke opium

Beat the rap

Escape criminal charges, be found not-guilty

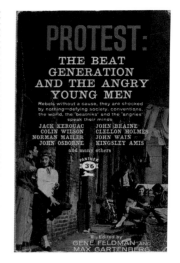

The bongo-banging Beat Generation meet the *Look Back in Anger* brigade, 1959.

Hollywood goes Beat, 1959.

Impersonate Charlie Parker in five easy lessons... a 1949 advert offering the secrets of jazz immortality for just $1.50.

Discover the magic of flush bracing, Daddy-O.

Frederick L.Nebel wrote a story called *Beat The Rap* for the May 1931 issue of *Black Mask* magazine

Beat the tubs

Play the drums

"It's all in the wrist n' I got the touch - dice, stud that's in the wrist too. Here - pick a card." FRANKIE MACHINE LISTS HIS ACCOMPLISHMENTS. FROM THE NOVEL *THE MAN WITH THE GOLDEN ARM*, NELSON ALGREN, 1949

Beat your chops

Talk

eg: "Say, is it a solid fact that you guys can beat your chops, lace the boots and knock the licks out groovy as a movie whilst jiving in a comin'-on fashion?" Bing Crosby to Nat Cole, US radio, 1945

Beat your gums

Talk

"You know, medicine's found ways to prolong some old squares' lives. You know how they spend it? Beating their gums..." FROM THE FILM *SHAKE, RATTLE AND ROCK*, 1957

Beatnik

A word coined by Herb Caen of the *San Francisco Chronicle* in 1958, for an article about the Beats. Sputnik, the Russian satellite, was much in the news at the time. Picked up by the media, it came to symbolize to the public the jazz-loving, Kerouac-reading, non-conformists of the 1950s, but it was a term hated by many of the Beats themselves

"She had her old beatnik costume on – the tight black pants, the bulky black sweater – and her hair was brushed and her lipstick was bright and straight." FROM THE NOVEL *THE WRECKING CREW*, DONALD HAMILTON, 1960

See also the scholarly, probing anaylsis of this phenomenon in the novels *The Beatniks*, Richard E Geis, 1960 ("The erotic and exotic – a lost world where naked sex flaunts its message to the sensuous beat of a drum") and *Beatnik Wanton*, Don Elliott, 1964 ("She Lusted in Sin Orgies and Reefer Brawls!")

The cover of the novel *A Real Cool Cat*, Jerry Weil, 1960, proclaimed "He was a faithful husband – until he found himself irresistibly attracted to a beautiful beatnik with a zest for love."

"Well I'm a bongo-beating beatnik / And I just don't dig rock'n'roll." FROM THE FRANKLY WIGGED-OUT RECORDING *BONGO BEATING BEATNIK*, JOE HALL & THE CORVETTES, 1959

See also the vocal group recording *Beatnik Girl*, The Bi-Tones, 1960

See also the 1959 exploitation film *The Beatniks* – "Their password was mutiny against society!" and the equally confused *The Rebel Set*, 1959 – "The drifters, the hipsters, the hot sisters! Today's big jolt about the beatnik jungle!"

Bebop

Modern jazz style developed by Charlie Parker, Dizzy Gillespie and others in the early 1940s.

Dizzy put out a single called *Bebop* in 1945

See also *He Beeped When He Shoulda Bopped*, Dizzy Gillespie & his Orchestra, 1946; *Poppa Stoppa's (Bebop Blues)*, Mr. Google Eyes & His Four Bars, 1949; *Be-Bop Wino*, a vocal group recording by The Lamplighters, 1953

Bedroom furniture

Dame, doll, gasser

eg: "She's a swell piece of bedroom furniture."

Beef

1. Complaint, grievance

"I'm not beefing about the Saratoga let-down. The guys we were fishing for just didn't bite." FROM THE NOVEL *KILLERS DON'T CARE*, ROD CALLAHAN, 1950

2. To talk
3. A criminal charge, or a crime

Behind

Under the influence of something

Behind the cork

Drunk, intoxicated

Behind the eight-ball

In trouble, in a difficult spot

"'I thought Augie was a particular friend of yours.' 'I thought so, too. And here he puts me behind the eight-ball with you...'" FROM THE NOVEL *LITTLE MEN, BIG WORLD*, W.R. BURNETT, 1951

Bill Haley recorded an unissued song called *Behind The Eight Ball* for the Cowboy label in 1949

Behind the parade

Old hat, out-dated, passé

Behind the stick

Working behind a bar - the stick being the wooden bar-top itself

Bells

Vibraphone

Belly fiddle

Guitar

Belly gun

Weapon with a short barrel, usually a 32.20, used for shooting someone at very close range

Bellyache

Complain

eg: "What are you bellyaching about?"

Belt of booze

A drink

Belting the grape

Drinking wine

Bend an arm

Have a drink

"Anyway, we haven't time to go to the Dutchman's, the finale is next. Let's run into Louie's. You can bend an arm there just as easy." FROM THE NOVEL *THE G-STRING MURDERS*, GYPSY ROSE LEE, 1941

Bend someone's ear

Talk, chatter

"Anway, thanks for the cheer, I hope you didn't mind my bending your ear." FROM *THE BALLAD ONE FOR MY BABY (AND ONE MORE FOR THE ROAD)*, FRANK SINATRA, LIVE AT THE SANDS, LAS VEGAS, 1966

Bent out of shape

1. Upset, disturbed
2. High on drugs or drink

Berries

Something mighty fine

"She had black hair an' black eyes an' a figure that looked like a serpent with nerve troubles. Except for the fact that she hadn't had her face lifted she mighta been your favourite film star. That baby was the berries." FROM THE NOVEL *YOUR DEAL, MY LOVELY*, PETER CHEYNEY, 1941

Better tune me in
and get my signal right

Understand what I'm telling you

Gypsy Rose Lee pictured hard at work writing her 1941 burleycue novel *The G-String Murders* – although it's often said to have been ghost-written by Craig Rice.

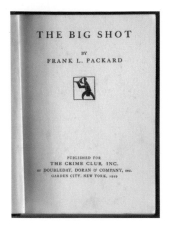

THE BIG SHOT

BY

FRANK L. PACKARD

PUBLISHED FOR
THE CRIME CLUB, INC.
BY DOUBLEDAY, DORAN & COMPANY, INC.
GARDEN CITY. NEW YORK. 1929

First edition title page of one of the earliest gangster novels, 1929.

"Better tune me in and get my signal right / Or there'll be no rockin' tomorrow night." FROM THE ROCKABILLY RECORDING *I GOT A ROCKET IN MY POCKET*, JIMMY LOGSDON (AKA JIMMY LLOYD), 1958

Bible-puncher

Clergyman

Big barracuda

An important guy

"'Got his name?' 'Morrison – big barracuda.' 'He was D.O.A.. Knife cut his heart in half.' 'Nobody did it, nobody saw it.'" FROM THE FILM *WHERE THE SIDEWALK ENDS*, 1950

Big chill

Death

Big house

Prison

In 19th century England, it was a slang name for the workhouse

Big house up the river

Sing Sing prison

Big shot

Boss, leader, important, carrying some clout

See the pioneering gangster novel *The Big Shot*, Frank L Packard, 1929

"'Listen! Do you know what a Big Shot is?' She nodded her head. 'I think I do,' she said. 'It's what the gangsters, or any mob for that matter, call their leader, isn't it?'"

See also the novel *Big Shot*, Laurence Treat, 1952

Big sleep

Death

Used by Raymond Chandler as the title of one of his most famous books, published in 1939, and filmed in 1946 with Humphrey Bogart as Philip Marlowe

Biscuit snatchers

Fingers, hands

Biters

Teeth

Blab

Talk, give the game away

Blab sheet

Newspaper

Black

Night time

"Say, you look ready as Mister Freddy this black." FREDDY SLACK TALKS HEP TO ELLA MAE MORSE DURING THE INTRO TO THEIR 1946 BOOGIE RECORDING *HOUSE OF BLUE LIGHTS*.

Black & white

Police car

Blackstick

Clarinet

Blast

Telephone call

"If you ever come to Riverport, how about giving me a blast on the phone?" FROM THE FILM *JAILHOUSE ROCK*, 1957

Blast the joint

Smoke dope

Blast yourself wacky

Go mad

Blasted

Drunk

See the novel *12.15 am: I'm Blasted* by McCall Horgan (n.d., early 1950s), the sensitive author of *The Lady Was Loaded*, *Blonde Hostage* and *Dames is My Undoing*

Blasting party

Dope party

Bleating your trap

Complaining

Blind staggers

Drunkenness

Blocked

Drunk or high on drugs

Blonde

"It was a blonde. A blonde to make a bishop kick a hole in a stained glass window." FROM THE NOVEL *FAREWELL, MY LOVELY*, RAYMOND CHANDLER, 1940

See also the novels *Blondes Are Skin Deep*, Louis Trimble, 1951 ("She taunted a dope-fiend killer"), and the entirely un-sensationalist *Stone Cold Blonde*, Adam Knight, 1951, billed as "The Case of the Nude Beauty's Corpse"

Blot out

Kill, assassinate

Blow

1. Leave, cut out, scarper
2. General term for playing a musical instrument, regardless of type

Blow a fuse

Go crazy, go wild

Blow for canines

High-pitched sax playing

Blow in on the scene

Arrive, make an entrance

Blow the box

Play the piano

Blow the joint

Leave the building

"Let's blow this joint, The music's dead..." FROM THE ROCKABILLY RECORDING *CAST IRON ARM*, JOHNNY PEANUTS WILSON, 1956

Blow the scene

Leave, disappear

"Look, baby, just don't you blow the scene on me! Stick in town or I'll chase you down to hell itself!" FROM THE NOVEL *TWO TIMING TART*, JOHN DAVIDSON, 1961

Blow the trap

Exit, vamoose

"I'm hungry. Maybe we can blow this trap. Go somewhere and eat. You game?" FROM THE NOVEL *RUN FOR DOOM*, HENRY KANE, 1960

Blow the works

Spill the beans, tell all

Blow up a storm

Cut loose during a musical number, get hot, play at your best

"Say Fats, a bunch of the kids would like to listen to you blowin' up a storm. Would you let them listen in?" FROM THE FILM *SHAKE, RATTLE AND ROCK*, 1957

See also the jazz novel *Blow Up a Storm*, Garson Kanin, 1959

Blow your jets

Get annoyed, lose your cool

McCall Horgan, the man who brought you *Dames is My Undoing*, *Blonde Hostage*, *The Lady Was Loaded*, and the immortal *12.15am: I'm Blasted*.

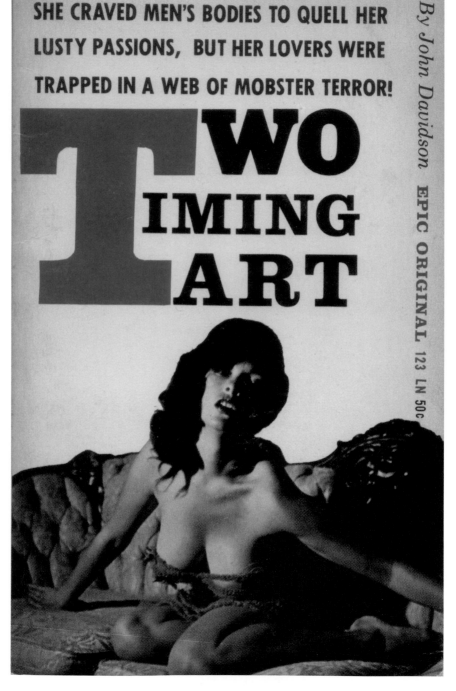

SHE CRAVED MEN'S BODIES TO QUELL HER LUSTY PASSIONS, BUT HER LOVERS WERE TRAPPED IN A WEB OF MOBSTER TERROR!

TWO TIMING TART

By John Davidson EPIC ORIGINAL 123 LN 50¢

Look, baby, just don't you blow the scene on me! Stick in town or I'll chase you down to hell itself!

Blowtop

1. A crazy or violent person, someone with a short temper

2. "Fellows who are excellent in their fields especially music and dancing." From the booklet *The Jives Of Doctor Hepcat* Lavada Durst, 1953

"Ain't that going to be kicks...listen will you to this old tenorman blow his top." FROM THE NOVEL *ON THE ROAD*, JACK KEROUAC, 1957

Boat

Automobile

"Capone motioned at a glossy black convertible job parked curbside. 'That your boat?'" FROM THE NOVEL *AL CAPONE*, JOHN ROEBURT, 1959

Bobby-soxer

Teenage girl, much given to screaming at Frank Sinatra

The name derives from the fashion for wearing short white socks

See also the rockabilly recording *Bop Bobby Sox Bop*, Alton Guyon, c. 1958

Body scissors

Having sex

"I knew by now that she was the kind of dame you couldn't turn your back on for five minutes without her having a body scissors on somebody." FROM THE NOVEL *KISS TOMORROW GOODBYE*, HORACE MCCOY, 1949

Boil my cabbage

Blues slang for sex, much used by the female blues singers of the 1920s

"He boiled my first cabbage / And he made it awful hot, / He boiled my first cabbage / And he made it awful hot, / When he put in the bacon / It overflowed the pot" FROM *EMPTY BED BLUES PART 2*, BESSIE SMITH, 1928

See also the blues recordings *Anybody Here Want To Try My Cabbage?*, Maggie Jones, 1924: *Good Cabbage*, Victoria Spivey, 1937

Boiled

Drunk, soused, juiced to the gills

"'Hard night ahead,' Gordon said, lifting his glass. 'If you think I'm going to get boiled...' 'Nobody's getting boiled.' Swallowing twice, Gordon emptied the glass. 'Just easing the tension. So we can think clearly.' He wiped his mouth with the back of his hand. 'Got a couple of ideas already.'" FROM THE NOVEL *THE MINK-LINED COFFIN*, JONATHAN LATIMER, 1959

Boiler

Automobile

"We're still talking when this boiler screeches up and stops on a dime. Out pops Cooch and walks towards us." FROM THE SHORT STORY *THE RITES OF DEATH*, HAL ELLSON, 1956

Boloney

Lies

"A bundle of first-class boloney straight off the ice." FROM THE NOVEL *CAN LADIES KILL?*, PETER CHEYNEY, 1938

Bomb

1. Automobile

"Give a listen. Power man! What a bomb!" FROM THE NOVEL *GO, MAN, GO!*, EDWARD DE ROO, 1959

"That red Thunderbird / Is the craziest bomb in town..." FROM *RED THUNDERBIRD*, A ROCK'N'ROLL RECORDING BY LYNN HOWARD & THE ACCENTS, 1958

See also the rockabilly recording *This Old Bomb Of Mine*, Howie Stange with Jim Flaherty's Caravan, c. 1958

2. A failure, such as a musical or theatrical performance

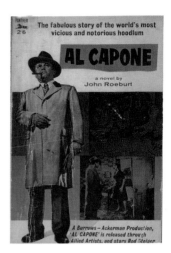

That your boat?

Tie one on like Dizzy. A solid (or polka dot) sender, 1949.

3. A cocktail, a jolt of juice, a serious shot of booze

Bone orchard

Cemetery

See *Bone Orchard Blues*, a blues recording by Ida Cox, 1928

Boneyard

1. Cemetery

See *Boneyard Shuffle*, a country recording by The Arkansas Travellers, 1927

2. Auto repair shop, garage

"It's in the boneyard, Molly... you know, the boneyard where the elephants go when they're tired of living." ie: I've smashed up the car FROM THE NOVEL *RUN TOUGH, RUN HARD*, CARSON BINGHAM, 1961

Bonnet-flipper

A gas, a knockout, something righteously hep

Boob trap

Clip joint, a place to fleece the suckers

"Ringo Martin operated the Spotted Leopard, a large, chromium-plated boob trap at the end of State Street" FROM THE NOVEL *ESPRIT DE CORPSE*, FRANK KANE, 1965

Boodle

Stash of money, a whole heap of folding green

See the novels *The Big Boodle*, Robert Sylvester, 1954, and *The Deadly Boodle*, J M Flynn, 1958

Booms

Drums

Booster

Shoplifter

Boots laced up tight

Hep, righteous, in the know, a suave customer

Booze fight

A drinking spree

There was a biker gang called the *Booze Fighters* in Los Angeles just after World War Two

Bop

1. To fight - the gang fights in the 1960 film *The Young Savages* are called bops rather than rumbles

2. To dance

"When I die don't bury me at all, / Just nail my bones up on the wall, / Beneath these bones let these words be seen: / 'The running gears of a boppin' machine.'" FROM *ROCKIN' BONES*, A ROCKABILLY RECORDING BY RONNIE DAWSON, 1958

3. Jazz movement originating in the early 1940s

The word Bebop was shortened to Bop with Charlie Parker's 1947 recording *Bongo Bop*

"The word bop was coined by none other than our old friend Fats Waller. It came about when Fats was playing with a small group at Minton's. Late one night some of the younger generation of musicians would bring along their instruments in the hope of jamming with the band. Waller would signal for one of them to take a chorus. The musician would start in to play, then rest for eight or twelve bars in order to get in condition for one of his crazy bop runs. Fats would shout at them, 'Stop that crazy boppin' and a-stoppin' and play that jive like the rest of us guys.'" HOT LIPS PAGE, QUOTED IN THE ORAL HISTORY *HEAR ME TALKIN' TO YA – THE STORY OF JAZZ BY THE MEN WHO MADE IT*, NAT SHAPIRO AND NAT HENTOFF, EDS., 1955

"At this time, 1947, bop was going like mad all over America. The fellows at

the Loop blew, but with a tired air, because bop was somewhere between its Charlie Parker Ornithology period and another period that began with Miles Davis." FROM THE NOVEL ON THE ROAD, JACK KEROUAC, 1957

See *Coppin' The Bop*, Jay Jay Johnson's BeBoppers, 1946 and *Bop's Your Uncle*, George Shearing, 1947

Jazzman Babs Gonzales had a band in 1946 called Babs' Three Bips And A Bop, and the Howard McGhee Boptet recorded for Atlantic in 1948. Artie Shaw opened a club in New York in 1949 called Bop City. By 1957, things had wigged-out in all directions, to the extent that United Artists were trying to cash in on the calypso craze by releasing a film called *Bop Girl Goes Calypso*

"See you tomorrow, cats. Same time, same channel, same bop beat…" FROM THE FILM *SHAKE, RATTLE AND ROCK*, 1957

Bop kick

"To play the new sound in music, the latest dance step." FROM THE BOOKLET *THE JIVES OF DOCTOR HEPCAT*, LAVADA DURST, 1953

Born tired

Lazy

Born under a bad sign

Fated, unlucky

Boss

Something really good, the best

Bottle babies

Drunks

From the autobiography *Really The Blues*, Mezz Mezzrow with Bernard Wolfe, 1946. In the short story collection *The Neon Wilderness* (1947), Nelson Algren has the variant bottle boy: "And the simple everyday bottle boy, who fights when he drinks, and he drinks all the time."

Bottle heister

A drunkard

Bottle the smart talk

Keep quiet, don't get wise with me

"Shut your mouth, you jerk. This is Drill's outfit. And he doesn't play with smart alecs. Save yourself some bruises and bottle the smart talk." FROM THE NOVEL *THE CRAZY MIXED-UP CORPSE*, MIKE AVALLONE, 1957

Bottle tipper

Heavy drinker

See *The Fiddlin' Bootleggers*, a country recording by The Monroe County Bottle Tippers, 1928

Bottle up and go

1. Hit the trail, cut out, vamoose, take a powder

2. Pick up your busking money and split before the cops arrive

See *Bottle Up And Go*, a vocal group recording by The Enchanters, 1957

Bottom dealer

Swindler, someone who deals from the bottom of the deck

Bought and sold and done for

Broke, down on your luck

Box

1. Vagina

See the shy, romantic 1950s vocal group performance *Baby Let Me Bang Your Box* by The Bangers, or *Hot Box Is On My Mind*, a piano blues by

Save yourself some bruises and bottle the smart talk.

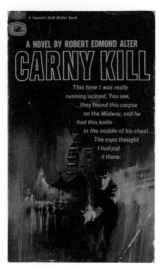

Can you bust a box if you have to?

Kingfish Bill Tomlin, 1929. By the late 1940s, however, jazz magazine *Down Beat* were calling their regular section devoted to hot news *The Hot Box*

2. A safe

"Can you bust a box if you have to?" ie: can you crack a safe? FROM THE NOVEL *CARNY KILL*, ROBERT EDMOND ALTER, 1966

3. *"A hopeless square to whom hip is hep and jazz means nothing."* FROM THE ARTICLE *THE ARGOT OF JAZZ* BY ELLIOTT HORNE, *NEW YORK SUNDAY TIMES*, 1957

4. Record player or phonograph

Box worker

Safe cracker

"He said that three or four years ago he was in another gang – box workers – safes, you know..." FROM THE NOVEL *THE BIG SHOT*, FRANK L PACKARD, 1929

Bozo

1. Idiot, square

Originating from Bozo The Clown, the traditional 19th century name for a type of circus performer whose main distinguishing characteristic is stupidity

2. Ordinary guy, all purpose term of address

eg: *"She is wearin' a lime-green frock that was cut by a bozo that could wield a mean pair of shears."*

Bracelets

Handcuffs

"One of the uniformed cops frisks me and snaps a pair of bracelets on my wrists." FROM THE NOVEL *KILLERS DON'T CARE*, ROD CALLAHAN, 1950

Brain guy

The organiser, the fixer, the smart cookie who lines up the deals and figures the angles

See the pioneering hard-boiled 1934 novel *Brain Guy* by Benjamin Appel

Brain it around

Think it over

Brass rail

Bar or saloon

Brawl

Wild party

Bread

1. Money

"In the bread department I am no-where..." FROM THE FILM *HIGH SCHOOL CONFIDENTIAL*, 1958

2. Penis

See *She's Your Cook, But She Burns My Bread Sometimes*, a blues recording by Bo Carter, 1930

Bread pan

Vagina

"She makes my bread rise / Late hours in the night, / I put my bread right in her pan / And I shoves it clean out of sight." FROM *BREAD PAN (JUST MY SIZE)*, A PIANO BLUES BY ROOSEVELT SYKES, 1937

Bread stasher

Working stiff, wage slave, someone who saves for a rainy day

Breadsville

A bank

Break it down

1. Musical term, defined by *Down Beat's Yearbook of Swing*, 1939 as "To get hot, swing it, go to town"
2. Spill the beans, speak your piece

"I'm listening," he said. *"Break it down."* FROM THE NOVEL *DEATH IS CONFIDENTIAL*, LAWRENCE LARIAR, 1959

Break it off

Stop talking

Break out like the measles

Go wild, play hot music, swing it

Breakfast uptown

A night in jail

Breathing natural gas

Hep, alert, knowing the score

Breeze

Leave, possibly in a hurry

eg: "Think I'd better breeze..."

Brew

An alcoholic drink

Bright

Daytime

Bright disease

To know too much

Bringdown

Something or someone depressing

See the R&B recording *Rain Is A Bringdown*, Ruth Brown, 1949

Broad

Dame, doll, gal, kitten

See the how-to handbook *A Guide For The Broad-Minded*, Jack Heller, ed., 1964

See also the novel *The Hot Pigeon*, Richard Lynford, n.d., mid 1960s

"Thirty million bucks and a couple of well stacked broads can really make life worth living... but brother, it's not so nice when they both bring a couple of knife-wielding killers."

Broadway battleship

New York streetcar

Brush

To ignore someone

Bucket

Prison

"I'll stay under cover. He's too stir-wise for me. I smell of the bucket" ie: He is sure to be able to tell that I've just come out of prison. FROM THE SHORT STORY *GOLDFISH*, RAYMOND CHANDLER, 1936

Bucket of blood

Cheap bar, spit & sawdust joint

See *Bucket of Blood*, a piano blues by Will Ezell, 1929

Bucket of suds

Takeaway beer, carried home in a bucket

Bug

To annoy or irritate

"I'm sorry baby, but don't bug me." FROM THE FILM *THE KILLERS*, 1956

See *Like, You Bug Me*, a vocal group recording by The Quarter Notes, 1958, and also the country recording *You Bug Me Bad*, Wanda Jackson, 1962

Bug juice

Moonshine liquor

Bug spray

Spirits, intoxicating liquor

"With his gun still on me, he brought the bottle up, jerked back his head quickly and finished off the whisky. Then he flipped the empty bottle across the rug. It stopped rolling near my shoe tips. 'Break out another bottle of that

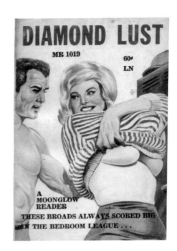

Home thoughts from a broad, 1960s-style.

Break out another bottle of that bug spray, shamus.

bug spray, shamus.'" FROM THE NOVEL *SLEEP NO MORE, SAM S TAYLOR, 1951*

Buggy

1. Automobile

2. Crazy, short for bughouse (see next entry)

"Take your buggy boy friend and clear out of here before I forget I'm a lady." FROM THE NOVEL *POP. 1280,* JIM THOMPSON, 1964

Bughouse

Crazy, insane, lost it completely

The mob nickname Bugsy derives from this – a crazy guy, a stone killer

Washington Square in Chicago has long been known as Bughouse Square, as has Union Square in New York

Build me a drink

Mix me a cocktail

Built

Someone with a good figure

"'You've got six weeks to make her a star.' 'Easy, Fats, it takes time. Rome wasn't built in a day.' 'She ain't Rome.'" ie: She's built already. FROM THE FILM *THE GIRL CAN'T HELP IT,* 1956

Bull

Cop, policeman

Bull fiddle

Double bass

Bullet binge

Getting frisky with firearms, shooting up the town

See the novelette *Dames On a Bullet Binge* by Frederick C Davis in the June 1941 issue of *Ten Detective Aces*

Bulletproof

Completely drunk

Bulling

Something good, mighty fine

Bum

1. A tramp, a hobo

2. A waster, a no-good, a freeloader, a chancer

See also the novel *Jazz Bum,* William Gwinn, 1954, 'An Evil Woman Drove Him Into An Underworld Of Dark Passions'

Bum steer

A bad deal, something wrong, an unlucky break

Bump

To kill

Bump your gums

Talk a lot

Bunco artist

Con man, swindler

Bundle

Bankroll, a quantity of money

Bunk habit

The practice of lounging around while others smoke opium, and inhaling the fumes

From the autobiography *Really The Blues,* Mezz Mezzrow with Bernard Wolfe, 1946

Burg

Town, city

Buried

1. As drunk as a skunk, plastered
2. A life sentence in jail

Burleycue

Burlesque, stripping

'I had a teacher once – guy was in love with me – and we developed my own routine for a solo. After that it was the wheel – L.A., Vegas, Frisco. Kind of the burleycue routine, you know? But as a single-o, solo performer.' FROM THE NOVEL *RUN FOR DOOM*, HENRY KANE, 1960

Burn

1. Die in the electric chair
2. Kill someone

"Max grinned genially. From his jacket pocket he produced a small-calibre pistol, then dropped it back again. 'We want you to burn him, Rick.' Rick stared at him with slowly growing comprehension. 'You mean kill him?' he finally asked in a husky voice. 'You got the scoop,' Max said." FROM THE SHORT STORY *A HOOD IS BORN*, RICHARD DEMING, 1959

Burn leather

1. Dance

See *The Joint is Jumping*, a jazz recording by Fats Waller

2. Walk fast or run

Burn me up

Go on, give it all you've got

"Burn me up this time, let's see if we can get a little fire into it." ELVIS TO HIS MUSICIANS, FROM THE FILM *JAILHOUSE ROCK*, 1957

Burn my clothes

An expression of surprise

"Burn my clothes if it isn't Romeo, our financial backer." FROM THE FILM *DAMES*, 1934

Burn rubber

1. Drive fast, make a quick getaway
2. Have sex

Burned

1. Annoyed
2. Robbed
3. Killed

Burning with a low blue flame

Drunk, swimming, sluiced to the gills

Bus

Car

Busier than a hustler with two bunks

Extremely busy

Bust

A washout, a drag, a failure

Bust your conk

Work hard, be thorough

Bust your vest

Be big, magnanimous

Busted

1. Arrested
2. Broke, poverty-stricken

"I'm busted, flat." FROM THE NOVEL *RED HARVEST*, DASHIELL HAMMETT, 1929

Busted flush

A bankrupt

Busting into a can

Cracking a safe

Butcher shop

Hospital

Butt me

Give me a cigarette

The good people at Kozy Books offer some deep philosophical insight into the burleycue world for just 50 cents.

Butter-and-egg man

Out-of-town big spender, the backer of a theatre show, free with his money and often a sucker

See *Big Butter and Egg Man from the West*, a jazz recording by Louis Armstrong's Hot Five, 1927

Button

The lookout in a criminal operation

Button-buster

A braggart or loudmouth

Button your gabber

Shut up

Button your lip

Keep quiet

Buy the farm

To die, peg out, cash in your chips

Buzz

To rob, to pick someone's pocket

"Tell you what I'll do, Tiger. I'll give you the names of eight cannons that fit the job and I'll bet you thirty eight dollars and fifty cents that one of them buzzed this moll's wallet." FROM THE FILM *PICKUP ON SOUTH STREET*, 1953

Buzz me

Give me a call on the telephone

"Buzz me, buzz me, buzz me baby, / I'm waitin' for your call..." FROM *BUZZ ME*, AN R&B JUMP-JIVE RECORDING BY LOUIS JORDAN & THE TYMPANY FIVE, 1946

See also *Buzz Me Babe*, a blues recording by Slim Harpo, 1960

Buzzer

Badge or ID, usually that of the police

By the handles

"Keep it up pal, and six of your best friends are gonna be carrying you by the handles..." DEAN MARTIN TO HECKLER, ONSTAGE AT THE SANDS, LAS VEGAS, FEBRUARY 1964

C-jag

Cocaine binge

Cornell Woolrich wrote a story called *C-Jag* for the October 1940 issue of *Black Mask* magazine, in which the murderer can't remember what he's done with the body due to an over-indulgence of snow

C note

One hundred dollars

"In a moment, Colosimo returned. He thrust money at Capone with a flourish. 'Five Cs, for a stake.'" FROM THE NOVEL *AL CAPONE*, JOHN ROEBURT, 1959

Cabbage

1. Money

"I'm looking for some guys with lots of cabbage and a certain amount of respectability... worth shaking down." FROM THE NOVEL *MURDER ON MONDAY*, ROBERT PATRICK WILMOT, 1952

2. 1920s blues slang for genitals

Cackle factory

Lunatic asylum

"'He'd be just the man who might try to con Torelli.' 'Con Torelli! You must have been sprung from the cackle factory. Not even Gunner would try that.'" FROM THE NOVEL *DARLING, IT'S DEATH*, RICHARD S. PRATHER, 1953

Café sunburn

Pallor

From the autobiography *Really The Blues*, Mezz Mezzrow and Bernard Wolfe, 1946

Cake cutter

Short-change artist, swindler

Calaboose

Prison

"The judge he pondered, / Then turned me loose, sayin' / 'Too many winos in my calaboose.'" FROM THE HILLBILLY BOOGIE RECORDING *THE WINO BOOGIE*, BILL NETTLES, 1954

Call some hogs

Snore

Call the children home

Cut loose on the bandstand, start wailing, open up and lay down some righteous music

"I used to hear Bolden play every chance I got. I'd go out to the park where he was playing, and there wouldn't be a soul around. Then, when it was time to start the dance, he'd say, 'Let's call the children home.' And he'd put his horn out the window and blow, and everyone would come running." KID ORY RECALLS THE GODLIKE GENIUS OF BUDDY BOLDEN, QUOTED IN THE ORAL HISTORY *HEAR ME TALKIN' TO YA – THE STORY OF JAZZ BY THE MEN WHO MADE IT*, NAT SHAPIRO AND NAT HENTOFF, EDS., 1955

Camisole

Prison slang for a strait-jacket

Can

1. Prison

"I'm fresh out of prison / Six years in the can..." FROM THE COUNTRY RECORDING *DRINK UP AND GO HOME*, CARL PERKINS, 1956

Mezz Mezzrow workin' on that café sunburn in *Really The Blues*, 1946.

Ditch that can and come back for your split.

2. Automobile

"'Tony,' said Rico, 'ditch that can and come back for your split.'" ie: dispose of the getaway car and then we'll divide up the money. FROM THE NOVEL *LITTLE CAESAR*, W.R. BURNETT, 1929

3. Backside, rear end

"Ira Borch - the grinning stranger, a slimy sonofabitch who'd been on my can for six months." FROM THE NOVEL *ALWAYS LEAVE 'EM DYING*, RICHARD S. PRATHER, 1961

Can it

Shut up

"'Mike, you surprise me. I thought you were keen on equal rights and all that jazz.' 'Can it,' he growled. 'You know where I stand at this late date.'" FROM THE NOVEL *THE BEDROOM BOLERO*, MICHAEL AVALLONE, 1963

Canary

1. Female singer

"You once had a great nose for finding new talent. Dug up some big canaries, but the booze got in your way." FROM THE FILM *THE GIRL CAN'T HELP IT*, 1956

See also the novel *The Hot Canary*, Joan Ellis, 1963 *"She sang for her supper, but did something else for her midnight snack."*

There were also many recordings of real canaries in the 1930s, often trained to whistle popular tunes of the day: "There must be a steady sale for 'actual canary bird recordings' somewhere, for there is seldom a month without at least one release by feathered warblers..." *Phonograph Monthly Review*, New York, November 1930

2. Police informer

Cancel someone's Christmas

Kill them

Canned heat

Cheap hooch made from a mixture of alcohol and methylated spirits, much favoured by hoboes and winos

See the blues recording *Canned Heat Blues*, Sloppy Henry, 1928

Cannon

1. Gun, firearm

See the short story *Cannon Kid* by Jack Compton in the August 1930 issue of *Detective Dragnet*

2. Gunman

"...Dave Moroni, Moron for short, who had been a minor cog in Murder, Inc. when Bugsy Siegel had been one of their top torpedoes. The other guy was a top-notch cannon who could kiss the dog and lift your wrist watch between ticks." FROM THE NOVEL *DARLING, IT'S DEATH*, RICHARD S. PRATHER, 1953

In the film *Pickup on South Street* (1953), the word is frequently used to describe a pickpocket or petty criminal

Can't see a hole in a ladder

Completely drunk

Cap

To shoot someone

Caper

Robbery, criminal enterprise

Capper

A shill, one who assists a card-sharp in swindling the suckers

Carve your knob

"To make you know, understand." FROM THE BOOKLET *THE JIVES OF DOCTOR HEPCAT*, LAVADA DURST, 1953

Cash in your checks

To die

"For the files, Blackie Glitz is just a mobster who cashed in his checks, via three slugs in his back, said slugs being non-self-inflicted." FROM THE NOVEL *THE CORRUPT ONES*, J C BARTON, CIRCA 1950

Cast iron arm

A punch like a steamhammer

See the rockabilly recording *Cast Iron Arm*, Johnny 'Peanuts' Wilson, 1956

Cat

Dude, hipster, a righteous groover

In 1953 *Doctor Hepcat* defined a cat as "A young man who is part of the modern social whirl, dresses in latest smart styles, understands all types of music dances and is accepted."

"There's a cat in town that you might know, / He goes by the name of Domino. / A long key chain and a diamond ring, / A blue sports car, he's a crazy king, / They love him so, that cat called Domino..." FROM THE ROCKABILLY RECORDING *DOMINO*, ROY ORBISON, 1956

See the jazz recording *That Cat Is High*, Tommy Powell & his Hi-De-Ho Boys, 1936

See also the R&B jump-jive recording *At The Swing Cats Ball*, Louis Jordan & The Tympany Five, 1939

Not surprisingly, *Down Beat's 1939 Yearbook of Swing* defines Cats as "Musicians in a swing orchestra, or people who like swing music."

See also the jazz recording *Stop The War (The Cats Are Killin' Themselves)*, Wingy Manone & his Orchestra, 1941

Cat clothes

Hipster threads – serious clothing, not for the squares

See the rockabilly recording *Put Your Cat Clothes On*, Carl Perkins, 1956

Cat house

Brothel

Cat's pyjamas

The best, top of the heap

Catch a handful of boxcars

Hop a freight train and leave town

Catting around

Playing the field, philandering

"All you married men / Take my advice / If you're cattin' around / You better have nine lives, / If you're cattin' around, / Yeah cattin' around, / Well I lost my baby / When she caught me cattin' around" FROM THE ROCKABILLY RECORDING *CATTIN' AROUND*, CHARLIE ADAMS 1954

See also the entry tomcatting around

Caught in a snowstorm

Addicted to cocaine

Century

One hundred dollars

Chalk-eater

A gambler who always backs the favourite in a horse race

Change the disc, kiddo

I've heard it all before, I don't believe you

"Change the disc, kiddo, and kid me not." FROM THE NOVEL *THE WYCHERLY WOMAN*, ROSS MACDONALD, 1961

Charging a bank

Robbing a bank

"Kid, we got us a little bank in Cedars just itchin' to be charged. It's all cased properly." FROM THE FILM *THEY LIVE BY NIGHT*, 1948

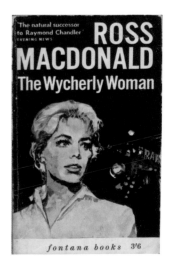

Change the disc, kiddo.

'See the death-defying fury of a head-on chicken race!' A double bill of dangerous dolls from 1956.

A shy, retiring Chippie, 1960.

Chassis

Body, limbs etc

Chat'n'chew

Restaurant, hash house

Cheaters

Eyeglasses, spectacles

Check the beat

Listen to the music

Check the character

Look at that person over there

From the film *High School Confidential*, 1958

Chew the scenery

Overact, make a big deal of something

Chicago lightning

Gunfire

Chicago overcoat

Coffin

Chicago piano

Machine gun

Chick

Girl, dame

"Dean had arrived the night before, the first time in New York, with his beautiful little sharp chick Marylou." FROM THE NOVEL *ON THE ROAD*, JACK KEROUAC, 1957

"Let me tell you bout my real gone chick, / She's got a different style..." FROM THE ROCKABILLY RECORDING *TONGUE TIED JILL*, CHARLIE FEATHERS, 1956

See the vocal group recording *That Chick's Too Young To Fry*, The Deep River Boys, 1945 (Also covered by The Prisonaires, from the Tennessee State Penitentiary, some of whom had wound up behind bars for exactly the same reasons spelt out in the song, who recorded for Sam Phillips' Sun label in the early 1950s.)

Chicken dinner

Pretty young girl

From the autobiography *Really The Blues*, Mezz Mezzrow with Bernard Wolfe, 1946

Chicken ranch

Brothel

Chicken run

Russian roulette-style race with cars

Chill

1. Kill, assassinate
2. Stop that, wait a minute

Chill your chat

Stop talking

Chime

The time of day, the hour

Chippie

1. Part-time prostitute

"My God! What did I ever think of to put in with a chippy like you?" FROM THE NOVEL *THE HIGH WINDOW*, RAYMOND CHANDLER, 1943

See the jazz recording *Chasin' Chippies*, Cootie Williams & his Rug Cutters, 1938

2. Occasional user of drugs

Chirp

Female vocalist

Chiseler

Swindler, cheat

Chiv

Knife

Choke dog

Rough moonshine liquor

Chop-beatin' session

Discussion

Chop suey

1. A messy death

"Some of the nicest people you ever took a gander at suddenly go daffy and make chop suey out of their best friends, with a meat axe." FROM THE FILM *SLEEP, MY LOVE*, 1948

2. Having sex

See the blues recording *Who'll Chop Your Suey When I'm Gone?*, Willie Jackson, 1926

For a firewood-themed rockabilly variant on the above, see the 1961 recording *Who's Gonna Chop (My Baby's Kindlin')* by Fred Maddox

Chopper

Machine gun, or machine-gunner

Choppers

Teeth

Chops

Any part of the body a musician uses to play his instrument

Chow

Food

Chuck

Food

Chuck horrors

Extreme reaction to food brought on by drug withdrawal

Chump change

Small change, a moderate amount of money, low wages

Cinder dicks

Railroad police

Clam up

Keep quiet, fall silent

Clam yourself

Be quiet, shut up

Clams

Dollars

"Nothin' a million clams won't cure." DANNY OCEAN GETS OPTIMISTIC, FROM *OCEAN'S ELEVEN*, THE NOVELISATION OF THE FILM SCREENPLAY, GEORGE CLAYTON JOHN-SON AND JACK GOLDEN RUSSELL, 1960

Claret

Blood

Claws

Fingers

Claws sharp

"The act of being well informed on all subjects." FROM THE BOOKLET *THE JIVES OF DOCTOR HEPCAT*, LAVADA DURST, 1953

Clean

1. Unarmed
2. Not carrying any stolen goods
3. Wealthy, rich

See the R&B recording Jack, *That Cat Was Clean*, Dr. Horse & His Musical Jockeys, 1958. Dr Horse, real name Al Pittman, was a former member of legendary combo Dr Sausage & his Five Pork Chops

Cliff dweller

Resident of a high-rise apartment block

Danny Ocean's crew - *Nothin' a million clams won't cure.*

William P McGivern, offering odds against tomorrow.

I clipped him good, and he busted his head on the bar railing.

Climb the six-foot ladder

To die, be buried

Clip

1. Kill someone
2. Punch someone

"A guy in the bar come at me with a bottle. I clipped him good, and he busted his head on the bar railing." FROM THE NOVEL *ODDS AGAINST TOMORROW*, WILLIAM P. MCGIVERN, 1957

3. Cheat someone

Clip joint

Club, bar or other business which routinely swindles its customers

See the novel *The Fabulous Clipjoint*, Fredric Brown, 1947 'Vice and Murder Prowl Chicago'

Clipster

Confidence man

Clout

1. Influence, authority
2. To steal

Clouting heaps

Stealing cars

Clown

Idiot, square, a waste of space

Clued-in

Aware, knowledgeable, on top of the situation

Clutch buster

Hot-rodder

Clyde

A square, a hick, a goon from Straightsville

Coal bin

Blues slang for a vagina

"I'll take your order / And fill your bin, / So get it cleaned out / And I'll put it right in, / Cause I'm just a coal man / Sellin' the hottest stuff in town." FROM THE BLUES RECORDING *THE HOTTEST STUFF IN TOWN*, BOB HOWE & FRANKIE GRIGGS, 1935

Cockroach joint

Cheap restaurant

Coffee grinder

Classic striptease act

Coffin nails

Cigarettes

"Get outta here with your coffin nails / Can't you see you're on the wrong trail / Go 'way, boy, don't wanna see one lit / Or I'll go into a nicotine fit." FROM THE COUNTRY RECORDING *NICOTINE FIT*, MISSISSIPPI SLIM, 1954

Coffin varnish

Rough liquor

Cold meat cart

Hearse

Cold meat party

A funeral

From the novel *Halo In Blood*, Howard Browne, 1946

Cold storage

Prison

Collar

1. To arrest someone
2. To acquire something

College

Prison

Comb your knowledge box

Comb your hair

Combed

Searched, frisked

"If a prowl went past, the coppers would comb them sure." FROM THE NOVEL *LITTLE MEN, BIG WORLD*, W.R. BURNETT, 1951

Come apart like a two-bit suitcase

Lose it, fall to pieces, dissolve into tears

Come clean

Tell all, speak up, confess

Jazz pioneer Buddy Bolden regularly played a venue in New Orleans around the year 1900 called Come Clean Hall

"You'd better talk, George. Come clean. Either you talk, or we'll get it out of the girl." FROM THE FILM *THE KILLING*, 1956

Come to life!

Get real, face the truth

Come-on

Inducement, bait, lure, encouragement

Come-on dame

Femme fatale, wolf trap, sucker bait

See the novel *Crime On My Hands*, Carl G Hoges, 1951 "A Sensational Suspense Story About Dope Peddlers – Hopped-up Gunmen – Come-on Dames!"

Comin' on

Hep, in control, confident – like a performer coming onstage and making an entrance

Community joy ride

Drug party

"Somebody was shooting up, and I walked over, and the guy finished with the spike and handed it to me, and I loaded it and blew my brains out, and then I passed the spike to somebody else, it was one of those affairs, a community joy ride, you know what I mean?" FROM THE NOVEL *SECOND ENDING*, EVAN HUNTER, 1952

Coney Island whitefish

Used condom floating in the sea

Continental

A damn, a curse

eg: "I don't give a continental..."

Cooch dancing

Hootchie-cooching, burlesque dancing, stripping

Cook

To do something well

Cookie cutter

Policeman's badge

Cool

1. In the know, A-ok, hep
2. Unworried, calm, relaxed

See the jazz recording *How You Gonna Keep Kool?*, The Georgia Melodians, 1924

That same year in the Presidential elections, Calvin Coolidge used the slogan "Keep Cool with Coolidge."

See also the jazz recordings *Look Hot, Keep Cool*, The Harmonians, 1933 and *Keep Cool, Fool*, Les Brown & his Orchestra, 1941. Among numerous 1950s examples, see the hunt-your-own-footwear-in-the-swamp-with-a-big-old-knife recording *Cool Gator Shoes*, Carl Belew,1959, the rock'n'roll recording *Cool Steppin'*

Baby, Steve Bledsoe & the Blue Jays, 1959 or the pop recording *Cool Drool*, Del Reeves, 1958

One of the all-time great juvenile delinquent films is the 1958 American International picture *The Cool and the Crazy*, advertised as "Seven Savage Punks on a Weekend Binge of Violence."

3. To kill, also known as to cool off

Cool, calm and a solid wig

Someone suave, a hepcat, a groover

Cool cat

A dude, a hipster, a real gone daddy

"Ubangi stomp with a rock'n'roll, / Beats anything that you ever been told. / Ubangi stomp, Ubangi style, / When it hits it drives a cool cat wild..." **FROM THE ROCKABILLY RECORDING** *UBANGI STOMP*, **WARREN SMITH, 1956**

Cool it

Calm down, don't worry, don't make a fuss

"They're ready to fight, but Elmo cuts in, 'Cool it, you studs,' he tells them. 'I said cool it!'" **FROM THE SHORT STORY** *THE RITES OF DEATH*, **HAL ELLSON, 1956**

See also the rock'n'roll song *Cool It, Baby* by Eddie Fontaine, as featured in the 1956 film *The Girl Can't Help It*, which contains the immortal lines: "I love your eyes, I love your lips, They taste even better than potato chips."

Cooler

Prison cell, solitary confinement

Cop

To obtain

Cop a drear

Die, expire, cash in your chips

Cop a nod

Go to sleep

Cop a plea

Plea bargain in order to get a lower sentence

See the jazz recording *Coppin' A Plea*, Gene Krupa & his Orchestra, 1941

Cop a slave

Get a job

Cop a sneak

Surreptitious look

Cop a squat

Sit down

Cop an attitude

Behave in a negative or aggressive fashion

Cop and blow

Easy come, easy go. You win some, you lose some

"He reconciled himself to the name of the game. Cop and blow." **FROM THE AUTOBIOGRAPHY** *I, PAID MY DUES*, **BABS GONZALES, 1967**

Copasetic

Good, in order, everything alright, sometimes spelt copacetic

"The highest compliment in the hep world, anything you can do you are a master of it." **FROM THE BOOKLET** *THE JIVES OF DOCTOR HEPCAT*, **LAVADA DURST, 1953**

Corn squeezings

Moonshine liquor

"Mighty, mighty pleasin' / Pappy's corn squeezings, / Mmm...white lightnin'." **FROM THE ROCKABILLY RECORDING** *WHITE LIGHTNING*, **GEORGE JONES, 1957**

Pappy's corn squeezings... George Jones hymns the hooch in 1959.

Cornball style

Square, boring, clichéd

Cornfed

From the country, coarse, unsophisticated

Cosmic goo

Metaphysics

"Don't worry me with all that cosmic goo, I've got practical problems." FROM THE NOVEL *BLOW UP A STORM*, GARSON KANIN, 1959

Cotton mouthed

Thirsty, ready to soak up the booze

"Alcoholic beverages were forbidden. Ergo: the people demanded them. It was a cotton-mouthed generation which ignored an irritating law by imbibing such commodities as bathtub gin and needled beer." FROM THE BOOK *THE UNTOUCHABLES*, ELLIOT NESS & OSCAR FRALEY, 1957

Couldn't find a fat man in a telephone booth

Unobservant, dumb, useless

"'But I do think you show an impressive lack of respect for our constabulary.' Liddell grunted. 'I don't think they could find a fat man in a telephone booth.'" FROM THE NOVEL *ESPRIT DE CORPSE*, FRANK KANE, 1965

County hotel

Local jail

Cover girl on the book of temptation

Irresistable dame, femme fatale

Crack some suds

Drink beer

Crack the books

Read

Crack wise

Joke, talk back, be sarcastic

Crack your jaw

Talk

Crap out

Be unlucky, fail

Crapshoot

A risky business, chancey undertaking

Crash-out

Prison break

Sometimes spoken as crush out. (To crush, in 19th Century English slang, meant to run away)

See the short novel *The Big Crush-Out* by George Bruce in the February 29 1936 issue of *Detective Fiction Weekly*

Crashing the ether

Broadcasting on the radio

Crazy

Good, superlative, wild, the best

"Ooh man, dig those crazy lips, / Ooh man, boy she really flips, / Ooh man, dig that crazy chick" FROM THE R&B JUMP-JIVE RECORDING *DIG THAT CRAZY CHICK*, SAM BUTERA & THE WITNESSES, 1958

See also the rock'n'roll recording *Crazy, Man, Crazy*, Bill Haley & The Comets, 1954

Richard S. Prather, author of numerous crime novels in the 1950s and 60s featuring private eye Shell Scott, wrote a book in 1961 called *Dig That Crazy Grave*. During the course

Don't worry me with all that cosmic goo.

Erle Stanley Gardner, also known as A A Fair.

of his million-selling career he also treated the public to *The Scrambled Yeggs*, *Have Gat Will Travel* and *The Wailing Frail*

Crease

1. To shoot

"Someone decided to crease Travis. He was shot last night." **FROM THE NOVEL** *YOU CAN ALWAYS DUCK*, PETER CHEYNEY, 1943

2. To hit or stun

Creep-joint

Brothel where the customers are likely to have their pockets picked

Crib

1. Home, apartment, residence
2. A safe

Croak

Die

Croak sheet

Life insurance policy

Croaker

1. Doctor

"'Is Burns bad?' 'Yeah, but the croaker says he'll survive.'" **FROM THE NOVEL** *THE FAST BUCK*, JAMES HADLEY CHASE, 1952

2. Murderer, ie: one who croaks someone

Crocked

Drunk

Croonette

Female singer

Cross-eyed

Drunk

Crossing the home plate

A successful seduction, going all the way

"I'd like to spend an afternoon with a man sometime. I'd like to visit and get acquainted with new people. I'd like to go ashore in Rio de Janeiro and prowl through the shops with some interesting man who wasn't thinking in terms of making your acquaintance, getting a pass to first base, stealing second and crossing the home plate, all within two hours." **FROM THE NOVEL** *TOP OF THE HEAP*, A A FAIR (ERLE STANLEY GARDNER), 1952

Crowd-pleaser

Police gun

Cruiser

Automobile

Cruising for a bruising

Looking for trouble

"Cruising – looking for my gal / I'm cruising – goin' don't know where / I'm cruising – looking for my gal / I'm cruising for a bruising that man / with her is gonna get..." **FROM THE ROCK'N'ROLL RECORDING** *CRUISING*, GENE VINCENT & THE BLUE CAPS, 1956

Cruising with your lights on dim

Stupid, bughouse, not all there

Crumb crushers

Teeth

Crummy

Unpleasant, poor quality, worthless

"I sniff at the odour of rotting chow and tell Nick, 'Crummy joint.' 'Yeah,' Nick says, 'and crummy people.'" **FROM THE NOVEL** *KILLERS DON'T CARE*, ROD CALLAHAN, 1950

Crunchers

Feet

Cuban candles

Cigars

Cubistic

Square, straight, boring

"Mother, you can be such a drag some-times, so utterly cubistic." **FROM THE FILM** *THE YOUNG SAVAGES*, 1960

Cuddle up on a nice cold slab

Die, step off, exit the big race

"They dashed out to the airport. The fellow she'd picked up cranked up his plane and made a blue streak to a field up north of San Francisco, where the plane let down and Maurine and George Bishop were scheduled to have a secret confab and lay plans so Gabby Garvanza would cuddle up on a nice cold slab in the morgue." **FROM THE NOVEL** *TOP OF THE HEAP*, A A FAIR (ERLE STANLEY GARDNER), 1952

Culture cave

Beatnik hangout, existentialist nitespot

In Ross Macdonald's 1959 novel *The Galton Case*, Lew Archer is advised to not to bother visiting a joint called The Listening Ear. ("It's a culture cave. One of those bistros where guys read poems to music. It ain't your speed at all."). When he goes there, this is what he finds: "... the audience was different from other nightclub crowds. A high proportion of the girls had short straight hair through which they ran their fingers from time to time. Many of the boys had longer hair than the girls, but they didn't run their fingers through it so much. They stroked their beards instead."

Cupcake

Term of endearment

Current concubine

Girlfriend, steady date

Cut

To outdo, to play better than another musician

Cut out

Leave, depart

Cut some rug

Dance

Pioneer Chicago DJ Jack L Cooper started a radio show in the early 1930s called *Rug Cutter's Special*

See the blues recording *Rug Cutter Swing*, Henry Allen, 1934

Cut the mustard

Get the job done

See *Too Old To Cut The Mustard*, by The Carlisle Brothers, as performed by a teenage Buddy Holly onstage at his school in Lubbock, Texas in 1953, and dedicated to his teachers: "Used to fight the girls off with a stick, / Now they say 'He makes me sick.'"

Cut the scene

1. Stop making a fuss
2. Leave, depart

Cut up

Have a laugh, fool around

Cut up rough

Get tough, start a fight

Cutie

A swell dame, a doll, a gasser, a knockout

See the novel *A Coffin for Cutie*, Spike Morelli, n.d. (1950s)

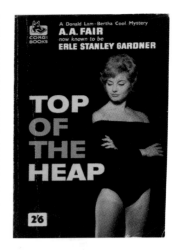

Cuddle up on a cold slab.

RADIO
STATION COPY
Publisher:
Acuff-Rose
Pub. (BMI)
Time: 2:13

COLUMBIA

45 RPM
4 - 42049
JZSP 54094

TOO OLD TO CUT THE MUSTARD
-W. T. Carlisle-
BILL CARLISLE

Used to fight the girls off with a stick / Now they say 'He makes me sick'.

D.O.A.

Dead on arrival, all washed up

"'D.O.A.,' said the intern. 'It looks to me like a stiff dose of cyanide in a cocktail, probably a sidecar.'" **FROM THE SHORT STORY *THREE WIVES TOO MANY*, KENNETH FEARING, 1956**

See the short story *D.O.A.* by Robert H Rohde in the July 2 1927 issue of *Detective Fiction* magazine

Rudolph Maté directed a film noir called *D.O.A* in 1950, from a novel by David Goodis (not to be confused with the 1978 documentary film of the Sex Pistols' USA tour)

Dabs

Fingerprints

Daddy-O

Term of address for a hipster

New Orleans DJ Vernon Winslow was broadcasting under the name Doctor Daddy-O in the late 1940s. He'd previously called himself Poppa Stoppa. Rock'n'Roll DJ Porky Chedwick of WAMO, Pittsburgh called himself "the Daddy-O of the radio, a porkulatin' platter-pushin' Poppa."

Billy Taylor put out a jazz recording in 1955 called *Daddy-O*, and the phrase was also used as the title of one of the great exploitation films in 1959 – "Meet the 'Beat' – daring to live, daring to love!"

"One little piggy liked to bop, / The other two did the stroll, / These little piggies, crazy little piggies / All they did
was rock'n'roll." **FROM THE ROCK'N'ROLL RECORDING *DADDY-O-GOOSE & THE THREE LITTLE PIGGIES*, FRED MICK WITH THE KINGSMEN, 1962**

See also the pop recording *Daddy-O*, Bonnie Lou, 1955, and the rockabilly recording *Take Up The Slack, Daddy-O*, The Sabres, 1959

"It was like being struck by lightning. It can happen to anyone any time and any place except that it mostly doesn't. But it did happen to Lester and, of all places, it happened to him in the crummiest little dump in the whole of the old precinct – a fly-blown chili parlor with beatnik overtones that, if your stomach can stand it, was archly named DADDYOS PADYO." **FROM THE NOVEL *THE BABE WITH THE TWISTABLE ARM*, HAMPTON STONE, 1962**

Dame

Woman

A selection of Frederick Nebel's stories for *Black Mask* magazine were published as a book in 1950 under the title *Six Deadly Dames*

See also the novels *All Dames are Dynamite*, Timothy Trent, 1935, and *Four Dames Named 'Sin'*, Mark Reed, 1952

Dancing on a dime

Dancing very close together

"Here at the ballroom young men and women come to dance rather than to listen. Preferably on a dime. To sock. In short, to rub bellies together and, thus, excite one another." **FROM THE AUTOBIOGRAPHY *TALKING TO MYSELF*, STUDS TERKEL, 1977**

A stirring story of desperate dope-skaters, early 1950s.

"If you think I'm going dancin' on a dime / Your clock is ticking on the wrong time." ELLA MAE MORSE TO FREDDIE SLACK FROM THE BOOGIE-WOOGIE RECORDING *HOUSE OF BLUE LIGHTS*, 1946

Dangle

Leave, get lost, scram

"Outside, then. Take the air. Dangle." FROM THE SHORT STORY *FLY PAPER*, DASHIELL HAMMETT, 1929

Date bait

1. Boyfriend or girlfriend
2. Someone attractive

See the 1960 exploitation film *Date Bait* - "Too young to know, too wild to love, too eager to say I will."

See also the rockabilly recordings *Date Bait*, Ronnie Self, 1958, and *Date Bait Baby*, Reggie Perkins, 1959

Dead man

Empty bottle

Dead on the vine

Worn out, exhausted

Dead on time

Hep, suave, in the know, on the beam

Dead presidents

Cash money, dollar bills

Dead soldiers

Empty bottles

"Get a load of them dead soldiers. Must have been some brawl last weekend." FROM THE FILM *THE DEVIL THUMBS A RIDE*, 1947

Deadfall

Nightclub or all-night restaurant that is really a clipjoint

Deal around me

Leave me out of this, I'm not interested

Deal him out

Kill him

"Right now, all I want is Coll. Deal him out — and no mistakes!" FROM THE NOVEL *'MAD DOG' COLL*, STEVE THURMAN, 1961

Deep-Sea Diving

Oral sex

"He's a deep-sea diver / With a stroke that can't go wrong, / He's a deep-sea diver / With a stroke that can't go wrong, / He can touch the bottom / And his wind holds out so long." FROM THE BLUES RECORDING *EMPTY BED BLUES PART 1.*, BESSIE SMITH, 1928

Deep six

Dispose of, kill

Delosis

"De-Lo-sis a young girl, pretty" FROM THE BOOKLET *THE JIVES OF DOCTOR HEPCAT*, LAVADA DURST, 1953

Detroit disaster

Automobile

Deuce

Two dollars

Diamond dust in her eyes

A gold-digger, a dame on the make

See the novel *Smuggled Sin*, Steve Harragan, 1953: "She had diamond dust in her eyes — lust in her heart — Steve in her arms!"

Dice-joint

Gambling hall

Dick

Detective

"I'm, just a square-toed dick. I can't match wits with you." FROM THE NOVEL *THE CLUE OF THE FORGOTTEN MURDER*, ERLE STANLEY GARDNER, 1934

In the early 1930s, Frederick Nebel wrote a series of stories for *Black Mask* featuring a detective called 'Tough dick' Donahue

See also Bernard G Priestley's charmingly-titled short story *When Dick Meets Dick* in the July 1929 issue of *The Dragnet Magazine*

Dig

1. Understand, comprehend, appreciate, approve of

See the jazz recording *I Don't Dig You Jack*, Blue Lu Barker, 1939

See also the jazz recording *I Dig You The Most*, Kenny Clarke with The Ernie Wilkins Septet, 1955. The flip-side was called *Cute Tomato*

"And indeed it is essential to dig the most, for if you do not dig, you lose your superiority over the Square, and so you are less likely to be cool (to be in control of a situation because you have swung where the Square has not, or because you have allowed to come to consciousness a pain, a guilt, a shame or a desire which the other has not had the courage to face). To be cool is to be equipped, and if you are equipped it is more difficult for the next cat who comes along to put you down." NORMAN MAILER HIPS THE HEP TO WHAT'S HAPPENING, FROM *THE WHITE NEGRO: SUPERFICIAL REFLECTIONS ON THE HIPSTER*, 1957

2. To notice, observe or look around

"I dug the square for Hassell; he wasn't there, he was in Riker's Island, behind bars." ie: I searched Times Square for him, but he was in jail. FROM THE NOVEL *ON THE ROAD*, JACK KEROUAC, 1957

3. General word used to punctuate a sentence to see if your audience is paying attention, dig?

Dig those mellow kicks

Enjoy yourself

Digging for dandruff

Racking your brains, trying to figure something out

Dime

Ten year jail sentence

Dime dropper

Police informer – ie: someone who drops a dime in the payphone to call up the cops. However, Harrison E. Salisbury's 1958 street-gang study *The Shook-Up Generation* says that the term "Drop a dime" was used by teenagers to mean simply "give me a dime"

Dime-grind palace

Cheap dancehall with girls available as paid dancing partners

"I work at the Palace Ballroom, / But gee that place is cheap... / Ten cents a dance, pansies and rough guys, / Tough guys who tear my gown." FROM THE JAZZ RECORDING *TEN CENTS A DANCE*, RUTH ETTING, 1930

Ding dong daddy

A dude, a hepcat

See the jazz recording *I'm a Ding Dong Daddy (from Dumas)*, Louis Armstrong, 1930 – also recorded by Slatz Randall & his Orchestra, 1930 and the country duo Zeb & Zeke, 1934

Characters in Nelson Algren novels have a habit of singing this song, for instance in *Never Come Morning*, 1941, and *The Man With The Golden Arm*, 1959

Dinner

Pretty young girl

Ruth Etting, a long way from the dime-grind palace.

A classic 1961 novel from million-selling author of *The Scrambled Yeggs, Have Gat Will Travel* and *The Wailing Frail*.

From the autobiography *Really The Blues*, Mezz Mezzrow and Bernard Wolfe, 1946

Dip your bill

Have a drink of booze

Dirty dozens

Trading insults back and forth, each one worse than the last

"'S'pose he tell you he was with you mama.' 'I don't play no dozens, boy,' Smitty growled. 'You young punks don't know how far to go with a man.'" FROM THE NOVEL *IF HE HOLLERS LET HIM GO*, CHESTER HIMES, 1945

"Ashes to ashes, sand to sand, I like your mama but she got too many men..." FROM THE BLUES RECORDING *THE DIRTY DOZENS*, SPECKLED RED, 1930

Dirty with money

Rolling in it, rich, wealthy

Dish

Good looking person

"You're a swell dish. I think I'm gonna go for you." JIMMY CAGNEY IN THE FILM *THE PUBLIC ENEMY*, 1933

Dish it out

Hand something out: punishment, information etc

See the jazz recording *I Can Dish It, Can You Take It*, Blue Scott & his Blue Boys, 1936

Dish out that mess

Play some solid music, lay it down so it stays down

Dish the dirt

Tell the story, give away secrets

Disk

Record, platter, waxing, a solid slab of sound

In the late fifties, *Mad* magazine did a parody of all the current rock'n'roll fan magazines and called it *Diskville*, which claimed "Frankie Avalon's new record is called *My Teenage Lips Are Chapped From Kissing An Ice Cold Chick*."

Dissolve

Leave in a hurry, disappear

The District

Storyville in New Orleans – the wide-open part of town below Canal Street, pre-1917, where whorehouses set the tone and jazz provided the soundtrack

"But the people I knew called all that was in Storyville 'The District.' I never heard it called Storyville. It got called that when somebody up here in the North read about it. It was never Storyville to me. It was always The District – the red light district." DANNY BARKER, QUOTED IN THE ORAL HISTORY *HEAR ME TALKIN' TO YA – THE STORY OF JAZZ BY THE MEN WHO MADE IT*, NAT SHAPIRO AND NAT HENTOFF, EDS., 1955

Dixie fried

Drunk

Dixie, as well as being the traditional name for the Southern states of the U.S., is also one of the most popular brands of beer in the region

"He hollered 'Rave on, children, I'm with ya, / Rave on, cats' he cried. / 'It's almost dawn and the cops are gone / Lets all get dixie fried...'" FROM THE ROCKABILLY RECORDING *DIXIE FRIED*, CARL PERKINS, 1956

Do a Brodie

Take a dive, flop

Named after Steve Brodie, a New York bar owner who jumped off the Brooklyn Bridge for a bet and lived to collect the money

Frankie Avalon – teenage lips chapped from kissing an ice cold chick.

Author Richard S Prather: *'She wore a V-necked white blouse, as if she were the gal who'd invented cleavage just for fun'.*

Do a Houdini

Disappear, leave in a hurry

Do a number on someone

Pull the wool over their eyes, deceive, con

Do right man

Someone who plays it straight, who wouldn't cheat on their partner

See the blues recording *Do Right Papa*, Butterbeans & Susie, 1925; the western swing recording *I'm a Do Right Papa*, Leon's Lone Star Cowboys, 1935; the country recording *I'm a Do Right Cowboy*, Tex Ritter, 1935

Dog around

1. Nag, verbally abuse

"Give me a break, Papa, / Don't throw your sweet mama down. / You've treated me so mean, / Ain't you tired of doggin' me round?" FROM THE BLUES RECORDING *GIVE ME A BREAK BLUES*, IDA COX, 1927

See also the blues recording *If You Don't Want Me (Stop Doggin' Me Round)*, Jan Garber, 1924

2. Following someone

"Who's the ugly lob at the end of the bar chilling us? He's dogging me. Doesn't seem to care if I know it or not." FROM THE NOVEL *DARLING, IT'S DEATH*, RICHARD S. PRATHER, 1953

Doghouse

Double bass

"The car radio gave me 'Whispers', very softly, with a lot of strings, a growling doghouse and a sobbing trumpet." FROM THE NOVEL *HALO IN BLOOD*, HOWARD BROWNE, 1946

Dogs

Feet

"Keep your dog on it." ie: Keep your foot on the accelerator. FROM THE NOVEL *RED HARVEST*, DASHIELL HAMMETT, 1950

See the blues recording *Got To Cool My Doggies Now*, Mamie Smith & her Jazz Hounds, 1922

Doing it all

Serving a life sentence in jail

Doing next week's drinking too soon

Those extra shots of booze that you really don't need because you're totally plastered already

Doing the book

Serving a life sentence in jail

"'He told me to tell you not to worry about him.' 'He's doing the book, I worry plenty.' 'Well, he's a tough kid, maybe he'll get a break.'" FROM THE FILM *THE KILLING*, 1956

Doll

Good looking girl

"It was a woman, a doll, a sensational tomato who looked as if she'd just turned twenty-one, but had obviously signalled for the turn a long time ago. She was tall, and lovely all over, maybe five-seven, and she wore a V-necked white blouse, as if she were the gal who'd invented cleavage just for fun." FROM THE NOVEL *ALWAYS LEAVE 'EM DYING*, RICHARD S. PRATHER, 1961

See Roger Corman's 1957 film *Teenage Doll* – "too young to be careful... too tough to care... now it's too late to say no!"

See also the novels *Tough Doll*, Peggy Gaddis, 1951 ("She went from good to bad – to worse") and *Dig A Dead Doll*, G.G. Fickling, 1960

Dollface

Term of endearment

Dome doc

Psychiatrist, headshrinker

Domino

To stop, to finish

Don't get your gauge up

Don't get excited, calm down

Don't let the grass grow in your ears

Don't be lazy or otherwise untogether

Don't let your mouth start something your head can't stand

Shut up or I'll hit you

Don't move a peg

Stay still

"When I say stop, / Don't move a peg..." FROM THE PIANO BOOGIE RECORDING *PINE TOP'S BOOGIE WOOGIE*, PINE TOP SMITH, 1928

Don't raise no needless dust

Don't make a fuss, don't go out of your way

Don't strip your gears

Be cool, don't blow your top

Don't sweat it

Don't worry about it

Don't take any wooden nickels

Be careful, watch your step

See the jazz recording *'Tain't Good (Like a Nickel Made of Wood)* Jimmy Lunceford & his Orchestra, 1936

A character in the 1960 Dolores Hitchens novel *Sleep With Slander* sends a telegram using the variant "Don't take any wooden blondes"

Don't vip another vop

Don't say a word

Dope

1. Heroin

See the novel *Lost House*, Frances Shelley Wees, 1938 "Dope, Danger and Dolls."

2. General term for various drugs, such as marijuana

On the cover of the paperback *Dope, Inc.*, (Joachim Joesten, 1953), a sinister hand can be seen offering a reefer to a nervous teenager

3. A drug user

"A dope's comin' up. You point out this McMann to'm. He's a good worker and'll go to hell for a snifter." (ie he'll kill anyone you want for a line of coke) FROM THE NOVEL *BRAIN GUY*, BENJAMIN APPEL, 1934

4. Information

eg: "What's the dope?"

Dope fiend

Habitual drug user

The strapline on the cover of the novel *Blondes Are Skin Deep*, Louis Trimble, 1951, is 'She Taunted a Dope-Fiend Killer'. In this case, the dope is cocaine

Dope it out

Reason things out, explain

"I tried to dope it out, a screwy thing like that. I added up and subtracted and tried to remember back to certain times and places, and all I got out of it was a headache." FROM THE NOVEL *SAVAGE NIGHT*, JIM THOMPSON, 1953

Dough

Money

"Plenty tough boy, and rolling in dough. Always had a bankroll that would choke a mule." FROM *LITTLE MEN, BIG WORLD*, W.R. BURNETT, 1951

See the jazz recording *What'll We Do For Dough?* Walter Anderson & his Golden Pheasant Hoodlums, 1927

Doughnut

1. Automobile tyre
2. Blues slang for vagina

See the blues recordings *Mama's Doughnut*, Spark Plug Smith, 1933, and *Who Pumped The Wind In My Doughnut*, Washboard Sam, 1935

Douse the Edisons

1. Put the lights out
2. Close your eyes

Douse the glim

Put the lights out

Down with the fish

Drunk

Drag

1. A bringdown, something depressing

"'Squares,' she said. 'Always squares. It's a nowhere drag. It hangs me up.'" FROM THE NOVEL *GENTLY GO MAN*, ALAN HUNTER, 1961

2. Influence

eg: He's got a lot of drag with the politicians downtown

3. *"Fun, killer, swinger, dumb."* FROM THE BOOKLET *THE JIVES OF DOCTOR HEPCAT*, LAVADA DURST, 1953

4. Dance

"Nothing braces me up like a good drag across the slag with a hag..." CHARMING SENTIMENTS FROM THE FILM *SHAKE, RATTLE AND ROCK*, 1957

5. Race a car on a drag strip

See the rockabilly recording *Drag Strip Baby*, Johnny Roane, 1958 and *Draggin'*, Curtis Gordon, 1956

Drag-and-eat pad

Restaurant

Draggin'-wagon

A hot car, something really fast

"He wanted to get out of the two-wheel class and own a draggin' wagon." FROM THE NOVEL *GO, MAN, GO!* EDWARD DE ROO, 1959

Dragging your rear axle

Beating about the bush, prevaricating

"Come to the point, you're dragging your rear axle in waltz-time." FROM THE FILM *HIGH SCHOOL CONFIDENTIAL*, 1958

Dragnet

Major police search, city – or even countrywide

"'Are you throwing out a dragnet?' 'Sorry, no dragnet Charlie. We've got a book full of names, addresses and phone numbers to check.'" FROM THE FILM *SIDE STREET*, 1950

Dragnet, starring Jack Webb, was one of the most successful police serials of all time, running on US radio from 1949–1951, and on TV from 1951–1970

Drape

1. A suit of clothes
2. *"To dress or to lounge."* From the booklet *The Jives Of Doctor Hepcat*, Lavada Durst, 1953

Draw a lot of water

To have a lot of influence

Draw one

I'd like a coffee

Draw one in the dark

I'd like a black coffee

Well, Be-Bop!

(Staff Photo by Got)
New York—Dizzy may play be-bop, but Cab Calloway *wears* it. The king of hi-de-ho poses backstage at the Strand theater in his be-bop suit, much more conservative than his previous zoot costumes. It is blue serge, no drape, no shape, just a belt in the back, pearl buttons and a hunk of watch chain.

'No drape, no shape' – Cab Calloway hips the hep to the new style in vines, 1947.

Drift

Get lost, go away, leave

"'Beat it,' he said. 'Drift. Take the air. Scram. Push off.'" FROM THE NOVEL *THE HIGH WINDOW*, RAYMOND CHANDLER, 1943

Drill

Shoot someone

Drilling

To walk, to move in a straight line

Drinking that mess

Tipping it back, sucking the bottle

"Drinking that mess is pure delight, / When they get drunk they start fighting all night, / Kicking out windows and knocking down doors, / Drink a half a gallon and holler for more..." FROM THE R&B RECORDING *DRINKIN' WINE SPO-DEE-O-DEE*, STICK MCGHEE, 1949

Drinking the town dry

A wild night, hitting the bottle high

Drinking your lunch out of a bottle

Being an alcoholic

Driving

Having sex

"I've been driving fourteen years, / Haven't had an accident yet..." FROM THE BLUES RECORDING *HENRY FORD BLUES*, ROOSEVELT SYKES, 1929

See the blues recordings *Hard Driving Papa*, Bessie Smith, 1926, and *Hitch Me To Your Buggy, And Drive Me Like a Mule*, Casey Bill Weldon, 1927

Drool

Rubbish, a waste of time, irrelevant

"All this was drool; we were waiting for Bix to cut loose." FROM THE AUTOBIOGRAPHY *WE CALLED IT MUSIC*, EDDIE CONDON WITH THOMAS SUGRUE, 1948

Drop a nickel or hang up

Out with it, say what you've got to say, put up or shut up

Drop that back into low and go by once more

Can you say that again please

Drop the veil

Stop pretending and come clean

"Drop the veil, sister, I'm in the business myself." FROM THE FILM *THE BIG SLEEP*, 1946

Drugstore cowboy

Young loafer on the street corner

Drunk tank

Holding cell for prisoners brought in drunk

Dryer than a cork leg

Thirsty, in need of some booze

Duck soup

In the writings of Dashiell Hammett this means a sure thing, something very easily accomplished. However, Nelson Algren uses it to mean something strange and not quite as it should be:

"'I hope he knows what he's doin' is all,' Mama T. observed dubiously. 'It looked queer as duck soup to me.'" FROM THE NOVEL *NEVER COME MORNING*, NELSON ALGREN, 1941

For the Marx Brothers, it meant whatever the hell they wanted it to mean...

Ducktail

Hepcat haircut, rockabilly style

See the rockabilly recordings *Duck Tail*, Rudy 'Tutti' Grayzell, 1956, *Duck Tail Cat*, Dan Virva, 1956, *King Of The Ducktail Cats*, Larry Nolen, 1957

'Drop the veil, sister...' Bogart and Bacall in *The Big Sleep*.

All this was drool; we were waiting for Bix to cut loose.

and *You Gotta Have A Duck Tail*, Billy Adams & The Rock-A-Teers, 1958

Dude

1. A suave cat, a hipster, well dressed

The U.S. Phonograph Company issued a wax cylinder in the early 1890s by Russell Hunting called *Casey And The Dude In A Street Car*

Raoul Whitfield wrote a story called *Sal The Dude* for the October 1929 issue of *Black Mask* magazine

One of Damon Runyon's regular characters in his stories of Broadway low-life was called Dave the Dude

"Well, the wide doll walks right up to the bunch under the arch and says in a large bass voice: 'Which one is Dave the Dude?' 'I am Dave the Dude,' says Dave the Dude, stepping up. 'What do you mean by busting in here like a walrus and gumming up our wedding?'" FROM THE SHORT STORY *ROMANCE IN THE ROARING FORTIES*, DAMON RUNYON, 1929

2. Guy, man, fella

Duded up

Well dressed, sharp

Duds

Clothes

Duked out

Dressed up, well turned out

"He was all duked out in a hard-boiled collar and a blue serge suit. There was a hatchet-faced dame with him in a stiff black satin dress and a hat that looked like a lamp shade." FROM THE NOVEL *SAVAGE NIGHT*, JIM THOMPSON, 1953

Dukes

Fists

"'You know how to handle your dukes, man,' he said. 'Shortest fight we've had

around here yet.'" FROM THE SHORT STORY *A HOOD IS BORN*, RICHARD DEMING, 1959

Dumb gat

A gun fitted with a silencer

Dummy-up

Fall silent, refuse to talk

Dump

Dwelling, building, apartment. It can be in any condition from well preserved to falling down. The phrase "Nice dump you've got here" is intended as a compliment, not an insult

Dungaree doll

Hip girl wearing jeans

"The flat top cats and the dungaree dolls / Are headed for the gym to the sock-hop ball, / The joint's really jumpin', the cats are going wild, / The music really sends me, I dig the crazy styles." FROM THE ROCK'N'ROLL RECORDING *READY TEDDY*, LITTLE RICHARD, 1956

Dust

1. Kill
2. Leave, depart

"Get moving: we may have to dust, and dust fast!" FROM THE NOVEL *THE FAST BUCK*, JAMES HADLEY CHASE, 1952

Dustin' the keys

Playing piano

"When Janis left, Lamont drained his glass and said 'Ruth, how about a little dusting off on the eighty-eight?' He nodded at a baby grand in a corner. 'No tonight, Rod. I haven't touched a key in weeks.'" FROM THE NOVEL *SLEEP NO MORE*, SAM S TAYLOR, 1951

Dutch milk

Beer

The eagle flies on Friday

Getting paid

Early bright

The early hours of the morning

Easy rider

Good at sex

See the blues recording *I Wonder Where My Easy Rider's Gone*, Tampa Red & his Hokum Jug Band, 1929

See also the blues recordings *Ride, Jockey, Ride*, Trixie Smith & her Down Home Syncopators, 1924, (billed as "exciting enough to stir up a dead man"); *Rider Needs A Fast Horse*, Ora Alexander, 1931; *Easy Ridin' Mama*, Washboard Sam, 1937; and the energetic vocal group recording *I'm Gonna Ride Tillie Tonight*, The Fortunes, 1948

Easy scratch

Money for old rope

Easy to pick for a human being cause he wears clothes

A lunk, a meathead, the caveman type

"Eddie Prank's his Deputy Sheriff, a hairy man, easy to pick for a human being because he wears clothes." FROM THE NOVEL *DRESSED-UP TO KILL*, E G COUSINS, 1961

Eat crow

Be humiliated, forced to apologise

Eat your mush and hush

Shut up and finish your food

Eats factory

Restaurant

Edisons

1. Eyes
2. Lights

Eggs in the dark

Eggs fried on both sides

Eighty-eight

Oldsmobile 88, a car from the early 1950s also known as a Rocket 88

"Got me a date and I won't be late, / Pick her up in my eighty-eight." FROM THE ROCK'N'ROLL RECORDING *RIP IT UP*, LITTLE RICHARD, 1956

See also the rock'n'roll recording *Rocket 88*, Jackie Brenston & his Delta Cats, 1951

Eighty-eights

Piano

Eighty-six

Ditch, dispose of, drop

Electric cure

The electric chair

"Ned Beaumont smiled tepidly and asked with mock admiration: 'Is there anything you haven't been through before? Ever been given the electric cure?'" FROM THE NOVEL *THE GLASS KEY*, DASHIELL HAMMETT, 1931

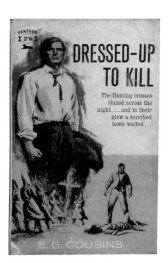

Eddie Prank's his Deputy Sheriff, a hairy man, easy to pick for a human being because he wears clothes.

Elephant teeth

Piano keys

"The cat that's pulling the elephant teeth is a bonnet-flipper and makes a gang of mad beats." ie: He's a damned good piano player. **FROM THE BOOKLET** *THE JIVES OF DOCTOR HEPCAT*, LAVADA DURST, 1953

Elevated

Drunk, high

Embalmed

Drunk, loaded

Embalmer

Bootlegger

Embalming fluid

Alcohol

Empty enough to steal the dog's dinner

Hungry

Enamel

Skin

From the autobiography *Really The Blues*, Mezz Mezzrow and Bernard Wolfe, 1946

Ends

Shoes, footwear

Enough bread to burn a wet mule

Very rich

From the autobiography *I, Paid My Dues*, Babs Gonzales, 1967

Enough to pass around

Very attractive, a knockout

"This dame was loaded with enough to pass around." **FROM THE NOVEL** *MORALS SQUAD*, SAMUEL A. KRASNEY, 1959

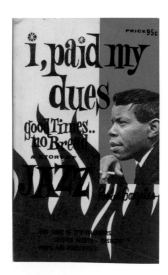

So sharp he's bleeding... author Gonzales ran a jazz combo in the late 1940s called Babs' Three Bips & a Bop.

Equalizer

Gun

Eternal checkout

Death

Evening rig

Formal dress, dinner jacket, black tie etc

Every-which-way drunk

Catatonic, totally plastered, drinking yourself insensible

"I was taken drunk that year — every-which-way drunk." **FROM THE SHORT STORY** *THE LOST DECADE*, F. SCOTT FITZGERALD, 1939

Everything is much straight

Things are fine, mellow, A-ok

Everything plus

Good-looking, the works

eg: *"She was a swell dame with everything plus."*

Executive session

Serious drinking

"I remembered the half bottle of scotch I had left and went into executive session with it." PHILIP MARLOWE IN THE SHORT STORY *TROUBLE IS MY BUSINESS*, RAYMOND CHANDER, 1939

Eyeball

1. Look at, observe

"For once no-one was looking at Trammell; all ten thousand or so were eyeballing me." **FROM THE NOVEL** *ALWAYS LEAVE 'EM DYING*, RICHARD S. PRATHER, 1961

2. Private detective

Face like the elevated railway

Ugly

Face like a Russian flag

Embarrassed

Fade out

Leave, often in a hurry

Fair shake

A decent chance, an equal opportunity

Fake some action

Do something, work, make an effort, pursue employment

"'What does he write?' Gently asked. 'Booksy jazz,' Maureen said. 'He fakes some action for the papers, but that's nowhere stuff, isn't it. Like he writes some wild poetry, jazz that really makes the touch. And he's writing a book too. Man, that book is the craziest.'" **FROM THE NOVEL GENTLY GO MAN, ALAN HUNTER, 1961**

Fall down, juvenile

Stop bothering me, you irritating youth

From the film *Beat Girl*, 1960

Fall guy

One who takes the blame for something, sometimes an innocent party

"'They got me measured for the fall guy.' 'Now just a minute...' 'Sure, I'm a fortune hunter that hypnotised Marsha, who

made her kill her father for his money.'" **FROM THE FILM TOUCH OF EVIL, 1959**

Fall in

Arrive

Fall in and dig the happenings

Come on in and have a good time, listen to this

Fall out

1. Depart
2. Go to sleep

Fan

Pick someone's pocket

Fan someone's baggage

Search their belongings

"I'm clean. Go ahead, fan me, c'mon..." **FROM THE FILM PICKUP ON SOUTH STREET, 1953**

Far out

1. Weird
2. Impressive, they don't run trains there anymore

Feeling no pain

Drunk, high, loaded

See the jazz recording *Feelin' No Pain*, The Charleston Chasers, 1927

Fess up

Speak up, give out some information, confess

Orson Welles in *Touch of Evil* – heading for a fall.

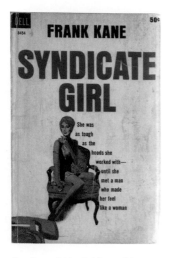

Syndicate Girl – fielding a big one.

Fetch me my liquid ham and eggs

Fats Waller calls for his morning whiskey

Field a big one

Take a serious bullet wound

"'How about his wife?' Lewis shrugged. 'Fielded a big one. The doc doesn't give her much of a chance.'" **FROM THE NOVEL** *SYNDICATE GIRL*, FRANK KANE, 1958

Filling station

Bar or off-licence

Fin

Five dollar bill

"When I turned to leave, he added, 'Got another fin on you?' I came around slowly. 'What do I look like, a halibut?'" **FROM THE NOVEL** *SLEEP NO MORE*, SAM S TAYLOR, 1951

Fine as wine

Good, the best

"They say it's fine as wine and really on the ball, / No windows, no doors, it's just a hole in the wall." **AMOS MILBURN DESCRIBES HIS IDEAL NIGHTCLUB, FROM THE BOOGIE-WOOGIE RECORDING** *CHICKEN SHACK BOOGIE*,1946

Fine frame, no parts lame

Good looking, having a good figure

Finger-man

Someone who sets up another person, either for arrest or assassination – puts the finger on them

Raymond Chandler published a short story called *Finger Man* in the October 1934 issue of *Black Mask* magazine

"They killed the Mover and they killed Anna, and they tried to kill me. They are now in bad trouble. I want the finger man. As soon as I figure out who he is, he's dead." **FROM THE NOVEL** *LITTLE MEN, BIG WORLD*, W.R. BURNETT, 1951

"I picked up the guy in a flea-bag hotel on Doncelos. His doll fingered him and picked up the swag with him." **FROM THE NOVEL** *DARLING, IT'S DEATH*, RICHARD S. PRATHER, 1959

Finger-popper

"A cat (musician or hipster) who is swinging." **FROM THE ARTICLE** *THE ARGOT OF JAZZ* **BY ELLIOTT HORNE,** *NEW YORK SUNDAY TIMES*, 1957

See also the R&B recording *Finger Poppin' Time*, Hank Ballard & the Midnighters, 1960

Fink

Informer, stool pigeon, all-round low-life

See the short novel *Fink* by Frederick C Painton in the February 26 1938 issue of *Detective Fiction Weekly*

First class bottle head

An alcoholic, a drunk

Fish

1. A sucker, a rube
2. A dollar
3. *"An erotic dance similar to the burlesque house grind."* **FROM** *THE SHOOK-UP GENERATION*, A BOOK BY HARRISON E. SALISBURY, 1958

Fish wrapper

A newspaper

Fishtail

Movement of car where the rear end swings from side to side

Flake

Unreliable, no good, a waste of space

Flap your ears

Listen

"Go right ahead baby, my ears are flappin'." FROM THE NOVEL *YOUR DEAL, MY LOVELY*, PETER CHEYNEY,1941

Flash your welcome sign

Give me some encouragement

"Your lips start me to burnin' / With a desire an' a yearnin', / To feel them cling to mine, / Well if you're with me flash your welcome sign." FROM THE ROCK'N'ROLL RECORDING *ARE YOU WITH ME*, MEL ROBBINS, 1956

Flat as a matzoh

Broke, out of cash

Flat on your can

Down on your luck

Flat top

Razored-flat teenage haircut, as mentioned by Little Richard in *Ready Teddy*, 1956

(see Dungaree Doll)

Not to be confused with Stanley Johnston's 1942 book, *Queen of the Flat-Tops*, which lays out the straight dope regarding the US aircraft carrier Lexington…

Flat tyre

1. A letdown
2. Impotent

"Couple of lightweights… yeah, flat tyres." JOAN BLONDELL TALKING ABOUT THE GUYS SHE'S WITH, WHO'VE BOTH PASSED OUT FROM DRINK. FROM THE FILM *THE PUBLIC ENEMY*, 1933

See also the country honkytonk recording *Cryin' In The Deep Blue Sea*, Hank Thompson, 1952: "When I went to see my baby, / She said stay away from me, / Cause I'm a live wire and you're a flat tyre / And I'm lettin' you go you see."

Fleabag

Cheap rooming house or hotel

Fleshpot

A joint where the action is

See the novel *Fleshpots Of Malibu*, C & G Graham, n.d. (1940s) "Days of temptation – nights of desire – and wild parties – in an exotic love colony"

Flimflam

Deception, con, swindle

Flip

Go wild, get excited, real gone

"I first began listening seven or eight years ago. First I heard Stravinsky's Firebird Suite. In the vernacular of the streets, I flipped." CHARLIE PARKER, QUOTED IN *THE ORAL HISTORY HEAR ME TALKIN' TO YA – THE STORY OF JAZZ BY THE MEN WHO MADE IT*, NAT SHAPIRO AND NAT HENTOFF, EDS., 1955

"I flipped my lid / I blew my top, / When I got roarin' / On a real cool bop…" FROM THE ROCK'N'ROLL RECORDING *I FLIPPED*, GENE VINCENT & THE BLUE CAPS, 1956

Flip your wig

1. Jump for joy, bust a gasket
2. Go insane, lose your cool

"I figured she was the type to flip good if she flipped." FROM THE NOVEL *ALWAYS LEAVE 'EM DYING*, RICHARD S. PRATHER, 1961

Flippers

Hands

"Get the hell out of here! I told you to blow! Beat it while you still got flippers to open the door with!" THE CUT AND THRUST

Get the hell out of here! I told you to blow! Beat it while you still got flippers to open the door with!

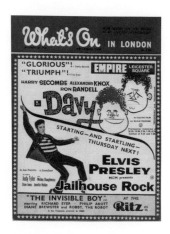

Elvis gets flippy as *Jailhouse Rock* replaces Harry Secombe at the Empire Leicester Square, January 1958.

OF PHILOSOPHICAL DISCOURSE, FROM THE NOVEL *SEARCH FOR A DEAD NYMPHO*, PAUL W FAIRMAN, 1967

Flippy

Really good, excellent, the most

"'Doll, where have you been?' 'Right in your little heart, Doll.' 'You didn't say a thing about my outfit...' 'Flippy... real flippy.'" ELVIS CHARMS HIS DATE, FROM THE FILM *JAILHOUSE ROCK*, 1957

Floating

Drunk

"I poured her a slug that would have made me float over a wall." FROM THE NOVEL *FAREWELL, MY LOVELY*, RAYMOND CHANDLER, 1940

Floozie

Tart, dancehall doll, streetwalker

Floozie-joint

Whorehouse

Flop

Somewhere to crash for the night

"That's Hardin. I hope he ain't in no trouble. He's a right guy that will always stake you to a flop and some crackers when the good things lose." FROM THE NOVEL *SHOOT A SITTING DUCK*, DAVID ALEXANDER, 1955

Flophouse

Cheap rooms, doss house

Florida honeymoon

A dirty weekend, a holiday affair

Fly

Smart, sophisticated, in the know

From the autobiography *Really The Blues*, Mezz Mezzrow and Bernard Wolfe, 1946

In England in the 18th century, the word was already in use as a term for someone who understood the latest slang

See the jazz recording *I Ain't Your Hen, Mr. Fly Rooster*, Martha Copeland, 1928

Fly it through to endsville

Bring it to a conclusion

Fly the coop

Leave, often in a hurry. Leave home

Foam

Beer

Focus your audio

Listen carefully

Fogged

Killed, rubbed out

"The smooth-faced young man had his pistol out again. 'I can fog him easy, Slats,' he said." FROM THE NOVEL *RED GARDENIAS*, JONATHAN LATIMER, 1939

Foggy

"Full, crowded, loaded." FROM THE BOOKLET *THE JIVES OF DOCTOR HEPCAT*, LAVADA DURST, 1953

Folding green

Banknotes

"Just put this hunk of the folding green back in your saddle bag and forget you ever met me." FROM THE NOVEL *THE LITTLE SISTER*, RAYMOND CHANDLER, 1949

For you and me the chill is on

Our relationship is over

Foul-up

A mistake

Four-flushing

Cheating, lying, untrustworthy

"...this goddam four-flushing town, all the viciousness and cruelty." HORACE MCCOY PRAISES GOOD OLD HOLLYWOOD, FROM THE NOVEL *I SHOULD HAVE STAYED HOME*, 1938

See the blues recording *Four Flushin' Papa, (You've Gotta Play Straight With Me)*, Lillian Goodner & her Sawin' Trio, 1924

A film called *The Four Flusher* starring Marion Nelson and George Lewis played the American theatre circuit in 1928

Fracture your toupee

Go crazy

Fractured

1. Drunk
2. Real gone, blown away, excited

"I'm fractured! fractured! / That music fractures me..." FROM THE ROCK'N'ROLL RECORDING *FRACTURED*, BILL HALEY & THE COMETS, 1953

Frail

Dame, doll, sweetheart, mainsqueeze

Eric Howard wrote a story called *The Fifty Grand Frail* for the November 1938 issue of *Black Mask* magazine

"She was the roughest, toughest frail, But Minnie had a heart as big as a whale" FROM THE JAZZ RECORDING *MINNIE THE MOOCHER*, CAB CALLOWAY & HIS ORCHESTRA, 1931

See also the novels *The Wailing Frail*, Richard S. Prather, 1956, and *The Fatal Frail*, Dan Marlowe, 1960

Frantic

Excellent, wild, solid gone

Frantic threads

Hip clothes, sharp apparel

Freak

1. Jazzman who uses mutes, cups, buckets etc to achieve different sounds on his horn
2. A fan of something, an enthusiast eg: a hotrod freak

Free to run for President

Out of work, unemployed

Fresh fish special

Bad prison haircut given to recent arrivals the fresh fish

"What about your haircut? Do you want a good one or do you want a fresh fish special – they hack it up. A good one'll cost you three packets of cigarettes." FROM THE FILM *JAILHOUSE ROCK*, 1957

Fresh from the farm

Innocent, gullible, a pushover

Fried

1. Given the electric chair
2. Drunk or high on drugs

Fried, dyed and swept to the side

Having your hair done, the full treatment: having it straightened, coloured and set

Friend of boys on the loose

Good-time girl, of the kind that frequently seem to show up in Mickey Spillane novels

"She was a taxi-dancer, a night club entertainer, friend of boys on the loose and anything else you can mention where sex is concerned." FROM THE NOVEL *KISS ME, DEADLY*, MICKEY SPILLANE, 1953

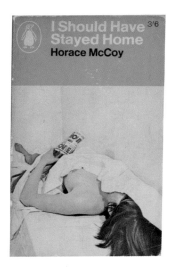

This goddam four-flushing town.

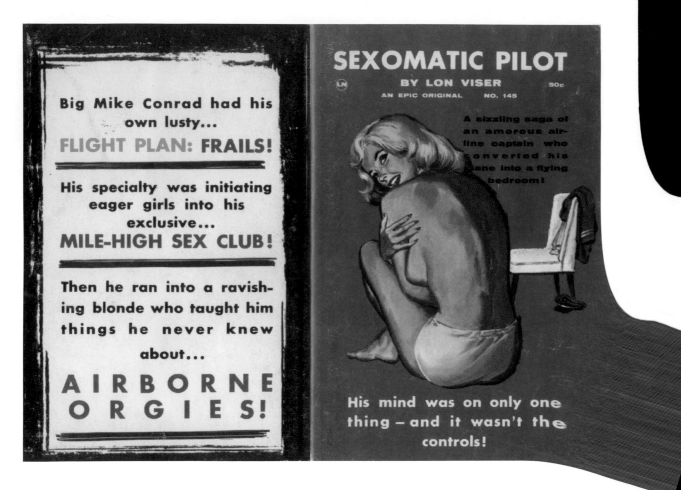

Flight plan: Frails – the one and only *Sexomatic Pilot*.

Friends in the bank

Money

"I've got a nice little joint at the Ambassador, with a built-in bar; I've got a swell bunch of telephone numbers and several thousand friends in the bank." FROM THE ULTIMATE HARDBOILED NOVEL *FAST ONE*, PAUL CAIN, 1933

Frill

Girl, dame similar to frail

"Half the guys in Hollywood was tryin' to marry this frill...the other half already had." FROM THE NOVEL *YOU CAN ALWAYS DUCK*, PETER CHEYNEY, 1943

From now until the fallout gets us

Forever

'... he's in, and he stays in, from now until the fallout gets us.' FROM THE NOVEL *RUN FOR DOOM*, HENRY KANE, 1960

From soup to nuts

Everything, the whole shooting match

Felix Arndt released a ragtime record in 1914 called *From Soup to Nuts*

Fronts

"Clothes, suits, money." FROM THE BOOKLET *THE JIVES OF DOCTOR HEPCAT*, LAVADA DURST, 1953

Fruitcake

Crazy person, weirdo

Fumigate your brains

Smoke a cigarette

Fungus among us

Punch-up, brawl, dispute, argument

"There was a fungus among us / There was a rumble in the jungle, / There was a static in the attic / A moaning an' a-groaning / A fungus among us" FROM THE ROCKABILLY RECORDING *THERE WAS A FUNGUS AMONG US*, TERRY NOLAND, 1958

Funky

Defined as "Smelly, obnoxious" in the autobiography *Really The Blues*, Mezz Mezzrow and Bernard Wolfe, 1946

Funky originally meant the smell of sex

Kenna's Hall, a New Orleans jazz hangout on Perdido Street, which was Buddy Bolden's regular gig venue in 1900, was known to everyone as Funky Butt Hall, or F.B. Hall for short

See also *Ain't Love Grand (Don't Get Funky)*, a jazz recording by John Hyman's Bayou Stompers, 1927

In 1950s jazz circles the word was quite common: for instance *Funk Junction* by King Pleasure and The Quincy Jones Band, 1954, or *Creme de Funk* by Phil Woods and Gene Quill, 1957. That same year, Gene Ammons' Allstars put out an album called *Funky*

Funnel

A heavy drinker

Funsville

A wild time, a gas, the most

"'Wow,' said Martin a couple of times. 'Funsville, huh?' I panted, working away.' FROM THE NOVEL *LUST, BE A LADY TONIGHT*, ROD GRAY, 1967

Fusebox

Head

Fuzz

Police, the heat, the city's finest

"'Why don't you bug off, I got work to do.' 'So have I.' 'Are you fuzz – from the police?' 'I'm a private detective.'" FROM THE NOVEL *THE WYCHERLY WOMAN*, ROSS MACDONALD, 1961

'Wow,' said Martin a couple of times. 'Funsville, huh?' I panted, working away.

Gg

G

One thousand dollars, a grand

G.I. Blues

Morbid fear of being in the army

"'He been reading in the paper where all the young men gonna be called to the Army,' Peaches said. 'He got the GI Blues.'" FROM THE NOVEL *IF HE HOLLERS LET HIM GO*, CHESTER HIMES, 1945

See also the jazz recording *Desperate G.I. Blues*, Cousin Jo with Pete Brown's Blue Blowers, 1946

G-man

Government agent, the Feds, the FBI

Dwight V. Babcock wrote a story for the January 1936 issue of *Black Mask* magazine called 'G-Man' Chuck Thompson

See the jazz recording G-Men, Cootie Williams & his Orchestra, 1941

Gabber

Radio commentator or D.J.

Gabfest

Argument, conversation

Gams

Legs

When Mildred Pierce hits the headlines, a press photographer yells at her in an effort to get a little more leg in the picture: *"The gams, the gams! Your face ain't news."* FROM THE NOVEL *MILDRED PIERCE*, JAMES M. CAIN, 1943

See also the short story *Case of the Gorgeous Gams* by John D MacDonald in the January 1952 British edition of *Black Mask*

Gargle

1. Drink
2. Sing

"...I don't mind if they hit it up a little – but no singing! They get paid a lot of dough – by me – to gargle their tonsils down on Second Avenue and I don't want they should throw around free samples." FROM THE NOVEL *THE SAVAGE SALOME*, CARTER BROWN, 1960

Gargle factory

Bar, alehouse

Gas

1. To talk

"He may have put it on for my benefit. If he did, he was a darn good actor. If he was just sitting there gassing with his sister, when he should have been taking it on the lam, he's just a hick. You pay your money and take your choice. Figure him either for a dumb guy with lots of beef and a sudden temper, or a bird who's as fast with his mind as he is with his fists, and that's plenty fast." FROM THE NOVEL *THE CASE OF THE CURIOUS BRIDE*, ERLE STANLEY GARDNER, 1934

2. Something really good

Skin magazine *Adam* issued a paperback of their *Swinging Party Humor* in the mid 60s, described on the cover as the "bawdiest, gassiest collection of rib-busting fun ever published"

The gams, the gams! Your face ain't news.

Gasser

Something or someone that takes your breath away

From the autobiography *Really The Blues*, Mezz Mezzrow and Bernard Wolf, 1946

"I copped a gig at Mintons and one night Alfred Lions came in to dig us. He said we gassed him, but we were too far out for the people." FROM THE AUTOBIOGRAPHY *I, PAID MY DUES*, BABS GONZALES, 1967

See the jazz recording *That's A Gasser*, Wingy Manone, 1945

"'Hey gasser, you lookin' for me?' 'Fall down, juvenile...'" FROM THE FILM *BEAT GIRL*, 1960

Gassing the slobs

Impressing your audience

Gassing your moss

Getting your hair straightened

Gat

Gun

"You know, you're the second guy I've met today that seems to think a gat in the hand means the world by the tail." HUMPHREY BOGART IN THE FILM VERSION OF *THE BIG SLEEP*, 1946

Gate

Hipster greeting for a fellow dude, short for *gate mouth*

In 1926 Columbia Records issued a record called *Gate Mouth* by The New Orleans Wanderers with an advert that read *"Gate Mouth* swings wide and handsome...this is the kind of mouth that stretches from ear to ear and buttons in the back."

Down Beat's 1939 Yearbook of Swing defines *gate* as a "Word of greeting between musicians."

See the jazz recording *Stomp It Out, Gate*, Rosetta Howard & The Harlem Hamfats, 1938

Jazz vocalist Martha Raye was known as Gate Mouth in the 1930s

Gator

In 1953 Doctor Hepcat defined the word *gator* as being interchangeable with the word cat

"The old jukebox was blowin' out the beat / The cats and the gators were shakin' their feet." FROM THE ROCKABILLY RECORDING *THREE ALLEY CATS*, ROY HALL, 1955

Geek

1. Lowest type of carnival sideshow performer, often featured in a cage, biting the heads off live chickens
2. Awkward person, weird looking

Geets

Money

See the vocal group recording *All My Geets Are Gone*, The Five Blazes, 1947

In *Carny Kill*, a 1966 crime novel by Robert Edmond Alter, the word is spelt slightly differently: "I got enough geetus that I don't have to live up here if I don't want."

Gentle up a drink

Add some more alcohol to the mixture, make it more potent

Germsville

A hospital

Get a boot

Get a blast, a charge, a jolt, get high

"If you don't get the fix, you begin to claw the damn walls down, but once you get it, once you get that quick boot,

New York DJ Murray The K aboard the USS Ling, getting down with fish in the hunt for underwater hipsters.

Martha " Gate Mouth '' Raye's kid brother is a plenty hot musician . . . Said Martha has plenty on the swing ball when she cuts the clowning . . . Did you notice how better she was in '' Double or Nothing? '' . . . Richard Himber conducting with one arm in a sling owing to abscess trouble . . . There's a new dark brown voice around called Maxine Williams that Broadway is inclining the ear to . . . She sings at the Onyx Club and no less a star than Ethel Waters can be seen there night after night putting the palms together for encore after encore . . . Don't say I didn't tell you now . . . Author Ben ('' Front Page '') Hecht and Louis Armstrong got together on a new jive song called '' Red Cap '' . . . You can latch on to the results on Decca . . . And that's that for the merry month of September . . . What did I think of the Farr-Louis fight? . . . A gorilla could have beaten them both !

Gate Mouth swings wide and handsome... the kind of mouth that stretches from ear to ear and buttons in the back.

Rockabilly daddy Charlie Feathers, hip to the tip, and ready to get with it.

and once you begin to nod, you're just normal, until it's time for the next fix." FROM THE NOVEL *SECOND ENDING*, EVAN HUNTER, 1952

Get a glow

Get drunk

Get both your eyes wet

Get drunk

Get fat

Get rich, become wealthy

Get hooked for your roll

Get robbed, have your wallet taken

Get in the wind

To leave

Get off the fence, Hortense

Make a decision, say what you mean

Get out of your fighting clothes and come to earth

Don't take offence so easily, calm down

From the novel *Little Caesar*, W.R. Burnett, 1929

Get my bread or I take your head

Babs Gonzales' time-honoured phrase designed to persuade club owners to pay his band at the end of the evening. From the autobiography *I, Paid My Dues*, Babs Gonzales, 1967

Get the blast put on you

Getting shot, having someone drill you a new navel

"Occasionally someone got the blast put on him – but only as a last resort." FROM THE NOVEL *LITTLE MEN, BIG WORLD*, W.R.BURNETT, 1951

Get well

"Become prosperous." FROM THE AUTO-BIOGRAPHY *WE CALLED IT MUSIC*, EDDIE CONDON WITH THOMAS SUGRUE, 1948

Get wise

Understand, learn something

Get with it

1. Be where it's at, make the scene, be aware

"We're gonna have a downbeat / We're gonna have a ball / Get 'em on their feet / Gonna rock 'em all / But we gotta get with it / 'Fore the night is gone" FROM THE ROCKABILLY RECORDING *GET WITH IT*, CHARLIE FEATHERS, 1956

See also the jazz recording *Git Wid It*, Paul Martell Orchestra, 1944

2. Have sex

"Let's get with it, please baby..." FROM THE NOVEL *GO, MAN, GO!*, EDWARD DE ROO, 1959

Get your hambone boiled

Have sex

"I'm going to Washington / To get my hambone boiled, / 'Cause these men in Atlanta / Bound to let my hambone spoil" FROM THE BLUES RECORDING *NOTHIN' BUT BLUES*, CLEO GIBSON & HER HOT THREE, 1929

Get your kicks

Have a wild time, become excited, enjoy yourself

"Get your kicks on Route 66" FROM THE R&B RECORDING *ROUTE 66*, ROY BROWN, 1946

Getting mighty crowded

Under pressure, tense

Getting the shakes

Becoming afraid, agitated, worked up

Gig

1. Musical engagement
2. Any job or occupation

Giggle water

Alcohol

Gimme some of that mud

I'd like a coffee

Gimme some skin

Hipster handshake

See the jazz recording *Give Me Some Skin*, Lionel Hampton & his Sextet, 1941

"Now gimme some skin, and ooze it out..." FROM THE FILM *THE WILD ONE*, 1954

Gimp

Lame, someone who walks with a limp

Eg: Moe The Gimp, 1920s mobster who married singer Ruth Etting

Damon Runyon wrote a story called *Madame La Gimp* for the October 1929 issue of *Cosmopolitan*

Ginhead

A drunk, an alcoholic

Ginmill

Bar, saloon, taproom, speakeasy

"One of the best Race releases is Okeh 8747, whereon the Hokum Boys discourse in haphazard and lighthearted fashion on the Folks Down South and the Gin Mill Blues..." PHONOGRAPH MONTHLY REVIEW, NEW YORK, FEBRUARY 1930

Ginmill cowboys

Bar regulars, bottle babies

Ginmill perfume

Alcohol breath

Gin palace

Bar

Give her a play

Make a pass, attempt to seduce

"Cherulli was giving her a play. Big, nice-lined moll. Came out of Harlem to the glitter spots. Makes it and spends it. She can wail." FROM THE NOVEL *GREEN ICE*, RAOUL WHITFIELD, 1930

Give him a permanent wave

Send someone to the electric chair

Give him the air

Tell him goodbye, finish the relationship, ignore him

"Dorothy Brock don't mean that to me. If it hadn't have been for me, she wouldn't have had a show to star in. She'd better not try to give me the air now." FROM THE FILM *42ND STREET*, 1933

Give him the heat

To shoot someone

From the novel *Dames Don't Care*, Peter Cheyney, 1937

Give him the works

Shoot him

"So you didn't try to make a deal before giving him the works?" FROM THE FILM *THE MALTESE FALCON*, 1941

Give it the gas

Step on it, get moving

"You can jump in my Ford and give her the gas / Pull out the throttle, don't give me no sass, / Take your foot, slap it on the floor, / When you get here we'll rock some more..." FROM THE ROCK'N'ROLL RECORDING *END OF THE ROAD*, JERRY LEE LEWIS, 1956

"A detective jumps in my car and says 'Follow that black sedan, it's full of

Jump in my Ford and give her the gas... Jerry Lee Lewis' debut single, 1956.

Give a listen. Power man! What a bomb!

thieves.' So I give her the gas..." **FROM THE FILM** *WHERE THE SIDEWALK ENDS*, 1950

Give it the go-by

Pass up the opportunity, decline

Give me an intro to this snake and I'll hitch up the reindeers for you

"Introduce me to this despicable person and I'll get the marijuana cigarettes for you to smoke." **FROM THE FILM** *HIGH SCHOOL CONFIDENTIAL*, 1958

Give out

1. Speak up, tell all, come across
2. Play music from the heart

Give the gate

Send someone away, fire them, send them packing

"I wondered whether there wasn't some safe way of getting Fay to give her the gate." ie: couldn't Fay find an excuse to sack her? **FROM THE NOVEL** *SAVAGE NIGHT*, JIM THOMPSON, 1953

Give the glad eye

Leer at, flirt with, look over

"'He doesn't look like a shamus,' he says. 'I've seen him trying to toss Ava the glad eye. He acts more like a hood on the loose.'" **FROM THE NOVEL** *KILLERS DON'T CARE*, ROD CALLAHAN, 1950

Give the hurry call

Telling someone to get here fast

Give the place the broom

Search the building

Glass or a funnel?

How would you like your drink?

Glasses

"She's a remarkable lady, she's seventy four years old and she don't need glasses. She drinks right out of the bottle, this cat..." DEAN MARTIN ONSTAGE AT *THE SANDS*, LAS VEGAS, FEBRUARY 1964

Glom

1. Acquire, obtain, steal

Dashiell Hammett in his novel *The Dain Curse*, 1928, spells it slightly differently: "Looks like him and another guy glaumed the ice..."

2. Observe, look at

Gobble pipe

Saxophone

Go, cat, go!

Exclamation of encouragement, hipster-style

"One for the money, / Two for the show, / Three to get ready / Now go, cat, go..." **FROM THE ROCKABILLY RECORDING** *BLUE SUEDE SHOES*, CARL PERKINS, 1956

See also the rockabilly recordings *Go Cat Go*, Bill Flagg, 1956, *Go Cats Go*, Texas Red Rhodes, 1958, and *Go Man Go, Get Gone*, Rex Zario, 1956

See also the novel *Go, Cat, Go!*, Edward de Roo, 1959

Go fry a hush-puppy

Get lost, vamoose

Go home and wrastle with that

That's what I can do – see if you can do better

Go into your dance, buddy

Alright, let's hear it, speak your piece

Go on a deep six holiday

To be buried, to die

Go pick yourself an orchid

Get lost, scram

Go press the bricks

Take a walk, get lost

Go put some more hair tonic on it

Stop worrying, shut up about it

"I just wanted to be sure." "Good. Then your mind's at rest. Go put some more hair tonic on it." FROM THE NOVEL *THE LONG SATURDAY NIGHT*, CHARLES WILLIAMS, 1962

Go the whole bundle

Take a chance

Go to a museum for your art lessons

Stop leering at me

Go to college

Serve a term in prison

God sure don't like ugly

You get what's coming to you

From the autobiography *Really The Blues*, Mezz Mezzrow with Bernard Wolfe, 1946

"I don't tell nothin' but the truth, because God don't like ugly." FROM THE NOVEL *A HEARSE OF ANOTHER COLOUR*, M.E.CHABER, 1959

God that's lousy stuff; I wisht I had a barrel

That's an excellent beverage, my compliments to the sommellier

Going commercial

Becoming a prostitute, selling it on the street

Going rotary

Blowing your top, losing it, going wild

Going steady with Mary Jane

Having a marijuana habit

Going to fist city

Going to have a fight

Going to hell in a handbasket

Turning bad, going to waste, going down the tubes

"Did that explain why I'm all mixed up? Why I'm a no-good bum...why I'm a delinquent slob going to hell in a handbasket?" FROM THE NOVEL *SAVAGE STREETS*, WILLIAM P. MCGIVERN, 1959

Going to slice city

Going to cut somebody up

Gold

Money

Gold digger

Someone looking for a rich partner

From the novel *Gentlemen Prefer Blondes*, Anita Loos, 1926

See also the film *Gold Diggers of 1933*, 1933

See also the novel *Gold Diggers*, Lois Bull, 1949, 'Meet the Come-On Girl with the Pay-Off Smile!'

Goldfish room

Police interrogation room, usually fitted with a one-way glass for observation purposes

Gone

Out of this world, superlative

"I have found the gonest little girl in the world and I am going straight to the Lion's Den with her tonight." FROM THE NOVEL *ON THE ROAD*, JACK KEROUAC, 1957

Busby Berkeley's dime-a-dance dames in search of the big boodle, 1933.

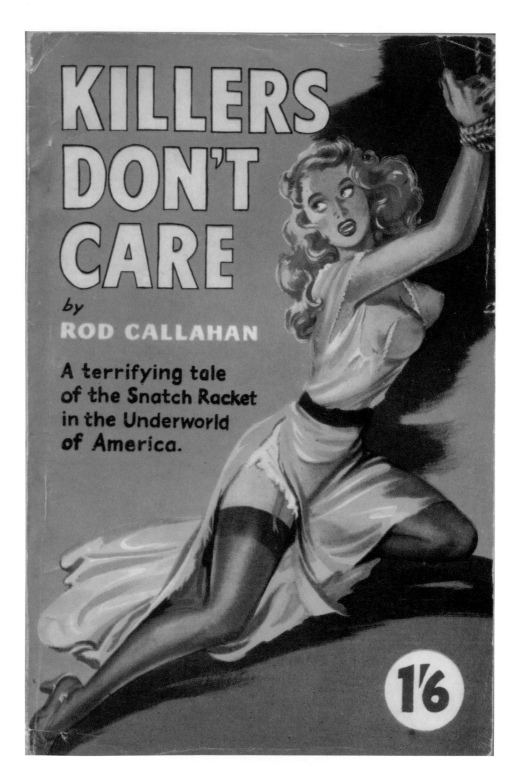

Two gorillas yank him to his feet and Merilli slugs him again… Rod Callahan's 'terrifying tale of Snatch Racket', 1950.

"Gee, Vince, when you sing it's really Gonesville." VINCE EVERETT (ELVIS PRESLEY) MAKES A BIG IMPRESSION ON A FAN, FROM THE FILM *JAILHOUSE ROCK*, 1957

Gone with the gin

Drunk, out of it, plastered

See the jazz recording *Gone With The Gin*, Hot Lips Page & his Band, 1940

Gong kicker

Opium addict

Good-gal

Girlfriend

"My good-gal loves me, / Everybody knows, / And she paid a hundred cash dollars, / Just bought me a suit of clothes." FROM THE COUNTRY RECORDING *BLUE YODEL NO. 9*, JIMMIE RODGERS, 1930

Good sauce from the gravy bowl

Alcohol

"We used to call booze 'sauce' and the gravy bowl was a cup." FROM THE AUTO- BIOGRAPHY OF *MINNIE THE MOOCHER AND ME*, CAB CALLOWAY, 1976

The goods

Good looking

"This dame is certainly the goods." FROM THE NOVEL *DAMES DON'T CARE*, PETER CHEYNEY, 1937

Goo-goo eyes and wolf whistles

Leering appreciation

Goof

Mistake, error

Satirising the writers of *Playboy* magazine in the early 1960s, the Reverend Roy Larsen came up with

the following: "Give us this day our daily Martinis – dry and smooth – and forgive us our goofs, even as we overlook the goofs of others..."

Goof syrup

Alcohol

"One thing more. Lay off that goof syrup. You've got to be in shape tomor- row." FROM THE NOVEL *SLEEP NO MORE*, SAM S TAYLOR, 1951

Goon from Saskatoon

An idiot, a square

Gorilla

Tough guy, mobster, strong-arm boy

"The two gorillas yank him to his feet and Merrill slugs him again. This time hard in the guts." FROM THE NOVEL *KILL- ERS DON'T CARE*, ROD CALLAHAN, 1950

Got it made in the shade

It's done, taken care of, I've got what I wanted

Gouge

1. Obtain

"I gouged twenty dollars out of her for expenses." PHILIP MARLOWE IN THE SHORT STORY *TROUBLE IS MY BUSINESS*, RAYMOND CHANDLER, 1939

2. Swindle or cheat

Grab a flop

Sit down, have a chair

Grab some air

Put your hands up, I have a gun

Grabbers

Hands

Grandstanding

Showing off

Author Peter Cheyney, delivering the goods.

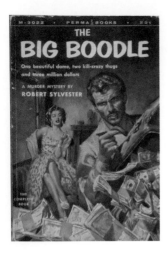

A whole heap of greenbacks – the biggest boodle in town.

Grape cat
Wino

Grass
Marijuana

Grasshopper
Marijuana smoker, weedhead

Graveyard shift
Night work

Gravy
1. Money

"Maybe the Guardians wanted the gravy, or the glory, or maybe Trammell was just too damned stinking to live – but they knocked their boy off." FROM THE NOVEL ALWAYS LEAVE 'EM DYING, RICHARD S. PRATHER, 1961

2. Sexual fluids

See *You Can Dip Your Bread In My Gravy, But You Can't Have None Of My Chops*, a shy, retiring blues recording from 1925 by Virginia Liston. The previous year she released a song called *You've Got The Right Key, But The Wrong Keyhole*

3. Something easy

eg: "It wasn't all gravy"

Graze on some grass
Smoke the weed

From the film *High School Confidential*, 1958

Grease
1. Protection money or a bribe
2. Sexual fluids

See the blues recordings *I Want Plenty Grease In My Frying Pan*, Margaret Carter, 1926; *Fat Greasy Baby*, Robert Peeples, 1930; *Take It Easy, Greasy*, Lil Johnson, 1936, and the rock'n'roll recording *Take It Easy, Greasy*, Peck Rowell, 1956

Grease joint
Cheap restaurant

Grease monkey
Mechanic

Grease your chops
Eat

Greased
1. Killed
2. Drunk

Greenbacks
Dollars

Greetings, gate, let's dissipate
The proper salutation when meeting a fellow hepster at the bar, according to Cab Calloway's Swingformation Bureau

Grift
A racket, swindle or other illegal means of making a few bucks, not usually involving violence

Grifter
Cheap crook, swindler

"By the time she was twenty-one in 1926, she definitely preferred Tenth Avenue to Fifth, grifters to bankers, and Hymie the Riveter to the Honourable Cecil Windown, who had asked her to marry him." FROM THE SHORT STORY FLY PAPER, DASHIELL HAMMETT, 1929

Probably the most famous use of the word came in 1963, when Jim Thompson published his novel *The Grifters*. The cover of the original edition explained the term thus: "The short-con men...the artists who take your cash and paint you foolish... are crooked as corkscrews...but they have their own laws. Law one is: keep moving. Law two... but these dark laws are revealed in this Regency original novel by Jim Thompson about a man who broke them..."

Grind

Striptease performance

Grind house

Striptease joint, or cheap cinema

Grinding

1. Slow, sexy dancing

"This is a real slow number playing, and one thing about China. She know how to do like a snake with them slow discs. I'm all for that, and we do some slow grinding." FROM THE SHORT STORY *THE RITES OF DEATH*, HAL ELLSON, 1956

2. Having sex

In his 1957 novel *A Walk On The Wild Side*, two of Nelson Algren's characters flirt with each other by discussing coffee grinding in a suggestive manner: "'It's always best do you grind your own, miss. For that way it's much fresher.' 'So you say. But what good is fresh if there ain't enough to satisfy? Mister, if you talkin' 'bout some little old scrawny-size pot I ain't interested. What I needs is a great big pot, enough for both morning and night.' 'So long as it make good cawfee, miss, size don't scarcely matter...'"

"Bought me a coffee grinder, / The best that I could find, / Bought me a coffee grinder, / The best that I could find, / Lord he can grind my coffee / Cause he has a brand new grind." FROM THE BLUES RECORDING *EMPTY BED BLUES PART 1.*, BESSIE SMITH, 1928

See also the blues recordings *Ain't Got Nobody to Grind My Coffee, (b/w Take Your Finger Off It)*, Mary Stafford, 1926; *Organ Grinder Blues*, Victoria Spivey, 1928; *My Georgia Grind*, Lucille Bogan, 1930; *Steady Grindin'*, James "Stump" Johnson, 1933

Grinding mill

1. Machine gun on tripod

"Tell him to set up his mill and start grinding." FROM THE NOVEL *RED HARVEST*, DASHIELL HAMMETT, 1950

2. Vagina

"She grinds my meal in the morning, / And she grinds it late at night, / She grinds my meal in the morning, / And she grinds it late at night, / She grinds it in a way / Suit any man's appetite." FROM THE BLUES RECORDING *GRINDING MILL*, JOHNNY TEMPLE, 1939

Groan box

Accordian

Groghound

Drunkard, alcoholic

Groove a tune

Cut a record, lay down some tracks, wax a platter

"We grooved a couple of tunes in New York and caught a wire at a nitery here in Chicago." ie: we recorded a couple of songs and then got a contract to broadcast from a nightclub. FROM THE NOVEL *THE LADY IN THE MORGUE*, JONATHAN LATIMER, 1936

Groover

Someone righteous, hep, solid, on the square

Groovy

"Really good, in the groove, enjoyable." FROM THE AUTOBIOGRAPHY *REALLY*

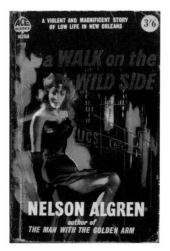

'It's always best do you grind your own, miss. For that way it's much fresher.' 'So you say. But what good is fresh if there ain't enough to satisfy? Mister, if you talkin' 'bout some little old scrawny-size pot I ain't interested. What I needs is a great big pot, enough for both morning and night.' 'So long as it make good cawfee, miss, size don't scarcely matter...' Nelson Algren's characters demonstrating the real meaning of the word 'grinding', 1957.

THE BLUES, MEZZ MEZZROW WITH BERNARD WOLFE, 1946

"'I decided at the last moment that I couldn't live without you.' 'You sound groovy...'" FROM THE NOVEL *IF HE HOLLERS LET HIM GO* CHESTER HIMES, 1945

"It's the Calloway Boogie, / Keeps you groovy / 24 hours a day" FROM THE JAZZ RECORDING *THE CALLOWAY BOOGIE*, CAB CALLOWAY & HIS ORCHESTRA, 1947

See also the jazz recordings *Boy, It's Solid Groovy*, Jimmy Smith & his Sepians, 1941, and *Groovy Like A Movie – Let's Get Groovy*, Bonnie Davis & the Piccadilly Pipers, 1944 (The B-side was called *I Don't Stand For That Jive*.)

See also the country recording *Groovie Boogie Woogie Boy*, Webb Pierce, 1949

Ground smashers

Shoes or feet

Gumshoe

1. Detective, private eye
2. To creep around, look for clues

Gunsel

Originally a term for a young person, punk, eventually it was used as a general word for a tough-guy or gunman

"Let's give them the gunsel. He actually did shoot Thursby and Jacobi, didn't he? Anyway, he's made to order for the part, look at him. Let's give him to them." HUMPHREY BOGART GIVING ELISHA COOK JNR A HARD TIME, FROM THE FILM *THE MALTESE FALCON*, 1941

Gut bucket

Lowdown dirty jazz. Earthy playing, custom-made for a slow grind

See the jazz recording *Gut Bucket Blues*, Louis Armstrong's Hot Five, 1926

Gut-ripper

Knife, shiv

"Double-edged double-jointed spring-blade cuts-all genuine Filipino twisty-handled all-American gut-ripper." FROM THE SHORT STORY COLLECTION *THE NEON WILDERNESS*, NELSON ALGREN, 1947

Gut scraper

Violinist

Guzzle shop

Bar, speakeasy

The Maltese Falcon – no place for a gunsel.

Hack

Automobile

Hack-jockey

Taxi driver

"You're a swell driver, Jakie. You should have stayed in the hack racket back in Brooklyn." FROM THE NOVEL *FAST ONE*, PAUL CAIN, 1933

Haemophilia of the larynx

Talkative, a blabbermouth

Half a yard

Fifty dollars

Half-hipped

Not very enlightened or sophisticated

From the autobiography *Really The Blues*, Mezz Mezzrow with Bernard Wolfe, 1946

Half-stiffed

Tipsy, under the influence

Hand in your dinner pail

Die

"He gives a big howl and hands in his dinner pail." FROM THE NOVEL *DAMES DON'T CARE*, PETER CHEYNEY, 1937

Hand it to them

1. Shoot at someone
2. Hit someone

"'Do you think it was the nut who socked you?' she asked. 'I couldn't see anything.' 'Why didn't you hand him one?' asked Burton Coffin. 'You could have nailed him as he ran out.' 'He nailed me first,' I said." FROM THE NOVEL *THE SEARCH FOR MY GREAT-UNCLE'S HEAD*, JONATHAN LATIMER, 1937

Hand out a line

Lie, bullshit

Hang out your hearing flap

Listen carefully

Hang your ears out in the breeze

Listen out for any news or gossip

"Drop by here about seven-thirty, eight o'clock. I'll show you some life you ain't seen before, and we can incidentally hang our ears out in the breeze." FROM THE NOVEL *THE TIGER AMONG US*, LEIGH BRACKETT, 1957

Hangin' it in

Having sex

A phrase very popular with Jerry Lee Lewis

Hanging paper

Passing forged cheques

Hangout

Pad, favourite spot, neighbourhood

See the short story *Hell is My Hangout* by W T Ballard in the September 1942 issue of *Ten Detective Aces*

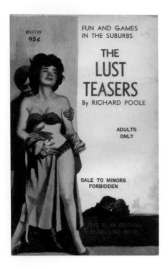

Harvesting a crop of lettuce was all in a days work for *The Lust Teasers*.

Hanky panky

1. Sex
2. A whore

"Helen wasn't no hanky-panky." FROM THE NOVEL *RED HARVEST*, DASHIELL HAMMETT, 1929

Hard-boiled

Tough, streetwise

"I like smooth shiny girls, hard-boiled and loaded with sin." PHILIP MARLOWE IN THE NOVEL *FAREWELL, MY LOVELY*, RAYMOND CHANDLER, 1940

"My God! For a fat, middle-aged, hard-boiled pig-headed guy, you've got the vaguest way of doing things I ever heard of..." PRAISE FOR THE CONTINENTAL OP, FROM THE NOVEL *RED HARVEST*, DASHIELL HAMMETT, 1929

Hulbert Footner wrote a story called *Hard Boiled* for the December 5 1925 issue of *Detective Story* magazine

A record by Lee Barth called *Onie Gagen* was described by a reviewer in August 1930 as "a comedy monologue in hard-boiled, tough-guy manner"

In 1946, a collection of stories from *Black Mask Magazine* was published under the title *The Hard-Boiled Omnibus*. It included stories by Dashiell Hammett, Raymond Chandler, Paul Cain, Raoul Whitfield and eleven other writers

See also the novels *The Hard-Boiled Blonde*, Glenn Watkins, 1946, *The Hard-Boiled Virgin*, Jack Woodford, 1947, *Hard-Boiled Mistress*, E T Keating, 1948, *Flash Casey, Hard-Boiled Detective*, George Harmon Coxe, 1948, and *Hard-Boiled*, Harmon Bellamy, 1950

Harlem sunset

Bloodletting, knife wounds

Harvest a crop of lettuce

Earn some money, score some of the long green

"Russ fidgeted.. He didn't like doing this sort of thing. It wasn't really what he was cut out for. But the chance to harvest himself a crop of lettuce had been too good to pass by. All he had to do to reassure himself was to think how long it would have taken him to make twenty-five thousand by working on some housing project, or breaking his back on a road-building job. Hell, he would never have been able to get that much loot together at one time by working for it." FROM THE NOVEL *THE LUST TEASERS*, RICHARD POOLE, N.D. (C.1964)

Hash

Food

Hash house

Cheap eating establishment, where standards are not exactly top-of-the-range

"'If it's that kind of job, I hoped you picked a five dollar house. You're too young for the two-dollar trade, and personally I wouldn't like sailors.' 'I'm a waitress in a hash-house.' 'It rhymes up the same way.'" FROM THE NOVEL *MILDRED PIERCE*, JAMES M.CAIN, 1943

"I'm sleeping in flophouses, eating in hash joints, mooching for dimes." FROM THE NOVEL *MURDER ON MONDAY*, ROBERT PATRICK WILMOT, 1952

I & M Ottenheimer published a pulp book of *Hash-House Jokes* in Baltimore in 1915

Hash-slinger

A cook, especially in a fast food joint

See the jazz recording *Slingin' Hash*, Zoot Simms, 1950

Hatchet man

Assassin, strong-arm guy

Have a firework

Would you care for a cigarette?

Have all your buttons on

To be smart, wise, firing on all cylinders

"He was an elderly guy, silver-haired and silver-tongued, but I could see at once he had all his buttons on. He had the kinda penetrating blue eyes that are the windows of a shrewd, alert brain." FROM THE NOVEL *NO DICE, SISTER!*, BART CARSON, N.D. (EARLY 1950s)

Have many coconuts

To be rich, rolling in money

Have one on the city

Drink some water

Have you seen my hat?

"Have you seen my girl, chick, broad, rib?" FROM THE ARTICLE *THE ARGOT OF JAZZ* BY ELLIOTT HORNE, *NEW YORK SUNDAY TIMES*, 1957

Have yourself a time

Go wild, push the boat out

Having your teeth pulled

Being disarmed

"I pulled his teeth, boss. He was carrying a .32 in the shoulder holster." FROM THE NOVEL *A HEARSE OF ANOTHER COLOUR*, M.E. CHABER, 1959

Hay

1. Marijuana

See the novel *It Ain't Hay*, David Dodge, 1946

2. Bed

"I was nuts about her then. Who wouldn't be? All the boys were anxious to nudge her into the hay." FROM THE NOVEL *DEATH IS CONFIDENTIAL*, LAWRENCE LARIAR, 1959

Hay parlour

Bedroom

He ain't worth the powder it'd take to blow his nose

I'm not impressed with him

He can tell you the pitch of a belch

He's a natural musician

"His folks wanted him to be a concert pianist. And has that kid got an ear! He can tell you the pitch of a belch!" HOAGY CARMICHAEL RECALLS HIS FRIEND GEORGE RECOMMENDING THE YOUNG BIX BEIDERBECKE, QUOTED IN *THE ORAL HISTORY HEAR ME TALKIN' TO YA – THE STORY OF JAZZ BY THE MEN WHO MADE IT*, NAT SHAPIRO AND NAT HENTOFF, EDS., 1955

He could stand one more greasing, he's not slick enough

He's not very impressive. A poor dresser or performer

He cut one that cooled all the boys

He played a solo that knocked out everyone in the band

He got it with the rats and mice

He won it in a crap game

See the novel *The Dain Curse*, Dashiell Hammett, 1928

He ought to have his wardrobe cleaned and burned

He dresses like a square

He'd put clothes on a fish

He's a smooth talker, a con artist, the kind that would sell you Christmas cards in June

All the boys were anxious to nudge her into the hay.

'All right dad, shed the heater' – Raymond Chandler talks that talk.

He's done more time than a clock

He's a regular jailbird, a career criminal

He's just like the man in the casket – dead in there

He's cool, he's a hepcat

He's so sharp he's bleeding

That is one well dressed dude

From the autobiography *I, Paid My Dues*, Babs Gonzales, 1967

He sure did speak

He played well

Head in a sling

Troubled, weighed down with worry

"I've been walking around with my head in a sling for years." FROM THE FILM *REBEL WITHOUT A CAUSE*, 1955

Head knock

The boss, the person in charge

Headache stick

Police baton

Headlights

Breasts

Headshrinker

Psychiatrist

Policeman: *"Do you know if the boy ever talked to a psychiatrist?"* Sal Mineo: *"You mean a headshrinker?"* FROM THE FILM *REBEL WITHOUT A CAUSE*, 1955

Heap

Automobile

eg: *"So I hopped in the heap and tooled it downtown."*

A heap of jack

Lots of money

Heaped to the gills

High on drugs

Heat

1. The law

"Somebody called the heat / They threw us all in jail. / We had a lot of rhythm / Nobody had their bail. / The judge gave us a hearing, / When he heard us play, / He shouted for an encore / In a real gone way, / He hollered 'Wail, man wail!'" FROM THE ROCKABILLY RECORDING *WAIL, MAN, WAIL*, KIP TYLER & THE FLIPS, 1957

2. Weapons

Heat-making gown

Low-cut dress

Heater

Gun

"All right dad, shed the heater..." FROM THE SHORT STORY *GOLDFISH*, RAYMOND CHANDLER, *BLACK MASK MAGAZINE*, JUNE 1936

Heavy sugar

A large amount of money

Heebie-jeebies

Fear, apprehension, the shakes

"Keep it up and you're going to have the heebie-jeebies for fair, a nervous breakdown." FROM THE NOVEL *RED HARVEST*, DASHIELL HAMMETT, 1929

See the jazz recording *Heebie Jeebies*, Louis Armstrong & his Hot Five, Feb 1926

Ethel Waters released a blues called *Heebie Jeebies* in 1926, for which the Columbia Records adverts read: "You all know the 'heebie jeebies'.

Perhaps you've had them before. You just can't keep still..."

When B.B.King was still a DJ in the early 1950s, he ran a radio show in Memphis called *Heebie Jeebies*

Heel

A louse, a punk, a bum

"Which one of you heels scratched the guy at West Cimmaron last night?" FROM THE SHORT STORY *FINGER MAN*, RAYMOND CHANDLER, *BLACK MASK MAGAZINE*, OCTOBER 1934

See also the novels *The Cuban Heel*, Steve Harragan, 1953, "A torrid tale of Cuban Intrigue, Cuban Cuties and Cuban Sin" and *So I'm a Heel*, Mike Heller, 1957 "Why shouldn't I be a wise guy in a world full of suckers."

Heel-beater

Dancer

Heel the joint

Leave without paying

Heeled

Packing a gun

Heist

A robbery or theft

Hell bent

Determined

Hen pen

Female prison

Hep

1. Hip, cool, righteous, in the know

"They said they were going to a real hep party, and that kind of party I'm still scared of, mister. I don't go to them." ie: A drug party. FROM THE NOVEL *VIOLENT NIGHT*, WHIT HARRISON, 1952

"Bill's heart pounded. Something was up. Even Madge, young as she was, was hep." FROM THE NOVEL *BRAIN GUY*, BENJAMIN APPEL, 1934

"'You're a thriller,' she told him. 'Where'd you get so hep?'" FROM THE NOVEL *GO, MAN GO!*, EDWARD DE ROO, 1959

Mitchell's Jazz Kings released a song called *Hep* in 1922, Cab Calloway & his Orchestra made a jazz record called *Hep Hep (The Jumping Jive)* in 1939, and even Fred Astaire put out a record in 1940 called *Dig It (I Ain't Hep To That Step, But I'll Dig It)* ie: I haven't seen that dance before, but I'll soon get the hang of it

The rockabilly recording *Homicide* by Myron Lee & The Caddies was released in 1958 by a St. Paul, Minnesota label called Hep

2. To inform someone, to put them wise

The word was being used in this sense by street gangs in the early years of the 20th century, as reported in the book *Apaches of New York*, A H Lewis, 1912

See the jazz recording *We The Cats Shall Hep Ya*, Cab Calloway and his Orchestra, 1944

Hepcat

One who is hep, totally uncubistic

Down Beat's 1939 Yearbook of Swing defined a *hepcat* as "1.A swing devotee who is 'hep' or alert to the most authoritative information, or 2. A swing musician."

Lavada Durst, a 1950s DJ with station KVET, Austin, Texas, broadcast under the name of Dr. Hepcat. He published a slang booklet in 1953 entitled *The Jives of Dr. Hepcat*

Lawrence Lariar describes a nightclub on Fifty Second Street in New

One who is well schooled in the hep world... Texas DJ Lavada Durst (aka Dr Hepcat) on the cover of his 1953 booklet of jive.

HEP

North Star
Publishing BMI

HEP 2146
JO8W-0289

HOMICIDE
(Myron Wachendorf)

MYRON LEE
and the Caddies

HEP RECORDS, SAINT PAUL, MINNESOTA

Rockabilly outfit Myron Lee & the Caddies were brought to you in 1958 by a real Hep label.

York in his 1959 novel, *Death Is Confidential*: "Hardly enough room to swing a hep-cat in. The last time I counted the tables, there were just two dozen. The take can't be much for Ziggi, unless he's selling reefers on the side."

"When we go dancin' on a Saturday night / She says 'real gone!' and she holds me tight, / She's always happy when she hears a band / She says 'dig this!' and she holds my hand, / I don't know what she's sayin' to me half the time / But I love that hepcat baby of mine." FROM THE COUNTRY RECORDING *HEPCAT BABY*, EDDY ARNOLD, 1954

See the jazz recording *Hep Cat Love Song*, Cab Calloway & his Orchestra, 1941, and also the rockabilly recording *Hep Cat*, Larry Terry, 1961, and the rock'n'roll recording *Rock'n'Roll Hep Cat*, The Rock-A-Tunes, 1959

On the other hand, Jack, try your hardest to avoid a slab of wax laid down by Tommy Sands in 1957 which shot itself square between the lamps with the title *Hep Dee Hootie (Cutie Wootie)*

Here's how

A toast when drinking

Here's your hat, what's your hurry?

Get lost, go away

Hey-hey

1. Sex
2. A disturbance, a fuss
3. Cheers, good health, down the hatch

Hi-pockets

Nickname for a tall guy (The corresponding nickname for someone short is Pee Wee.)

In 1953, country music DJ Hi-Pockets Duncan from KDAV Lubbock, Texas, gave Buddy Holly his first radio exposure, and briefly became the singer's first manager

Hick

Country bumpkin, unsophisticated

"Whadda you hicks do around here for kicks?" FROM THE FILM *THE WILD ONE*, 1954

Hide

A set of drums

High, fly and too wet to dry

Something, or someone, very good, pleasing

High-hat

Stuck up, putting on airs

"Look here gal don't you high-hat me / I ain't forgot what you used to be / When you didn't have nothin' / That was plain to see, / Don't get above your raisin' / Stay down to earth with me." FROM THE BLUEGRASS RECORDING *DON'T GET ABOVE YOUR RAISIN'*, LESTER FLATT, EARL SCRUGGS & THE FOGGY MOUNTAIN BOYS, 1951

High roller

Ostentatious or heavy gambler

High tone

Fashionable, expensive

High sign

Signal, significant gesture, ok, warning

"One of his yegg men sat by the doors has seen me and has given his boss the high sign." FROM THE NOVEL *KILLERS DON'T CARE*, ROD CALLAHAN, 1950

High-tail it

Run away, leave in a hurry

Whadda you hicks do around here for kicks?

High, wide and handsome

Doing well, everything A-ok

"Jake married her after he left here and moved to New York – after he was riding high, wide and handsome. It must be quite a comedown for her, living like she has to now." FROM THE NOVEL *SAVAGE NIGHT*, JIM THOMPSON, 1953

See the country recording *High, Wide and Handsome*, Tex Ritter, 1935

Highball

Spirits and a mixer – a tall shot of booze

See virtually every US crime novel written between 1930 and 1960, or, if you're hipped on a specific example, try the short story *The Devil's Highball* by Madeleine Sharps Buchanan in the May 10 1930 issue of *Detective Fiction Weekly*

Hills and dales

Figure

"She tightened her robe around her, the one that was doing such a poor job hiding her hills and dales." FROM THE NOVEL *THE CRAZY MIXED-UP CORPSE*, MIKE AVALLONE, 1957

Himalayas

Chest

"Baby, you got the Himalayas knocked into a sombrero." FROM THE NOVEL *GRIN AND DARE IT*, RICKY DRAYTON, 1953, which concludes in the following vein: *"She had the kind of curves to make 3D seem flat; however drunk she got she could never have fallen flat on her face; she couldn't have stood against a wall without opening a window."*

Hincty

Paranoid, nervous

Hip

In the know, worldly wise, clever, enlightened, sophisticated

See the jazz recordings *Hip! Hip!*, Jack Stillman's Orioles, 1925; *Hip Chic*, Duke Ellington & his Famous Orchestra, 1938; *Stop Pretending (So Hip You See)*, Buddy Johnson & his Band, 1939; and the blues recording *You Done Got Hip*, Roosevelt Sykes, 1942

See also the novel *Hip Chick*, Joan Ellis, 1966

"One is Hip or one is Square (the alternative which each new generation coming into American life is beginning to feel), one is a rebel or one conforms, one is a frontiersman in the Wild West of American night life, or else a Square cell, trapped in the totalitarian tissues of American society, doomed willy-nilly to conform if one is to succeed." FROM *THE WHITE NEGRO: SUPERFICIAL REFLECTIONS ON THE HIPSTER*, NORMAN MAILER, 1957

Hip to the tip

The pinnacle of hipness, a righteous dude

Hip your ship

To inform, to tell you something

Hipped

To understand, to possess knowledge, to be convinced of something

"You're still hipped on Medley as a killer? Hell, Frank, it doesn't make sense." FROM THE NOVEL *THE LENIENT BEAST*, FREDRIC BROWN, 1957

Hippy

"Generic for a character who is supercool, overblasé, so far out that he appears to be asleep when he's digging something the most." FROM THE ARTICLE *THE ARGOT OF JAZZ* BY ELLIOTT HORNE, *NEW YORK SUNDAY TIMES*, 1957

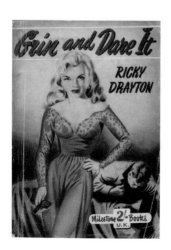

Baby, you got the Himalayas knocked into a sombrero.

Ethel Boileau wrote a novel called *Hippy Buchan* in 1925, about a jazz-era romeo who becomes heir to a dukedom: "The Gods were both kind and unkind to Hippy. They gave him the faculty of visioning others' minds and motives. For a while he had a lot of fun, transcribed without dilution in many breezy pages."

Hipster

"*Someone who's in the know, grasps everything, is alert.*" FROM THE AUTOBIOGRAPHY *REALLY THE BLUES*, MEZZ MEZZROW AND BERNARD WOLFE, 1946

"*One who is well schooled in the hep world.*" FROM THE BOOKLET *THE JIVES OF DOCTOR HEPCAT*, LAVADA DURST, 1953

Bo Diddley's first band, in the late 1940s, was called Ellas McDaniel & the Hipsters

Allen Ginsberg's poem *Howl*, 1956, talked of "angelheaded hipsters burning for the ancient heavenly connection to the starry dynamo in the machinery of night."

In 1957, Norman Mailer published an essay called *The White Negro: Superficial Reflections on the Hipster*, included in his 1959 collection *Advertisements for Myself*

Down Beat columnist Ira Gitler wrote this definition circa 1959: "The hipster is a groovy guy / colourful and laughable / always fallin' by / The hippy is overdone / over-hip and he ain't no fun / But one who is hip / now he's the man / he's always cool / and never a flip / I'm wise to you cats / you'll skip one and two / focus on three / and nod, 'That's me.'"

See also the novel *Sin Hipster*, Don Holliday, c. 1964, advertised with the immortal words: "Life was an orgy for these passion bums!"

Hit

Underworld contract killing

Hit man

Assassin

Hit the bottle high

Get drunk

"*Before you start hittin' that bottle over there, I want to do you a small favour, if you'll let me.*" FROM THE NOVEL *THE MAN WITH THE GOLDEN ARM*, NELSON ALGREN, 1949

See the jazz recordings *Hittin' The Bottle*, Frankie Trumbauer, 1930, and *Hittin' The Bottle Stomp*, Mississippi Jook Band, 1936

Hit the bricks

1. Leave
2. Walk the streets

Hit the hay

1. Go to sleep

"*Alright, precious, you'd better hit the hay. You sound all-in.*" FROM THE FILM *THE MALTESE FALCON*, 1941

2. Smoke marijuana

Hit the skids

To be down on your luck, busted and generally behind the eight ball

Hit the wall

To break out of prison

Hitched up

1. One night stand
2. Married

"*I went out last night, / An' I got hitched up...*" FROM THE ROCKABILLY RECORDING *SHE SAID*, HASIL ADKINS, 1964

Hittin' the hop

On drugs

Harry 'The Hipster' Gibson climbing sideways up the north face of a piano, 1947.

Hittin' the jug

Serious drinking

"Well out to the dance hall / And cut a little rug, / Oh we're runnin' like wildfire, / An' a hittin' that jug..." FROM THE ROCKABILLY RECORDING *WE WANNA BOOGIE*, SONNY BURGESS & THE PACERS, 1956

Hobo jungle

Tramp settlement or camp

Hoister

Pickpocket

Hold onto your chair and don't step on no snakes

Listen up, get ready, brace yourself

Hole in the wall

Low class joint, cheap bar

"No windows, no doors, / Just a hole in the wall..." FROM THE BOOGIE RECORDING *CHICKEN SHACK BOOGIE*, AMOS MILBURN, 1946

Holed up

In hiding

Holding

In possession of drugs

Holding down a package

Intoxicated, plastered, several drinks past the point of no return

"I was holding down a lovely package." COMMENTS DASHIELL HAMMETT'S CONTINENTAL OP IN THE 1924 STORY *THE GOLDEN HORSESHOE*

Holding on

"Just remember the words of the great Joe E. Lewis. He said 'You're not drunk if you can lay on the floor without holdin' on.'" DEAN MARTIN ONSTAGE AT *THE SANDS*, LAS VEGAS, FEBRUARY 1964

Holler

Yell

"I wiggled and I hollered, / Screamed and I cried, / Don't shoot me baby I'm too young to die..." FROM THE ROCKABILLY RECORDING *DON'T SHOOT ME BABY*, BILL BOWEN & THE ROCKETS, 1956

Honey

Good looking woman, a real doll

Honky tonk

Bar, juke joint, spit and sawdust club

"The honk-a-tonk last night was well attended by ball-heads, bachelors and leading citizens." FROM *THE DAILY ARDMORITE*, ARDMORE, OKLAHOMA, FEBRUARY 24TH 1891 QUOTED BY NICK TOSCHES IN *THE BLACKWELL GUIDE TO RECORDED COUNTRY MUSIC*

One of the most popular songs on the Mississippi riverboats during the First World War – particularly on boats such as the J.S. and the Bald Eagle, where the bands were run by legendary bandleader Fate Marable – was a number called *Honky Tonky Town*

The Emerson Military Band released the *Honky Tonk Rag* in 1917, and Bennie Moten's Kansas City Orchestra put out a record in 1925 called *Sister Honky Honk*

See also the country recordings *Honky Tonk Blues*, Al Dexter, 1936 and *I'm Going To Get Me A Honky Tonky Baby*, Buddy Jones, 1941, and the rockabilly recording *Honky Tonk Stomp*, Hal Payne, 1958

"I'm a honky tonk man, / And I can't seem to stop. / I love to give the girls a whirl / To the music of that old jukebox..." FROM THE ROCKABILLY RECORDING *HONKY TONK MAN*, JOHNNY HORTON, 1956

Sophie Tucker starred in a film called *Honky Tonk* for Warner Brothers in 1929

The undisputed king of suave, Dean Martin: *'You're not drunk if you can lay on the floor without holdin' on'.*

See also the novel *They Don't Dance Much*, James Ross, 1940, billed as "The Hard-Boiled Story of a Roadside Honky-Tonk"

Honky tonk angel

Good-time girl

"Let them honkytonkin' angels / Be the girls I'll never love, / Let 'em know it's you I'm cravin', / It's you I'm thinkin' of..." FROM THE COUNTRY RECORDING *LET THE JUKEBOX KEEP ON PLAYING*, CARL PERKINS, 1955

Honky tonk hotel

A low class flophouse

"It's funny, anyway. That girl had class, yet she was living in that honky tonk hotel." FROM THE NOVEL *THE LADY IN THE MORGUE*, JONATHAN LATIMER, 1936

Hooch

Alcohol

"Keep away from bootleg hooch / When you're on a spree, / Take good care of yourself / You belong to me." FROM THE JAZZ RECORDING *BUTTON UP YOUR OVERCOAT*, RUTH ETTING, 1929

Hooch hound

Drunkard

Hoochie-coocher

Striptease artist

"Folks now here's the story / 'Bout Minnie The Moocher / She was a red-hot / Hoochie-coocher." FROM THE JAZZ RECORDING *MINNIE THE MOOCHER*, CAB CALLOWAY & HIS ORCHESTRA, 1931

See also the blues recording *Hoochy Coochy Blues*, Lemuel Fowler, 1926, and the rockabilly recording *Hootchie Coochie Gal*, James Mask & His Impalas, 1959

Hood

Hoodlum, mobster, tough-guy

"The crime climate had changed greatly since the wild and lunatic Twenties. The big hoods were now businessmen and owned hotels and summer resorts and distilleries." FROM THE NOVEL *LITTLE MEN, BIG WORLD*, W.R. BURNETT, 1951

See also the novels *The Hoods Take Over*, Ovid Demaris, 1957, and *The Young Hoods*, Joe Castro, 1959, "A pounding novel of the gangs that thrive on dames and dope – and spread the bitter poison of delinquency."

Hoodlum

See Hood.

See the jazz recording *March of the Hoodlums*, Eddie Lang, 1930

See also the novel *The Hoodlums*, John Eagle, 1953 'These are the Hoodlums... and violence is their business.'

See also the R&B recording *Hoodlum Joe*, Lee Dorsey, 1963

Hooey

Lies, rubbish

Hoof

1. Feet
2. Dance

Hoofery

Dancehall

Hoofing it

1. Walking
2. Dancing

Hooked through the bag and back again

Totally addicted to drugs

"Helen know the score all right. Helen was hooked through the bag and back again." FROM THE NOVEL *SECOND ENDING*, EVAN HUNTER, 1952

Vice Squad magazine telling it like it is – from back in the days when Mickey Cohen was the mainbrain wise guy in L.A., and 'hood' meant something other than your home turf.

The Killer getting ready to hop in his kemp and take off for the casbah, 1958.

Dorothy Baker's 1939 jazz novel *Young Man With A Horn*, hit the big screen in 1950. In England, the distributors were so worried by the unintentional double-entendre in the title that they released it as *Young Man Of Music*.

Hooks

Hands, fingers

Hoosegow

Prison

"Trundle him off to the hoosegow – he'd look nice in a pair of bracelets." WALDO LYDECKER IN THE FILM *LAURA*, 1944

Hop

1. Drugs

"... some were habitual drunkards and some were dope fiends as follows: opium, heroin, cocaine, laudanum, morphine, et cetera. I was personally sent to Chinatown many times with a sealed note and a small amount of money and would bring back several cards of hop. There was no slipping and dodging. All you had to do was walk in to be served." JELLY ROLL MORTON REMEMBERING HOW EASY IT WAS TO MAKE A CONNECTION IN 1902 IN NEW ORLEANS, QUOTED IN *THE ORAL HISTORY HEAR ME TALKIN' TO YA – THE STORY OF JAZZ BY THE MEN WHO MADE IT*, NAT SHAPIRO AND NAT HENTOFF, EDS., 1955

2. A dance party

"You know I got my hot-rod down the shop / Gotta meet my baby at the Teen Town hop." FROM THE R&B JUMP RECORDING *TEEN TOWN HOP*, THE PHILHARMONICS, 1961

See the jazz recording *Wednesday Night Hop*, Andy Kirk & his Twelve Clouds Of Joy, 1937, the same outfit who cut a tune called *What's Your Story, Morning Glory?* in 1938

See also the vocal group recording *At The Hop*, Danny & The Juniors, 1957, and the rockabilly recording *Granny Tops 'Em At The Hop*, Bob Grady, 1959

Hop in my kemp and take off for the cashbah

"Get in my car and go to Lovers' Lane" FROM THE FILM *HIGH SCHOOL CONFIDENTIAL*, 1958

Hop joint

Place where drugs are bought or smoked

"Went in the hop joint / Smoking the pills, / In walked a sheriff from Jericho Hill..." FROM THE HILLBILLY BOOGIE RECORDING *COCAINE BLUES*, ROY HOGSHED, 1948

Hophead

Drug addict

See the jazz recording *Hop Head*, Duke Ellington & The Washingtonians, 1927

Hopped up

1. Intoxicated, drugged up

"You're a friend of mine, remember? You got the brass down on you. A hopped-up hood tried to kill you." FROM THE NOVEL *VIOLENT NIGHT*, WHIT HARRISON, 1952

2. Customised car

"Say, this baby really rolls along, is she hopped up?" FROM THE FILM *THE DEVIL THUMBS A RIDE*, 1947

See also the rockabilly recording *Peroxide Blonde & A Hopped Up Model Ford*, Gene Simmons, 1958

Hopper

Drug addict

Hopping a freight

Hitching a ride on a freight train

"'During the depression,' said the cowboy to me, 'I used to hop freights at least once a month. In those days you'd see hundreds of men riding a flatcar...'" FROM THE NOVEL *ON THE ROAD*, JACK KEROUAC, 1957

Horn

1. Trumpet

See the jazz novel *Young Man With a Horn*, Dorothy Baker, 1938 – (very) loosely based on the career of Bix Beiderbecke: "But a piano wasn't exactly right for him, and he turned to brass finally; he earned enough money to buy himself a horn. And then he learned to play a horn – a trumpet, if there's anybody here who doesn't know what kind of horn a horn is."

This title (which would undoubtedly have given Peter Cook and Dudley Moore considerable entertainment), clearly had the UK distributors worried when it was filmed with Kirk Douglas and Lauren Bacall in 1950. In the US they went with the original name, in Britain it became *Young Man of Music*

2. Telephone

Horse of a different colour

Something else again, another matter entirely

"'Do you think someone else was in the room?' 'Like Peter,' said George Coffin, 'I wouldn't come back if I were a madman.' 'Who do you think was in here?' 'Horse of a different colour. No idea.'" FROM THE NOVEL *THE SEARCH FOR MY GREAT-UNCLE'S HEAD*, JONATHAN LATIMER, 1937

See also the novel *A Hearse of a Different Colour*, M E Chaber, 1958

Horse feathers

Rubbish, bullshit

See the jazz recording *Horse Feathers*, Cliff Jackson & his Krazy Kats, 1930

Chico: "There's a man outside with a big black moustache." Groucho: "Tell him I've got one." FROM THE MARX BROTHERS FILM *HORSE FEATHERS*, 1932

"'We pretended to be struggling for the gun. I fell over the carpet.' 'Ah, horse feathers!'" JOEL CAIRO FAILS TO CONVINCE THE POLICE. FROM THE FILM *THE MALTESE FALCON*, 1941

Hosed down

Riddled with bullets

Hot car

1. Fast car

See the 1958 exploitation film *Hot Car Girl*, produced by Roger Corman, originally part of a double bill with *Cry Baby Killer*

2. Stolen car, one the police are looking for "My Cad would be hotter than a strip-teaser's tassel by now..." Shell Scott realizes that the cops have a description of his car – from the novel *Always Leave 'Em Dying*, Richard S. Prather, 1961

Hot circle

A great record, a wild waxing, one of the platters that matter

Hot Dames on Cold Slabs

A landmark in hipster sleaze from Michael Storme, the sensitive author of *Make Mine A Shroud*, *Make Mine A Harlot*, *Make Mine Beautiful*, *Make Mine A Virgin*, *Make Mine Dangerous*, *Make Mine A Corpse* and *Sucker For A Redhead*

Hot little mouse

Good looking woman, a real gone chick

"He told me he was running around with a hot little mouse named Leona Sandmark." FROM THE NOVEL *HALO IN BLOOD*, HOWARD BROWNE, 1946

Hot in the zipper

Sexually aroused, amorous

The hot lead treatment

Getting shot

I pulled his teeth, boss. He was carrying a .32 in the shoulder holster.

Hot man

1. A good jazz musician, capable of playing the hippest music

There was a jazz band in the Storyville district of New Orleans in 1910 called The Four Hot Hounds, and Joe 'King' Oliver was one of the members

2. A wanted criminal

Damon Runyon's 1930 story *The Hottest Guy in the World* is someone who is sought after by cops, rather than music fans

Hot number

1. Solid-sent piece of music
2. Good looking dame

See the short story *Hot Number* by Stewart Sterling in the November 1953 British edition of *Black Mask*. See also the novel *Shameless Love*, Ross Sloan, 1959 "The alluring girl in the French bathing suit was more than just a hot number. She turned out to be a man-hungry sinner!"

Hot pillow joint

Cheap motel renting rooms by the hour

Hot rod

1. Fast or customised car

"… the newspapers were between the wars at the time, and looking for something to print and they thought up the phrase 'Hot-Rod Hoodlums.' Innocent people were being attacked by packs of youngsters who escaped in what the papers called hot-rods. Every car with the hood off is a hot-rod to the papers. Chrome plating doesn't make a rod, or steel-packed mufflers, or a driver with goggles." FROM THE NOVEL *THUNDER ROAD*, WILLIAM CAMPBELL GAULT, 1952

"O'Brian got out of the car. He said 'You ought to drive hot rods, Ed.' 'I

would. Except for my mother. She's queen of the dirt tracks. She'd be jealous if I muscled in.'" FROM THE NOVEL *VIOLENT NIGHT*, WHIT HARRISON, 1952

"Dig that crazy driver, / Yeah dig that fool a hole. / Dig it down by the side of the road, / He can hear them hot rods roll…" FROM THE ROCKABILLY RECORDING *DIG THAT CRAZY DRIVER*, WILLIAM PENNIX, 1958

See also the rockabilly recording *Devil's Hot Rod*, Johnny Tyler, 1955, and a special prize for finding his theme and sticking to it should surely go to hillbilly boogie singer Arkie Shibley, who released *Hot Rod Race*, 1950, *Hot Rod Race No. 2*, 1951, *Arkie Meets The Judge (Hot Rod Race No. 3)*, 1951, *The Girl In The Mercury (Hot Rod Race No. 4)*, 1951 and *Hot Rod Race No. 5 (The Kid In The Model A)*, 1951

See the 1958 exploitation film *Hot Rod Gang*, which features Gene Vincent & The Blue Caps, who also released an EP of the same name. See also the films *Hot Rod Girl*, 1956 ("Teen-age terrorists on a speed-crazy rampage") and *Hot Rod Rumble*, 1957 ("Revved-up youth in a jungle of thrills"), *Hot Rods to Hell*, 1967 ("Call them punks… call them animals… but you'd better get out of their way!") and the pioneering 1950 film *Hot Rod*

2. Stolen or illegal gun

See the short story *Hot Rods* by John Whitmore in the August 13 1932 issue of *Detective Story* magazine

Hot-seat fodder

Criminal

Hot squat

The electric chair

Erle Stanley Gardner wrote a story called *The Hot Squat* for the Octo-

Robert Mitchum starring in the film of William Campbell Gault's hot rod novel, *Thunder Road*.

Dig that crazy driver, Yeah dig that fool a hole. Dig it down by the side of the road, He can hear them hot rods roll…

ber 1931 issue of *Black Mask* magazine

Hotcha

Expression of enjoyment in hipster circles, popular in the twenties and thirties

There was a venue in Harlem in 1932 called Club Hotcha, and that same year James P Johnson and Andy Razaf wrote the music for a stage show called *Harlem Hotcha*

Hotcha number

A good looking woman

Hotsy-totsy

Fine and dandy, really good

The word hotsy was originally a slang term for a prostitute

Prolific jazz bandleader Irving Mills ran an outfit in the late twenties called Irving Mills & his Hotsy Totsy Gang

See the jazz recording *Everything Is Hotsy Totsy Now*, The California Ramblers, 1925

Hotter than a two-dollar pistol

1. Sought-after, in demand, whether for reasons of popularity or because you're wanted by the police

"I was dead broke, on the lam, and as hot as a two-dollar pistol with the authorities everywhere." FROM THE AUTOBIOGRAPHY *RAP SHEET*, BLACKIE AUDETT, 1955

2. Steamed-up, enthusiastic

"Well, there was her first trick. Her being fresh from the farm, I was supposed to keep an eye on her. She had the room next door there and I kept the door open a crack, the mark hotter than a two-dollar pistol for the kid and not even noticing." FROM THE NOVEL *SEARCH FOR A DEAD NYMPHO*, PAUL W FAIRMAN, 1967

Hottest nymph that ever backed into a mattress

A swell dame, a sex bomb

"You couldn't tell about women. They might look like cardboard dolls and at the same time be the hottest nymph that ever backed into a mattress." FROM THE NOVEL *A KILLER IS LOOSE*, GIL BREWER, 1954

Hotwire

To start a car without the use of keys

House hop

Rent party, a dance in someone's apartment

House peeper

Hotel detective

How about that mess?

Hey, look at that. What do you reckon?

See the R&B recording *Floor Show (How 'Bout That Mess)*, Frank Culley & His Orchestra, 1949

How come you do me like you do?

Why do you treat me this way?

See the jazz recording *How Come You Do Me Like You Do?*, Rudy Vallee, 1930

How do you like them apples?

How does that grab you? What do you think of that?

How's the grouch bag holding?

Do you have any money on you?

Hum Dum Dinger From Dingersville

Beautiful girl, a total knockout

A hotcha hipster sideswiping his suitcase, mid-1930s.

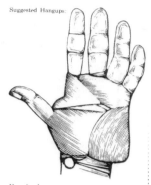

Suggested Hangups:

Your hand.

Your foot.

Reach over the back of your head and feel one of your eyes from above and behind—upside down. Try to think of something you can't remember.

Tune your television set to an empty channel and watch the specks. (This is "Channel X".)

Complete this list: Ford Maddox Ford, Jerome K. Jerome, William Carlos Williams. . . .

Sound advice for the confused beatnik, from the sleeve of the LP *How To Speak Hip*.

See the country recordings *She's A Hum Dum Dinger*, Buddy Jones, 1941, and *She's A Hum Ding Mama*, Jack Hilliard and Leslie Palmer, 1938

Hung up

1. Worried, anxious
2. Fascinated

Harlan Ellison wrote a book in 1961 entitled *Gentleman Junkie And Other Stories of the Hung-Up Generation* "A startling collection of 'hip' stories by an impressive young writer, torn from the shadows of a twilight world"

Hungry

"I'm so hungry I could eat the raw right stump of General Sherman." FROM THE NOVEL *KISS TOMORROW GOODBYE*, HORACE MCCOY, 1949

Hunky dory

Ok, in order, fine

"There was I talking to myself, / Feeling hunky dory, / A pretty girl passed by, / I tried to catch her eye, / She seemed to sigh / 'Hey, what's his story?'" FROM THE JAZZ RECORDING *WHAT'S HIS STORY*, HARRY "THE HIPSTER" GIBSON, 1946

The Columbia Orchestra released a record called *Hunky Dory* in 1901

Hush house

Speakeasy, illegal gin-joint

Hush-hush

Secret

Hymn-hustler

Priest, sky pilot, bible-basher

I

I ain't comin' on that tab

I don't agree with you

I ain't saying you're wrong, but I ain't saying you're right either

Diplomacy, the Jim Thompson way, from the novel *Pop. 1280*, 1964

I am cable and able to wake you

I'm about to let you know what's happening

I dig your lick

I understand what you're saying

I don't know beans

I haven't a clue, your guess is as good as mine

I don't mean maybe, baby

That's right, I really mean it, that's what I want to do

See the rockabilly recording *Don't Mean Maybe, Baby*, Alvis Wayne, 1957

I don't go for that magoo

Don't hand me that line, I'm not falling for that kind of talk

I don't sound you

I don't understand you

I feel like Death Valley

I'm thirsty

I get it, but I don't want it

I hear what you're saying, but I don't like it

I got a lot of room in my ears yet

Keep talking, I'm listening

I got your signal clear and cool

I understand you perfectly

From the film *High School Confidential*, 1958

I had a bee on my tail. Thought I could drown it

I had a raging thirst

"Had a couple before I left Phoenix. Couple of more in Wickenberg. Same for Blythe. For Indio. In Riverside I bought a pint. Usually I don't drink like that. Had a bee on my tail. Thought I could drown it." FROM THE NOVEL *THE DEADLY SEX*, JACK WEBB, 1959

I have heard the wind blow before

You're bluffing, don't hand me that line

I tried to carry a moose head through a revolving door

Somebody beat me up

From the novel *The Bedroom Bolero*, Michael Avallone, 1963

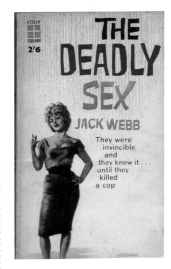

Had a bee on my tail. Thought I could drown it.

I wanna jump your bones

I'd like to sleep with you

Ice

1. Jewels

See the novel *Hot Ice*, Robert J Casey, 1933

2. To kill someone

Iceberg act

Playing it cool

Iceman

Professional killer

Ickie

"One who does not understand swing music." FROM *DOWN BEAT'S YEARBOOK OF SWING*, 1939

"One of the upper crust, big shot, bankers, money people." FROM THE BOOKLET *THE JIVES OF DOCTOR HEPCAT*, LAVADA DURST, 1953

I'd rather drink muddy water, and sleep in a hollow log

I'm not interested

"Rather drink muddy water, / Sleep in a hollow log, / Than to be in Atlanta / Treated like a dirty dog." FROM THE COUNTRY RECORDING *T FOR TEXAS (BLUE YODEL NO. 1)* JIMMIE RODGERS, 1927

If I'm lyin' I'm flyin'

I'm telling the truth, I swear

If she don't bake, she doesn't get dusted

If she doesn't pay, she doesn't get any narcotics

From the film *High School Confidential*, 1958

If that don't turn you on, brother, you ain't got no switches

That should impress you - if not, then you're probably dead already

If that's good then my feet are kippers

I'm not impressed

If you were a shotgun, baby, I'd be dead

You're trouble

I'm fresh out of a chatterbox

I don't have a machine gun

I'm gonna tear your playhouse down

You're in trouble, I'm going to make you pay, you'll be sorry

"I caught you out, runnin' round, / Now I'm a-gonna tear your playhouse down." FROM THE ROCKABILLY RECORDING *NOTHIN' BUT A NUTHIN*, JIMMY STEWART & HIS NIGHTHAWKS, 1957

See the blues recording *I'm Gonna Tear Your Playhouse Down*, Hazel Myers, 1924

I'm like a bear from the fair, I ain't nowhere

I'm lost, I don't know what I'm doing

Fats Waller, contributing an article to a magazine about his music, wrote "Give me a piano to beat up and that's me; but as to this writing business, I'm like a bear from the fair, I ain't nowhere," quoted in the oral history *Hear Me Talkin' To Ya – The Story Of Jazz By The Men Who Made It*, Nat Shapiro and Nat Hentoff, eds., 1955

Jimmie Rodgers: *'Rather drink muddy water / Sleep in a hollow log'.*

High School Confidential's Mamie Van Doren: *'If she don't bake, she don't get dusted'.*

I'm scoring it straight for you

This is the truth, I'm laying it on the line

'You're a nice normal-type fella. You'll get the whole deal handed to you – with the marriage bit. Believe me, I'm scoring it straight for you, pally-boy. If I seen it any different, I'd have married her myself.' FROM THE NOVEL *RUN FOR DOOM*, HENRY KANE, 1960

In a bluesey groove

Depressed, low down

In a heap

Completely drunk

In a pig's eye

That's rubbish, I don't agree with you

In dutch

In trouble with someone, in their bad books

"We ain't never been in dutch / We don't browse around too much. / Don't bother us, leave us alone / Anyway we almost grown." FROM THE ROCK'N'ROLL RECORDING *ALMOST GROWN*, CHUCK BERRY, 1959

In like Flynn

A certainty, a sure thing, deriving from popular stories of Errol Flynn's success with women

In my book you're way upstairs

I really like you, I'm impressed

In the bag

Drunk

"He had been drinking steadily since his return from the Arizona Club nearly twenty four hours earlier and yet one who did not know him well could never have told from his speech, his walk, or his visible reflexes that he was in the bag." FROM THE NOVEL OF THE SCREEN-PLAY OF *OCEAN'S ELEVEN*, GEORGE CLAYTON JOHNSON AND JACK GOLDEN RUSSELL, 1960

In the grip of the grape

Drunk

In the groove

Just right, solid, A-ok, righteous

Defined in *Down Beat's 1939 Year Book of Swing* as "1. Playing genuine swing, and 2. Carried away by the music"

"She's in the groove, right on the ball / She's reet, petite and gone..." FROM THE R&B JUMP JIVE RECORDING *REET, PETITE AND GONE*, LOUIS JORDAN & THE TYMPANY FIVE, 1947

In there

Groovy, fine as wine, hip

"Now I'd say this chick is really in there..." FROM THE JAZZ RECORDING *THE HIPSTER'S BLUES, OPUS 71/2*, HARRY "THE HIPSTER" GIBSON, 1944

Indoor aviator

Elevator attendant

Interviewing your brains

Thinking

Iron

1. Kill

eg: "To iron someone out"

2. Gun

"'I'm keeping your gun,' Rudy went on. 'I'm taking any iron that Carol has when she shows.'" FROM THE NOVEL *THE GETAWAY*, JIM THOMPSON, 1958

Iron bungalow

Prison

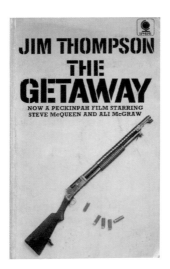

A serious piece of iron decorating the cover of Jim Thompson's *The Getaway*.

Clara Bow, the original 'It' Girl.

Iron cure

Death, a fatal bullet wound (cures most things...)

See the novelette *Iron Cure* in the September 1941 issue of *Black Mask*

Iron men

Dollars

"'Hundred dollars,' I said. 'Iron men, fish, bucks to the number of one hundred...'" FROM THE NOVEL *FAREWELL MY LOVELY*, RAYMOND CHANDLER, 1940

It

1. Sex appeal

Clara Bow, one of the most famous movie stars of the 1920s, had huge success with a film called *It* (1927), based on a book by Elinor Glyn. The sign on her grave at Forest Lawn cemetery reads: "Hollywood's 'It' Girl"

See the jazz recording *I've Got 'It', But it Don't Do Me No Good*, Helen Kane, 1930

See also the country recording *There Ain't No Sales Tax On It In Idaho*, Dick Smith, 1956

2. Sex organs

"You gotta wet it, / You gotta wet it, / Dampen it so it can grow, / You gotta wet it, / You gotta wet it, / Dampen it farmer you know, / Sprinkle it and dampen it / And let the good work go on." FROM THE BOOGIE-WOOGIE RECORDING *WET IT*, FRANKIE "HALF-PINT" JAXON, 1937

"You didn't want it when you had it / So I got another man, / Keep your hands off it, / It don't belong to you." FROM THE BLUES RECORDING *TAKE YOUR HAND OFF IT*, LIL JOHNSON, 1937

See also the blues recordings *She Done Sold It Out*, The Memphis Jug Band, 1934; *Try And Get It!*, Bea Foote, 1938; *I Want Every Bit Of It*, Bessie Smith, 1926

3. Virginity

See the jazz recording *She Really Meant To Keep It*, Johnny Messner & his Orchestra, c.1940

It ain't hay

That's quite something, it's valuable, not to be sneezed at

Abbot & Costello made a film called *It Ain't Hay* in 1943, very loosely based on the 1935 Damon Runyon story *Princess O'Hara*

See also the novel *It Ain't Hay*, David Dodge, 1946, where it sure ain't hay, it's marijuana

It ain't the meat it's the motion

It's not what you've got that counts, it's what you do with it

It could out-whistle Whistler's Mother

It's sensational

It doesn't bother me

That's great, I'm really impressed

Eddie Condon's response when first seeing Louis Armstrong play. From the autobiography *We Called it Music*, Eddie Condon with Thomas Sugrue, 1948

It fits in with the beat

That suits the occasion, that's appropriate

It fries my wig

It blows my mind, I'm impressed, I'm astonished

It looks like rain

Someone is about to get arrested

It melts your fingernails

That's rough liquor, bootleg hooch

It turns my crank

I like it, I approve, it turns me on

It will pull you dead to the curb

It'll knock you out, you'll love it

It wound up in smoke

It ended in gunfire

It's a natural gas that you can't zig a zag

You can't mend something that's broken, you can't fight City Hall, it's a hopeless case

It's all right, I make it fresh every morning

I'm paying the bill. Don't worry, I've got plenty of money

From the film *Johnny O'Clock*, 1947

It's git down time

This is it, something's about to happen

Git down time is traditionally the time of the evening when prostitutes start work

It's got guts and it don't make you slobber

It's good, I approve

It's my game right down the alley

I know what I'm doing

I've got to take a rub-down in water

I need a bath

Ivories

1. Piano keys

"Here's a cat that lays down a group of ivory talking trash and strictly putting down a gang of jive." ie: He's a really good piano player. FROM THE BOOKLET *THE JIVES OF DOCTOR HEPCAT*, LAVADA DURST, 1953

James P. Johnson, the blues, stride and boogie pianist was billed as "King of the Ivories" when appearing at the New Star Casino in New York in February 1922

2. Teeth

Ivory from the ears up

Stupid, a blockhead

"If you're dumb enough to think that the police haven't suspected you of having a young lover, and planning to get rid of your stodgy, middle-aged husband so you could inherit his money and go places with the boy you really like, you're ivory from the ears up." FROM THE NOVEL *TOP OF THE HEAP*, A A FAIR (ERLE STANLEY GARDNER), 1952

Ixnay

No (backslang for nix)

Izzatso?

Really, you don't say? (Is that so?)

'It wound up in smoke' – Rico gets ventilated in *Little Caesar*.

J

J.D.

Juvenile delinquent

"The rock'n'rollers, the Twisters, the hipsters, the teenage J.D.s, all inside with their black leather, black denim, black hair, black eyes and black hearts." **FROM THE NOVEL** *TWILIGHT GIRLS*, **JUDSON GREY, 1962**

See also the novel *Juvenile Delinquents* (a.k.a. *The Lower Part Of The Sky*), Lenard Kaufman, 1952, and the rockabilly recording *Juvenile Delinquent*, Ronnie Allen, 1959

Jack

1. Money

"The place is lousy with jack..." ie: There's lots of money at that nightclub we're going to rob. **FROM THE NOVEL** *LITTLE CAESAR*, **W.R. BURNETT, 1929**

"All the jack he'd made in the rackets was gone. The state had latched on to part of it and the federal government had taken another big bite and lawyers had eaten up the rest." **FROM THE NOVEL** *SAVAGE NIGHT*, **JIM THOMPSON, 1953**

2. All-purpose term of address between hipsters, sometimes lengthened to Jackson

Jack rabbit blood

Habitual prison escaper, said to have jack rabbit blood because of their continual tendency to run away

Jacket

1. A prisoner's file, both positive and negative, kept throughout the duration of their sentence

2. The sentence for a particular crime

"He'd been in short pants in the days when Louie Fomorowski was beating two murder raps. They'd gotten a one-to-life jacket on him for the second one, of which he'd served nine months in privileged circumstances." **FROM THE NOVEL** *THE MAN WITH THE GOLDEN ARM*, **NELSON ALGREN, 1949**

Jackroller

Pickpocket, mugger, purse-snatcher

Jailbait

1. Underage girl

See the book *Jailbait*, William Bernard, 1951, a study of juvenile delinquency advertised somewhat over-enthusiastically by the publishers of the 1956 reprint: "Here at last is the real story of teen-age sin the headlines have never dared reveal! Of teen-age girls entertaining men in cheap hotel rooms. Of sexual misconduct raging like a plague from Maine to California! Of secret trysts between high school girls and men in their forties! And here is the startling truth about what goes on behind the walls of reformatories after dark!"

2. Someone destined for prison

"'Are you interested in that?' 'What's it to you?' 'That's jail bait.' 'He's just a kid.' 'Yeah, that's what I said once. Maybe you'll be lucky. Maybe they won't send him back to prison. Maybe he'll get himself killed first.'" **FROM THE FILM** *THEY LIVE BY NIGHT*, **1948**

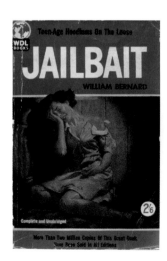

The real story of teen-age sin the headlines have never dared reveal!

See also the short story *Jail Bait* by Roger Torrey in the October 1936 issue of *Black Mask*, and the juvenile delinquent novel *Jailbait Jungle*, Wenzell Brown, 1962

Jalopy

Automobile, not usually of the newest variety

"We got a ride from a couple of fellows wranglers, teenagers, country boys in a put-together jalopy." FROM THE NOVEL *ON THE ROAD*, JACK KEROUAC, 1957

See also the 1953 Bowery Boys film *Jalopy*

Jake

1. Correct, alright, in order, ok

"'Stick-up,' he said. 'Be very quiet and everything will be jake.'" FROM THE NOVEL *FAREWELL, MY LOVELY*, RAYMOND CHANDLER, 1940

2. All purpose term of address between hipsters

See the R&B jump jive recording *Jake, What a Shake*, Louis Jordan & The Tympany Five, 1939

3. Moonshine liquor

Jam-up

Something really good

Jane

Woman, girl

"You said he or she – do you think maybe it was a jane did the croaking?" FROM THE NOVEL *THE CORRUPT ONES*, J.C. BARTON, C. 1950

"I can't let you in just now. Ya see, I got a jane inside..." FROM THE FILM *THE PUBLIC ENEMY*, 1933

Jass

Jazz music, written both ways from 1913 up until around 1920, when the word Jazz became the accepted spelling

In New Orleans in the 1890s there was a snappily-titled proto-jazz outfit called The Razzy Dazzy Spasm Band. The first New Orleans band to head north arrived in Chicago in 1915, and were initially billed as Tom Brown's Band from Dixieland, but soon changed their name to Brown's Dixieland Jass Band. Nick La Rocca's Original Dixieland Jazz Band were formed in 1915, and they put out the *Dixie Jass Band One-Step* in January 1917. In November 1917 they released *At The Jass Band Ball*, which by March 1918 had become *At The Jazz Band Ball*. W.C. Handy put out a record called *That Jazz Dance* in 1917, credited to Handy's Orchestra of Memphis. In June 1917 The Frisco Jazz Band put out a song called the *Johnson 'Jass' Blues*. Whichever way you spelt it, the word started out with a king-size double meaning: originating in the brothels of Storyville, jazz music was sex music, pure and simple

The first British band claiming play jazz was the Murray Club Jazz Band (the featured act, not surprisingly, at the Murray Club in London), who formed at the end of 1917. As jazz slowly took hold in Britain, one theory advanced in the press by a distinctly unimpressed critic was that this music and the dances that went with it were the result of 'grotesque and indecent movements invented by drunken cowboys in the Argentine'

See also *Jazzin' Around*, Theodore Morse, September 1917; *Jazzbo Jazz (Jazz Deluxe)*, Earl Fuller's Famous Jazz Band, March 1918; *The Jass 'Lazy Blues'*, Dabney's Band, November 1917 and *Tack 'Em Down*, The Creole Jass Band, 1918

Nick La Rocca's Original Dixieland Jazz Band.

The great Bessie Smith: 'Nobody in town can bake a jelly roll like mine'.

Annette Mills' British music hall song *Boomps-a-Daisy* gets the jitterbug treatment from Nat Gonella, 1939. What the hepcats made of this is anybody's guess.

Java

Coffee

eg: *"Gimme a shot of java, nix on the moo-juice"* ie: a cup of coffee, no milk FROM THE AUTOBIOGRAPHY *REALLY THE BLUES*, MEZZ MEZZROW AND BERNARD WOLFE, 1946

See the vocal group recording *Java Jive*, The Ink Spots, 1946

Jazz

1. Music (see Jass)
2. Having sex, or sexual fluids

"'Jesus!' she jeered. 'The nicest looking guy I ever saw and you turn out to be a lousy snooping copper. How much? I don't jazz cops.'" FROM THE NOVEL *THE KILLER INSIDE ME*, JIM THOMPSON, 1952

See the shy retiring recordings *The Jazz Me Blues*, Lucille Hegamin, 1920; *I Want A Jazzy Kiss*, Mamie Smith, 1921; *I Wanna Jazz Some More*, Kitty Brown, 1924

Jazz baby

Jazz fan, usually a girl or flapper of the 1920s

See the jazz recordings *Jazz Baby*, Jim Europe's 369th Infantry "Hell Fighters" Band, March 1919 and the *Jazz Babies Ball*, Maceo Pinkard, 1920

Jazz water

Bootleg alcohol

John Joseph wrote a story called *Jazz Water – By Special Delivery* for the May 1924 issue of *Black Mask* magazine, which advertised it as "The romance of the hooch"

Jazzbo

Boyfriend

Jelly roll

Sex organs

"Jelly roll, jelly roll, / Laying on the fence, / If you don't try to get it / You ain't got no sense..." FROM THE BLUES RECORDING *YOU'VE GOT TO SAVE THAT THING*, ORA ALEXANDER, 1931

See the blues recordings *I Ain't Gonna Give Nobody None Of This Jelly Roll*, Dabney's Novelty Orchestra, 1919; *Nobody In Town Can Bake A Jelly Roll Like Mine*, Bessie Smith, 1923; *Jelly Whippin' Blues*, Tampa Red, 1928; *You'll Never Miss Your Jelly Till Your Jelly Roller's Gone*, Lil Johnson, 1929; and the disarmingly modest *I Got The Best Jelly Roll In Town*, Lonnie Johnson, 1930

See also the R&B recording *Jelly Roll*, Richard Berry & the Dreamers, 1955

Jerks & fillies

Boys and girls, cats and kittens, studs and sisters

"Jerks and Fillies" was DJ Gene Noble's all-purpose name for callers to his show on WLAC Nashville in the 1950s

Jet jockey

Airline pilot

Jim

All-purpose hipster term of address, usually uncomplimentary

Jitterbug

1. Jazz dance which became popular in the late 1930s
2. Someone who dances to jazz

Defined rather snottily by *Down Beat's 1939 Yearbook of Swing* as "A swing fan (not a true swing music lover) who expresses his fondness for swing music by eccentric dancing or emotional gestures and gyrations."

See the jazz recordings *Lullaby to a Jitterbug*, The Andrews Sisters, 1938, and *Jitterbugs Broke It Down*, Ollie Shepard, 1940

Jive

1. *"v. To kid, to talk insincerely or without meaning, to use an elaborate or misleading line n. Confusing double-talk, pretentious conversation, anything false or phony."* FROM THE AUTOBIOGRAPHY *REALLY THE BLUES*, MEZZ MEZZROW AND BERNARD WOLFE, 1946

Down Beat's Yearbook of Swing, 1939 defined the word merely as "the language of swing", however, they also list "Jive artist" as "an elegant nothing, a ham who sells out"

Cab Calloway publicised his own booklets of jive slang with the jazz recordings *Jive (Page One of the Hepster's Dictionary)*, Cab Calloway & his Orchestra, 1938, and *Jiveformation Please*, Cab Calloway & his Orchestra, 1938

The word shows up in numerous jazz and blues recordings, for instance: *Don't Jive Me*, Louis Armstrong's Hot Five, 1928; *State Street Jive*, Cow Cow Davenport & Ivy Smith, 1928; *Sweet Jivin' Mama*, Blind Blake, 1929; *Jive Man Blues*, Frankie "Half-Pint" Jaxon, 1929; and the succinctly-titled *Jive*, Duke Ellington & his Famous Orchestra, 1932

See also *Jive Bomber*, recorded in London during the Blitz by Stephane Grappelli & his Quartet. Another jazz-related response to the Luftwaffe came in 1941 from Una Mae Carlisle with a song called *Blitzkrieg Baby (You Can't Bomb Me)*

Many rock'n'roll DJs of the fifties used the name Doctor Jive, the most famous being Tommy Smalls of WWRL, New York City

2. Marijuana

See the jazz recording *Here Comes The Man With The Jive*, Stuff Smith & his Onyx Club Boys, 1936

3. Insulting term of address, short for jive-ass motherfucker

Jive stick

A marijuana cigarette

Jive that makes it drip

Clouds that produce rain

From the autobiography *Really The Blues*, Mezz Mezzrow and Bernard Wolfe, 1946

Joe below

"A musician who pays less than union scale" FROM *DOWN BEAT'S YEARBOOK OF SWING*, 1939

John Hancock

Signature

Johnny-on-the-spot

Right place, right time

eg: "say the word and I'll be Johnny-on-the-spot." ie: I'm there when you need me

"Friend you go out in a hall / Want the joint to rock, / All you do is give us a call / We'll be johnny on the spot." FROM THE ROCK'N'ROLL RECORDING *ROCKIN' IS OUR BIZNESS*, THE TRENIERS, 1956

See also the rockabilly recording *I'm Johnny On The Spot*, Glenn Reeves, 1955

Joint

Place, venue, establishment

See the rockabilly recording *Knocked Out Joint On Mars*, Buck Trail, 1957

Jolt

1. A shot of alcohol

"Sighing heavily I walked to the liquor cabinet and refilled my glass – this time with

The Andrews Sisters get hep, 1940.

straight booze. I needed a good jolt and I planned on getting it." FROM THE NOVEL *TWO TIMING TART*, JOHN DAVIDSON, 1961

2. A shot of dope

"Once they get used to the jolts, they need four or five of them in a day. That'll cost anywhere from five dollars to ten dollars. I've found kids who spent their lunch money for dope." FROM THE NOVEL *THE DEADLY LOVER*, ROBERT O. SABER, 1951

Joy ride

Having sex

Judas hole

Small hole in the door of a speakeasy

Juice

Alcohol

See the jazz recording *Buy Me Some Juice*, Blue Lu Barker, with Danny Barker's Fly Cats, 1939

Juice jolt

Electrocution, the hot squat

"He's looking for a pat on the back from his paper, and maybe a few extra dollars, and everybody telling him how smart he is because he was able to get the goods on the Big Shot of New York that nobody else couldn't do. Get me? He's trying to nominate Norry for the juice jolt up the river..." FROM THE NOVEL *THE BIG SHOT*, FRANK L PACKARD, 1929

Juiced

Drunk

"Let's drink some juice / Let's all get loose..." FROM THE R&B RECORDING *JUICED*, JACKIE BRENSTON & HIS DELTA CATS, 1952

Juke joint

Cheap bar with dancing facilities

"Your nerves are jumping like a juke joint on Saturday night" FROM THE NOVEL *HALO IN BLOOD*, HOWARD BROWNE, 1946

A decade before he co-starred with a chimp in *Bedtime For Bonzo*, 1942 saw Ronald Reagan hanging out in the juke joints.

Gene Vincent's 1957 tribute to that rockin' juke joint on the outskirts of town.

"Now I work all the week / And I draw my pay, / I hit a juke joint / And I throw it all away." FROM THE HONKYTONK RECORDING *JUKE JOINT JOHHNY*, LATTIE MOORE, 1952

"Well there's a little juke joint / On the outskirts of town, / Where the cats pick 'em up / And they lay them down..." FROM THE ROCK'N'ROLL RECORDING *DANCE TO THE BOP*, GENE VINCENT & THE BLUE CAPS, 1957

Jump street

The beginning of something

Jumping

Wild, uninhibited

"Check your weapons at the door, / Be sure to pay your quarter, / Burn your leather on the floor, / Grab anybody's daughter. / The roof is rockin', / The neighbours are knockin', / We're all bums when the wagon comes, / I mean this joint is jumpin'." FROM THE JAZZ RECORDING *THE JOINT IS JUMPIN'*, FATS WALLER & HIS RHYTHM, 1937

Jumped up

Arrested, cornered by the police

Jungled up

Living arrangements

eg: "He's jungled up over in the Bronx" ie: he's got a room somewhere in the Bronx

Just a hop ahead of the undertaker

Unwell, not in good shape, hungover

Just for kicks

For a laugh, for the hell of it

Juvie

Juvenile delinquent

See the novel *The Juvies*, Harlan Ellison, 1961 'Life and Death of the Gutter Kids'

Keep plant

Keep watch, act as lookout, stay in one place

Keep your lamps on the prowl

Keep a lookout, keep your eyes peeled

Keep your nickel out of it

Keep your opinions to yourself, stay out of this

"Keep your nickel out of this, wise guy." FROM THE NOVEL *RED GARDENIAS*, JONATHAN LATIMER, 1939

Kick

"The kind of music you like, dance, cigarette or movie." FROM THE BOOKLET *THE JIVES OF DOCTOR HEPCAT*, LAVADA DURST, 1953

See the advertising for the 1961 exploitation film *Wild Youth* – "The 'way-out' guys and the 'make-out' gals... what is their latest kick?"

Kick off

To die, expire, bite the dust

"'Another one kicked off on us, Captain.''How many times do I have to tell you that a man can die in jail just the same as in hospital?'" FROM THE NOVEL *A WALK ON THE WILD SIDE*, NELSON ALGREN, 1957

This term was in use in 18th century English slang, describing the movement of a condemned man's legs during a hanging. Another expression for death on the gallows in those days was to 'kick the clouds before the hotel door'

Kicking the gong around

Smoking opium

See the jazz recording *Kicking The Gong Around*, Cab Calloway & his Orchestra, 1931

Kicks

Thrills, excitement, a good time

"'I don't like you when you're with them.''Ah, it's all right, it's just kicks. We only live once. We're having a good time.'" FROM THE NOVEL *ON THE ROAD*, JACK KEROUAC, 1957

"When we went ridin' in my new sports car / Just me and my baby and my old guitar, / Down the road and over the hills / Gettin' our kicks and havin' our thrills, / I said 'How do you like it?' and she said / 'Wow, man!'" FROM THE ROCKABILLY RECORDING *WOW, MAN!*, BOBBY JACKSON, 1957

"Anything for kicks," she said. *"That used to be my philosophy of life. It doesn't work out the way you expect it to. Kicks include getting kicked in the head by a horse."* FROM THE NOVEL *THE WYCHERLY WOMAN*, ROSS MACDONALD, 1961

Meanwhile, back in the world of drugs, the soon-to-expire Mr. Birk is explaining his philosophy: *"'And you take it for kicks?' 'Kicks. Experience. Knowledge. Or sometimes, just plain old euphoria. You do dig euphoria, don't you?' he leered."* FROM THE NOVEL *THE ICEPICK IN OLLIE BIRK*, EUNICE SUDAK, 1966

Just for kicks: *The Icepick In Ollie Birk*.

Fifteen years before Raquel Welch's fur bikini, the Chinchilla Killer-Diller attempts to take the world by storm, 1950.

Hammer's version of *The Mummy* hailed as a 'Killer-Diller Chiller' by the *Sunday Pictorial*, 1959.

See also the novel *Marijuana Girl*, N R DeMexico, 1950 "She traded her body for drugs – and kicks!"

Kicksville

Something enjoyable, a blast, the state of getting your kicks

"A voiceless roar issued from a half-dozen throats. The excitement of it, the thrill of it, spread through the group like wildfire. This was Kicksville! This was the utmost!" FROM THE NOVEL *RUN TOUGH, RUN HARD*, CARSON BINGHAM, 1961

Killer Diller

A knockout, the best, something truly hep

"Every band has a favourite killer-diller, which is sure to be included on almost every programme they broadcast." FROM PROFESSOR CAB CALLOWAY'S *SWINGFORMATION BUREAU*, EARLY 1940s

"'They call him Zand. He's a killer.' Joe and the other boys laughed. Reisman eyed them steadily. 'How do you mean?' 'Sharpest dresser in town. Poiple shoits! He'll moidah ya, ya bum!'" FROM *LITTLE MEN, BIG WORLD*, W.R. BURNETT, 1951

See the jazz recordings *Killer Diller*, Benny Goodman & his Orchestra, 1937, and *Killer Diller*, Gene Coy & his Killer Dillers, 1948

See also the short story *The Case of the Killer-Diller* by Cornell Woolrich in the May 1939 issue of *Dime Detective*

In 1950, some genius with more money than taste attempted to corner the high end of the swimwear market by designing a fur bikini known as the Chinchilla Killer-Diller (see illustration)

King bee

A stud, a ladykiller, top of the heap

"I'm a king bee baby, Buzzin' round your hive. I can make honey, Let me come inside..." FROM THE ROCKABILLY RECORDING *GOT LOVE IF YOU WANT IT*, WARREN SMITH, 1957

King Kong

Moonshine, bootleg whiskey

"On the second floor was a King Kong speakeasy, where you could get yourself five-cent and ten-cent shots of home-brewed corn." FROM THE AUTOBIOGRAPHY *REALLY THE BLUES*, MEZZ MEZZROW AND BERNARD WOLFE, 1946

Kiss-off

1. Reject, get rid of, say goodbye to
2. Kill

See the novel *The Kiss Off*, Douglas Heyes, 1951 "Murder in a Love Nest"

Kisser

Mouth or lips

"Chuck had the kisser of a clown, the wide-open, honest, boyish smile of the natural buffoon." FROM THE NOVEL *DEATH IS CONFIDENTIAL*, LAWRENCE LARIAR, 1959

Kitten

Girl

"Where are you carrying the heater, kitten?" FROM THE NOVEL *KISS ME, DEADLY*, MICKEY SPILLANE, 1953

See also the novel *Kitten With A Whip*, Wade Miller, 1959

Kitty

All-purpose term of address between hipsters

Knee pad

To beg

Knock a scarf

To eat

Knock a statue act

Hold on, wait a minute

Knock fowl soup

To die

Knock me a kiss

Kiss me

Knock off the gab

Shut up, keep quiet

Knock over

Rob

See the 1927 Dashiell Hammett short story *The Big Knockover*

Knock the polish off your toes

To dance

"Well my old gal's slow and easy, / All the hepcats know. / She gets that boppin' beat / She knocks the polish off her toes." FROM THE ROCKABILLY RECORDING *PUT YOUR CAT CLOTHES ON*, CARL PERKINS, 1957

Knock someone bow-legged

Hit them square in the kisser, a mighty punch

Knocked out

1. Drunk, intoxicated
2. Wild, real gone, the most

See the rockabilly recording *Knocked Out Joint On Mars*, Buck Trail, 1957

Knockin' a jug

Getting drunk

See the jazz recording *Knockin' a Jug*, Louis Armstrong & His Orchestra, 1929, and the blues recording *Let's Knock A Jug*, Frankie "Half-Pint" Jaxon, 1929

Know where the beat is

"To understand Swing." FROM *DOWN BEAT'S YEARBOOK OF SWING, 1939*

Know your groceries

To be hip, aware, alert to the situation, to do things well, be accomplished

Peter Cheyney has a variant on this in his 1943 novel *You Can Always Duck*: "The guy who threw this Chez Clarence dump together knew his vegetables."

Knowledge box

Head, brain

Knowledge box hitting on all cylinders

Intelligent, a smart customer

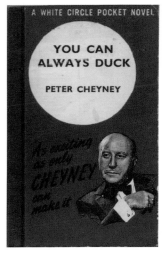

You Can Always Duck – a dead-cert as far as vegetables are concerned.

L

L7

A square, totally cubistic.

A shape that can be made using both thumbs and both forefingers

Lacquer crackers

Records, waxings, platters, discs

Lam out of it

Get lost, leave, go away

"Why the hell don't you lam out of here, bud? Before I throw a handful of fat coppers in your lap." **FROM THE NOVEL** *THE LITTLE SISTER*, RAYMOND CHANDLER, 1949

Lame

1. Something bad, poor quality, disappointing
2. "Can't understand, dumb, not able." From the booklet *The Jives of Doctor Hepcat*, Lavada Durst, 1953

Lamps

Eyes

"I didn't think of anything but the blonde in my arms, and the .45 in my fist, and the twenty-six men outside, and the four shares of Consolidated I'd bought that afternoon, and the bet I'd made on the fight with One-Lamp Louie, and the defective brake-lining on my Olds, and the bottle of rye in the bottom drawer of my file cabinet back at Dudley Sledge, Investigations." Evan Hunter takes a sideswipe at Mickey Spillane's tough-guy style. **FROM THE SHORT STORY** *KISS ME, DUDLEY*, 1954

Lamping

Looking or staring

"The customers were still lamping him and the doll like they were fillum stars. To one and all, such a drama could only have one end. Outsize Romeo rescues doll. Doll dates up. Nine months, she has a lil baby goil to match." **FROM THE NOVEL** *CROOKED COFFINS* BY GRIFF, 1930S

Last word

Perfection, nothing better, the ultimate yelp

"Holly Hill was the last word in women. And the last word was Yes." **FROM THE NOVEL** *THE CRAZY MIXED-UP CORPSE*, MIKE AVALLONE, 1957

Latch on

Become aware, understand

Late bright

Late in the evening

Later

1. Goodbye
2. A putdown

eg: "Later for that Lawrence Welk music, buddy."

Lay it down

Speak your piece

"When he laid it, wham! it stayed there..." **FROM THE SPOKEN WORD PERFORMANCE** *THE NAZZ*, LORD BUCKLEY, 1951

Lay it on me

Tell me, say what you've got to say, give it to me

The customers were still lamping him and the doll like they were fillum stars.

Let's go Bedsville, what do you say?

Lay some hot iron

Dance really well

Laying track

Lying

Layout

Living quarters, residence

"They lead us into Merilli's private apartment, which is a swanky layout." FROM THE NOVEL *KILLERS DON'T CARE*, ROD CALLAHAN, 1950

Lead poisoning

Getting shot

Leaky

Prone to tears

"'She's a little red around the eyes.' Oh, Christopher, a weeper. If there's anything I hate, it's a leaky dame.'" The dames married to Glen Miller's band get bitchy about a newcomer. FROM THE FILM *ORCHESTRA WIVES*, 1942

Let it hang

Wait a minute, hold on

Let me wake you, Jack

Let me put you straight, let me tell you something

Let's brush it hard and see where the dandruff falls

Let's discuss this carefully

From the novel *Murderer's Row*, Donald Hamilton, 1962

Let's flat git it

Let's get real gone, let's go wild

See the rockabilly recording *Let's Flat Git It*, Danny Wolfe, 1958

Let's get out of the wheatfields, Mabel, we're going against the grain

Dean Martin alfresco at *The Sands*, Las Vegas, february 1964

Let's go Bedsville

Would you care to become amorously involved?

"She giggled. 'Let's go Bedsville, what do you say?''Much as I'd like to, uh, go Bedsville, doll, I really am here for other purposes. 'She arched an eyebrow and teasingly began to fold back the covers. 'We'll see.'" FROM THE NOVEL *JOHNNY HAVOC AND THE DOLL WHO HAD 'IT'*, JOHN JAKES, 1963

Let's keep the dead leaves off the lawn

There's no use dragging up old arguments

Let's kick this thing around and see what we stub our toe on

Let's discuss this

"Now," she said, "as they say on Madison Avenue, let's kick this thing around and see what we stub our toe on." FROM THE NOVEL *THE LONG SATURDAY NIGHT*, CHARLES WILLIAMS, 1962

Let's tear

Let's get in the car and drive fast

Let's you and me nibble one

Would you like a drink?

From the novel *Farewell My Lovely*, Raymond Chandler, 1940

Letting the air out of someone

Stabbing them

Lettuce

Dollar bills, money, the folding green

"Arson, fraud, forgery – even murder. I knew all the tricks in the book. All the capers insurance-happy goons still think they can slip over on the underwriters. I figured if I could earn eighty-five per running down Coastal's toughest cases, I was good for twice that kind of lettuce hanging out my own shingle." FROM THE NOVEL *SLEEP NO MORE*, SAM S TAYLOR, 1951

Lick

"A hot phrase in rhythm." FROM *DOWN BEAT'S YEARBOOK OF SWING*, 1939

Lid

Head, brain eg: "Stash that idea in your lid, dad..."

Lift the dogs

Pick your feet up, get a move on

"Lift the dogs, Janson...we ain't got all night." FROM THE NOVEL *CHICAGO CHICK*, HANK JANSON, 1962

Lifter

Pickpocket

Jazzman Danny Barker remembered a New Orleans character in the pre-First World War days named Good Lord the Lifter, along with other Storyville regulars such as Bird Leg Nora, Stack O Dollars, Jack the Bear, Miss Thing, Three Finger Annie, Stingaree, and Bull Frog Sonny. There was also a singer called Bodidily, a name later adopted in a slightly different spelling by the late, great Ellas McDaniel. Bodidily had a huge hit in the 1920s entitled *Someday Sweetheart.*

Like a rough night on the ocean

The worse for wear, bedraggled, not at your best

"He found himself feeling sorry for the broad. She really looked like a rough night on the ocean." FROM THE NOVEL *NAKED IN VEGAS*, JOHN DENTON, 1962

Lip locking

Kissing

Liquid grocery

Store selling alcohol

Liquorice stick

Clarinet

Line your flue

Eat

From the autobiography *Really The Blues*, Mezz Mezzrow and Bernard Wolfe, 1946

Livin' end

1. The best, superlative, righteous

See the advertising for the 1959 film *Speed Crazy* – "From juke joint to drag strip... it's the livin' end."

2. The last straw, the limit

"Christ, he thought. This was the goddam living end. The kid in hot water again. Molly wise to Irene. He was sick and tired of the whole stinking rat race." FROM THE NOVEL *RUN TOUGH, RUN HARD*, CARSON BINGHAM, 1961

Living room gig

Musician's TV appearance

Loaded

1. Drunk or full of drugs

"'What's the matter with you, anyhow?' 'He's just loaded, honey...'" FROM THE FILM *REBEL WITHOUT A CAUSE*, 1955

2. Armed, packing a weapon, often written as loaded for bear

"Both of them had a bulge on the right hip that meant just one thing. They were

She really looked like a rough night on the ocean.

Look like Tarzan, sing like Jane...

She let him have the sultry, sideways glance and the lifted eyebrow. 'Well, well. Look what comes in when they leave the doors open.'

loaded." FROM THE NOVEL *KISS ME, DEADLY*, MICKEY SPILLANE, 1953

3. Rich, having plenty of money

Locoweed

Marijuana

"He was raised on locoweed, / He's what you call a Swing halfbreed." FROM THE BOOGIE-WOOGIE RECORDING *COW COW BOOGIE*, ELLA FITZGERALD & THE INK SPOTS, 1942

Long bread

A large amount of money

Long gone daddy

1. Headin' for the hills, outta here

"I'm leavin' now, I'm a long gone daddy / I don't need you anyhow." FROM THE COUNTRY RECORDING *LONG GONE DADDY*, HANK WILLIAMS, 1947

2. In love, totally sent

"I'm a long gone daddy / And I'm long gone for you." FROM THE ROCKABILLY RECORDING *LONG GONE DADDY*, PAT CUPP & HIS FLYING SAUCERS, 1956

Long goodbye

Death

Long green

A large amount of money

See the novel *The Long Green*, Bart Spicer, 1952 The cover of the novel *One for the Money* (a.k.a. *Black Wings Has My Angel*, Elliott Chaze, 1953), features the strapline 'Virginia would walk through fire to get her hands on the long, cool green.'

Longhairs

Highbrows, non-hipsters, squares, fans of straight music

Down Beat's Yearbook of Swing, 1939, defines a longhair as "A sym-

phony man, one who likes classical music."

Look like Tarzan, sing like Jane

Little Richard's recipe for rock'n'roll success

Look what comes in when they leave the doors open

Hipster greeting, look who's here, good to see you

"She let him have the sultry, sideways glance and the lifted eyebrow. 'Well, well. Look what comes in when they leave the doors open.'" FROM THE NOVEL *DEATH OF A STRAY CAT*, JEAN POTTS, 1955

Looker

Beautiful woman

Loon-lounge

Asylum, cackle factory

Looped

Drunk, soused, awash, plastered

"The lady was looped, if you want my opinion. I don't mean falling-down looped. She could probably walk a chalk-line and handle herself physically. But she had that varnished look they get when they've been drinking hard, maybe stayed up a couple of nights drinking." FROM THE NOVEL *THE WYCHERLY WOMAN*, ROSS MACDONALD, 1961

Loose as a goose

Relaxed, at ease, intoxicated

See the jazz recording *Loose Like A Goose*, Bennie Moten's Kansas City Orchestra, 1929

Loose brains

Stupidity

Loose wig

1. Open-minded, receptive to new ideas
2. A wild performer

Lounge lizard

Sharp-dressed dude with an easy line in patter

Louse up

Make a mistake

Lousemachine

Limousine

Lousy

1. Something rotten, low class, no good
2. Full, replete, plentifully supplied

"The town's lousy with dames." ie: There are lots of good-looking women here FROM THE NOVEL *THE DEAD DON'T CARE*, JONATHAN LATIMER, 1937

Lowdown

1. The full story, the inside dope
2. Feeling blue, depressed
3. Something treacherous or deceitful

Lower than a snake's belly

Depressed

Lower than the belly of a cockroach

Down, way down

Lubrication

Alcohol

Lug

Big guy, heavyweight

Lunch hooks

Fingers

Lupara sickness

Mafia-inflicted shotgun wounds

"The words 'lupara sickness' always sent a chill coursing up his spine. Today, lupara sickness is a figure of speech. In the early days of the organization in Sicily, when the Council handed down a sentence of death, the executioners used a shotgun loaded with hand-made, triangular pellets honed to razor sharpness. The pellets, called 'lupara,' were fired from close range and sliced the condemned's face and throat to ribbons." FROM THE NOVEL *ESPRIT DE CORPSE*, FRANK KANE, 1965

Lush

1. Alcoholic, heavy drinker

"Never saw this motherless lush in my life before, Captain. Ain't them blood stains on his jacket?" FROM THE NOVEL *THE MAN WITH THE GOLDEN ARM*, NELSON ALGREN, 1949

For a suitably lurid pulp treatment of the evils of the demon booze, see *The Lady Is A Lush*, Orrie Hitt, 1960

See the jazz recording *Nix on those Lush Heads*, Blue Lu Barker, with Danny Barker's Fly Cats, 1939

"You crummy, one-eyed lush!" FROM THE FILM *THEY LIVE BY NIGHT*, 1948

2. Good looking

"A lush little miss said 'Come in, please.'" FROM THE R&B JUMP JIVE RECORDING *SATURDAY NIGHT FISH FRY*, LOUIS JORDAN & THE TYMPANY FIVE, 1945

Lush dive

Cheap bar or gin joint

Lush hound

Drunkard

Esprit De Corpse – watch out for lupara sickness.

Mm

Mahogany

The bar, the stick, behind which stands the bartender

"I flopped my porkpie on the mahogany, ordered a bomb, paid with a ten spot and shoved all the change back to the booze clerk." FROM THE NOVEL *JOHNNY HAVOC AND THE DOLL WHO HAD 'IT'*, JOHN JAKES, 1963

Main brain

Expert, scientist, the one with the grey matter

'He was quite a good dresser, I thought, for a main brain.' FROM THE NOVEL *LUST, BE A LADY TONIGHT*, ROD GRAY, 1967

Main drag

Main street or thoroughfare

"I walked a couple blocks without sighting a bar, either on the main drag or the side streets." FROM THE NOVEL *SAVAGE NIGHT*, JIM THOMPSON, 1953

Mainsqueeze

Girlfriend

Main stem

Main street or thoroughfare

In Horace McCoy's 1937 novel *No Pockets in a Shroud*, magazine editor Mike Dolan writes a regular column called *The Main Stem*

Make

1. To see, recognise
2. To seduce

Make a bulldog hug a hound

Very persuasive

"Big legged woman. / Keep your dresses down, / You got somethin' baby. / Would make a bulldog hug a hound." FROM THE JERRY LEE LEWIS RECORDING *BIG LEGGED WOMAN*, 1958

Make like a fish

Have a bath

Make like a tree and leave

Quit the scene, take off, vamoose

"Well let's make like a tree and leave, / Let's make like a storm and blow, / Let's make like a chicken and fly this coop, / Let's make like a rock and roll..." FROM THE ROCKABILLY RECORDING *MAKE LIKE A ROCK'N'ROLL*, DON WOODY, 1955

Make out like a foreign loan

To do well, be successful

Make the scene

1. To be there, to arrive or attend
2. To comprehend the situation, to dig something

Make with a mouthful of Hi-Fi

Sing me a song

Make with the feet

Get moving, speed up, go away

"On your way, dreamboat. Make with the feet." FROM THE NOVEL *THE LITTLE SISTER*, RAYMOND CHANDLER, 1949

Horace McCoy: he knew his way around the main stem.

Making time

1. Becoming acquainted, necking, getting off with someone

"Chuck would make time with any broad on my payroll. He's a young girl's dream, isn't he?" FROM THE NOVEL *DEATH IS CONFIDENTIAL*, LAWRENCE LARIAR, 1959

See also the novel *Pound Of Flesh*, Simms Albert, 1953, "Kitty made time with the boss behind his wife's back – and with everybody else behind the boss's back!"

"We were making good time, / Getting in the know, / When the captain said Son, we gotta go' / I said 'That's alright, / You go right ahead, / I'm gonna Ubangi Stomp / Till I roll over dead.'" FROM THE ROCKABILLY RECORDING *UBANGI STOMP*, WARREN SMITH, 1956

2. Hurry up, travel fast

Man

1. All-purpose hipster form of address
2. A policeman, ie: the man
3. Drug connection or supplier

Marble city

Cemetery

Mark

A victim, a sucker

Maryjane

1. Marijuana, or a marijuana user

""You know what a maryjane is? You know what a mainliner is?' 'I think so. Are you trying to tell me these boys are drugged?'" FROM THE FILM *TOUCH OF EVIL*, 1959

2. Lesbian

"'Your little Edie is a Mary Jane – a chicken for some dyke.' 'He means,' Stretch explained, 'a les-bi-an. A girl that likes girls.'" FROM THE NOVEL *TWILIGHT GIRLS*, JUDSON GREY, 1962

Maryjanes

Shoes

"She was wearing pink cotton half socks and black patent leather Mary-Janes and a white dress with a pink ribbon tied around the middle." FROM THE NOVEL *YOUNG MAN WITH A HORN*, DOROTHY BAKER, 1938

"My Maryjane's been bitin' me for the past few minutes...this one's bitin' my instep." FRANK SINATRA ONSTAGE AT *THE SANDS*, LAS VEGAS, 1966

Mash

Alcohol

eg: "Drinkin' mash and talkin' trash."

Mash me a fin, gate, so I can cop a fry

Lend me five dollars, I want to get my hair straightened

Mashed

Drunk, blasted, out of your gourd

Mason-Dixon line

Anywhere out of bounds when necking, smooching or parking and petting

See the jazz recording *That's Her Mason-Dixon Line*, Will Bradley & his Orchestra, 1941

Match me

Give me a light

"Match me, Sidney..." BURT LANCASTER TO TONY CURTIS, FROM THE FILM *SWEET SMELL OF SUCCESS*, 1957

Mattress route

Sleeping your way to the top

"Gloria Clarke had made the big time by way of the mattress route. She was fruit for the newsmen, always hot

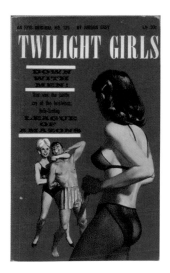

Your little Edie is a Mary Jane – a chicken for some dyke.

copy..." FROM THE NOVEL *DEATH IS CONFI-DENTIAL*, LAWRENCE LARIAR, 1959

Max out

To serve your entire prison sentence, with no parole

Maybe you got something there, but I wouldn't squeeze it too hard

Don't push your luck, watch what you're saying

"He stopped and looked at me care-fully. 'Maybe you got something there,' he said, 'but I wouldn't squeeze it too hard.'" GOOD ADVICE FROM MOOSE MAL-LOY, FROM THE NOVEL *FAREWELL, MY LOVELY*, RAYMOND CHANDLER, 1940

Mazuma

Money, the folding green

Meadow mayonnaise

Bullshit

"'You think the kind of stuff that sells real estate in Los Angeles will get you by with the San Francisco police de-partment.' 'What do you think sells the real estate in Los Angeles?' I asked. 'Meadow mayonnaise,' he said." FROM THE NOVEL *TOP OF THE HEAP*, A A FAIR (ERLE STANLEY GARDNER), 1952

Meal ticket

1. Job
2. Sugar daddy or benefactor

Meat

Blues slang for penis

"I'm going downtown / To old butcher Pete's, / Cause I want a piece / Of his good old meat..." FROM THE BLUES RECORD-ING *TAKE IT EASY, GREASY*, LIL JOHNSON, 1936

Meat show

Strip show, burlesque performance

A blonde set him up for a pigeon, slipped him a Michael F and flew off with his bankroll.

Meat wagon

1. Police vehicle
2. Ambulance
3. Hearse

"There's your customer, everything else is for the meat wagon." POLICEMAN TO DOCTOR AFTER SHOOT-OUT, FROM THE FILM *SIDE STREET*, 1950

Melting the gold fillings in your mouth

Kissing like you mean it

Memphis umbrella

A head full of serious hair grease or pomade, generally water-resistant

Mess Around

1. Have sex
2. Dance

"When I say git it, / Want you all to mess around..." FROM THE DADDY OF ALL BOOGIE-WOOGIE RECORDINGS, *PINE TOP'S BOOGIE WOOGIE*, PINE TOP SMITH, 1928

See also the jazz recording *Don't For-get To Mess Around*, Louis Armstrong's Hot Five, 1926, and also the blues re-cordings *That Dance Called Messin' Around*, Sara Martin, 1926, and *Messin' Around* Trixie Smith, 1926

Mickey Finn

Knockout drug, often disguised in an alcoholic drink

"He was hooked on the Irish Pigeon Racket last night. A blonde set him up for a pigeon, slipped him a Michael F and flew off with his bankroll." FROM THE NOV-EL *MORALS SQUAD*, SAMUEL A KRASNEY, 1959

This was also the name of the investi-gator in the novel *Mysterious Mickey Finn*, Elliot Paul, 1953 'Tingling Sus-pense and Gay Doings of a Private Detective in Thrill-Crazed Paris'

Midnight ramble

Late night show or dance. Popular in blues circles during the 1920s

See also the rock'n'roll recording *Midnight Ramblin' Tonight*, H-Bomb Ferguson, 1961

Misery

1. Coffee

"They's a jernt on Market Street belongs to a guy used to be a pal of mine in the field artillery. He'll set us up to coffee an'. He's a Greek, an' his misery's the hottest stuff in cups." FROM *SOMEBODY IN BOOTS*, NELSON ALGREN, 1935

2. Gin

Miseries

The blues, depression

"Sam, you sure do look like you've got the miseries." FROM THE COUNTRY RECORDING *LOVESICK BLUES*, EMMETT MILLER & HIS GEORGIA CRACKERS, 1928

"Gonna tell Aunt Mary 'bout Uncle John, / He claimed he had the miseries / But he's havin' lots of fun..." FROM THE ROCK'N'ROLL RECORDING *LONG TALL SALLY*, LITTLE RICHARD, 1956

Mitt

Hand

"No, buddy. No you won't. Keep your mitts off that desk." FROM THE NOVEL *RED GARDENIAS*, JONATHAN LATIMER, 1939

Mix it

To fight

Modernistic

With it, switched on, up to date

See the jazz recording *You've Got To Be Modernistic*, Jimmy Johnson and Clarence Wilson, 1930

Mojo

1. Penis

See the blues recording *My Daddy's Got The Mojo, But I Got the Say-So*, Butterbeans & Susie, 1926

2. Hard drugs
3. Voodoo charm

Moll

Girlfriend, usually tied up with a gangster

In 18th century English underworld slang, the word simply meant "whore". Erika Zastrow wrote a story called *A Moll And Her Man* for the September 1928 issue of *Black Mask* magazine, who billed it as "A romance of the Underworld." See also the novels *Night Club Moll*, Nick Baroni, c.1950, *Confessions Of A Chinatown Moll*, Jeff Bogar, 1953, and *Baby Moll*, Steve Brackeen, 1958 'She was the kind of woman a man would die for... and usually did.'

Monday morning quarterback

Know-all, braggart

Moniker

Name

Monogram in lead

Bullet wound

Monkey

"A music critic (He sees no music, hears no music, digs no music)." FROM THE ARTICLE *THE ARGOT OF JAZZ* BY ELLIOTT HORNE, *NEW YORK SUNDAY TIMES*, 1957

Mooch

1. An early jazz dance

The Edison company issued a recording by Collins and Harlan in

His misery's the hottest stuff in cups.

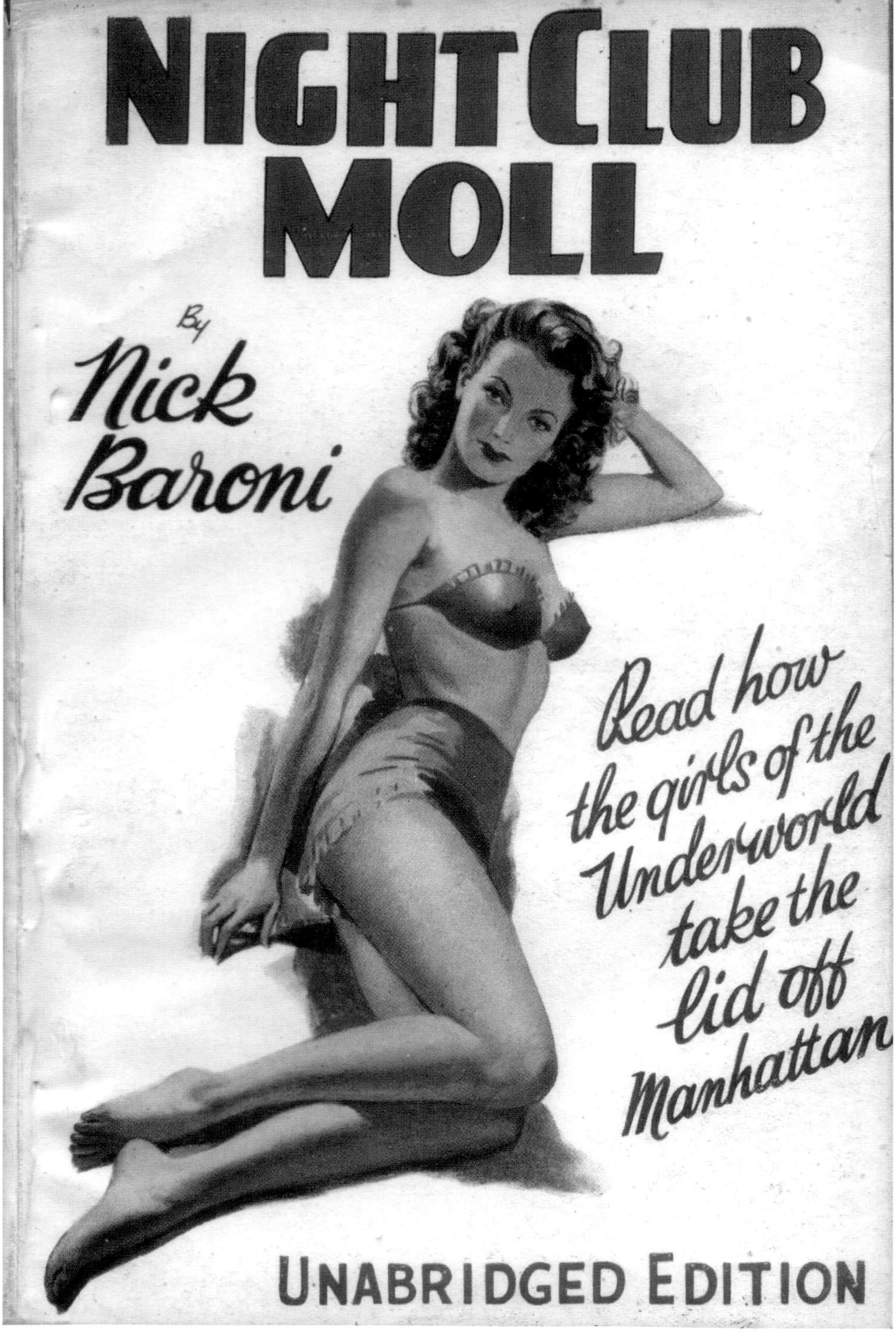

NIGHT CLUB MOLL

By

Nick Baroni

Read how the girls of the Underworld take the lid off Manhattan

UNABRIDGED EDITION

Ludco's rat-like puss twisted into a grin…

1914 called *Mootching Along*, accompanied by the following explanation: "For a long time, way back in the days before the war, the negroes did a shuffling or lazy man's dance. They could do it for hours at a time without tiring. They called it The Mootch. The shuffle explains the movement of the feet, and the 'mootch' defines the lazy movement of the shoulders, and the sway and rhythm of the body. Professor Charles H. and Mrs. Anderson will present their latest ballroom dance The Honolulu Mooch, Saturday October 15th, 1915." From an advert in the Harlem press, New York, 1915

See also the jazz recording *Shake It Up, Mooch It Up*, Eddie Heywood's Kansas City Blackbirds, 1927

2. To beg
3. To swindle or cheat

"Somebody said that Danny mooched Sam out of something like a hundred thousand bucks." FROM THE NOVEL OF THE SCREENPLAY OF *OCEAN'S ELEVEN*, GEORGE CLAYTON JOHNSON AND JACK GOLDEN RUSSELL, 1960

4. To walk around aimlessly

Moocher

Small time panhandler or beggar

Mooching the stem

Begging on the street

Moo-juice

Milk

From the autobiography *Really The Blues*, Mezz Mezzrow and Bernard Wolfe, 1946

Moonshine

Bootleg hooch, usually made out in the hills

See the short story *Moonshine* by Arthur Mallory in the August 6, 1921 issue of *Detective Story* magazine

Moonshiner

One who makes bootleg hooch

Early country star Fiddlin' John Carson, singer of classics such as *Who Bit The Wart Off Grandma's Nose* and *It's A Shame To Whip Your Wife On Sunday*, was described in a 1920s publicity handout as a "Moonshiner"

Moose-eyes

A leering dude

Mootah

Marijuana

"If you ever want the real truth about drugs just get me talking sometime. I'll tell you stories about it, but not what the papers said. That was for the birds. Like what they said about mrijuana, hell, Buddy, mootah never hurt a fly, I mean it. I know guys who bust a joint before each meal. Like taking a cocktail, you know?" FROM THE NOVEL *SECOND ENDING*, EVAN HUNTER, 1952

Morals of an alley cat

Someone who has little difficulty overcoming their shyness, a good time had by all

See the novel *Sing A Song Of Sex*, Hilary Hilton, 1963 "She's long-legged, sloe-eyed and her black hair reached down to here. She's beautiful, sensual and talented. She's queen of the folk singers. She has the morals of an alley cat!"

More dough than an army baker

Lots of money

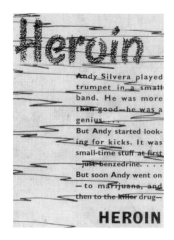

Second Ending – beware the mootah, brothers and sisters.

She got a lot of what they call the most... Jayne Mansfield starring in the Daddy-O of all rock'n'roll flicks, 1956.

More fun than a hot transfusion

Really wild, the best, a knockout

"Well, crazy, you have just destroyed three thousand of my corpuscles...Lady, you're more fun than a hot transfusion, you're really plasma. I think we could swing if I knew the music." SHELL SCOTT TALKS THAT TALK. FROM THE NOVEL *THE KUBLA KHAN CAPER*, RICHARD S. PRATHER, 1966

Moss

Hair

Most

The best

"She's got a lot / Of what they call the most" FROM THE ROCK'N'ROLL RECORDING *THE GIRL CAN'T HELP IT*, LITTLE RICHARD, 1956

"Look, y'know, you could be the most, but all that old-style jive you got written up on the board is nowhere." GANG LEADER J.I. TALKING TO THE TEACHER. FROM THE FILM *HIGH SCHOOL CONFIDENTIAL*, 1958

See also the vocal group recording *She's The Most*, The Five Keys, 1956, and the rockabilly recording *You Mostest Girl*, Bobby Lee Trammell, 1958

Most burnt

Excellent

Most monster

Mighty fine, the best

Motivate your pie chopper

Start talking

Motormouth

One who talks a lot

Moth's chance in a nudist colony

Doomed, no chance at all

Mothbox

Piano

Mount

Race car, designated rod, personal heap

"Of all the crust. That takes it for sheer ego. Do you realize how many really hot wheelers are looking for a mount?" FROM THE NOVEL *THUNDER ROAD*, WILLIAM CAMPBELL GAULT, 1952

Mountain dew

Bootleg liquor

Mouse

1. Black eye
2. Girl

"'A mouse I've never seen before saves me from the cops and asks me to go to a conference in her hotel room. Would I walk in cold?' She hesitated, and asked curiously, 'What's a mouse, Jim?' 'Don't act dumb. A mouse is a broad.'" FROM THE NOVEL *MURDERER'S ROW*, DONALD HAMILTON, 1962

Mouthpiece

Lawyer

"'Polly, this is Morrie Tannenbaum, the famous criminal lawyer from Chicago...' 'Are you really a mouthpiece?' Polly demanded eagerly." FROM THE NOVEL *THE DEADLY LOVER*, ROBERT O SABER, 1951

See also the book *The Great Mouthpiece – The Life of William J Fallon*, Gene Fowler, 1931, and the novelette *The Mouthpiece Martyr* by S J Bailey in the August 1937 issue of *Ten Detective Aces*

Mouthwash

Alcohol

Much beamy

Convivial, pleasant

Mud

Coffee

Mudkicker

Prostitute, streetwalker

Muffin

Girl

"That muffin you grifted — she's ok. Stuck her chin way out for you." FROM THE FILM *PICKUP ON SOUTH STREET*, 1953

Mug

1. Face, visage
2. A guy, a palooka, an ordinary Joe

Muggles

Marijuana

See the jazz recording *Muggles*, Louis Armstrong & His Orchestra, 1928

Mugshots

Photos in the police files of criminals' faces

Mugsnapper

Photographer

Mulligan stew

Cheap meal, poor man's food

Murderistic

Mighty fine

See the jazz recording *Murderistic*, Jimmy Dorsey & his Orchestra, 1941

Mush

Sloppy sentiment

"The world will pardon my mush / But I have got a crush on you." FROM THE LIVE RECORDING *I'VE GOT A CRUSH ON YOU*, FRANK SINATRA, AT THE SANDS, LAS VEGAS, 1966

Must be tough on your mother, not having any children

I don't know what you are, but you don't impress me

Mutt

Dog

My finger's itching

Keep quiet or I'll shoot you

My meat, Jack

That's right up my street, that's the one for me

See the novel *Killers Are My Meat*, Stephen Marlowe, 1957

My solid pigeon, that drape is a killer-diller, an E-flat Dillinger, a bit of a fly thing all on one page

How to compliment a young lady on her new, and pretty dress, according to Cab Calloway's Swingformation Bureau

My tonsils are dry

I'm thirsty, I could use a drink

Frankie and the Count slay Vegas on the suavest live album of them all.

N n

Nab

Arrest

"You nabbed his brother on a narcotics rap." FROM THE FILM *TOUCH OF EVIL*, 1959

Nabbers

Police, the forces of law

Naturally buzzin' cuzzin

A lively guy, a switched-on dude

Neck

To kiss, to jointly exercise the tonsils

Neck oil

Alcohol, booze

Necking party

A kissing session

See the novel *Sex Life Of A Cop*, Oscar Peck, n.d., late 1950s "This was no ordinary necking party. Before them stood their enraged boss – the Chief of Police – and some woman."

Necktie

The hangman's noose

"Well, they're gonna put a necktie on Gus he won't take off." FROM THE NOVEL *LITTLE CAESAR*, W.R. BURNETT, 1929

Necktie party

A lynching

"It sure looked as if I was about to be the guest of honour at a necktie party." FROM THE NOVEL *POP. 1280*, JM THOMPSON, 1964

Nickel

Five year jail sentence

Nickel-nurser

Stingy, a tightwad

Nickel rat

Cheap crook

"'We've had twelve more legitimate citizen complaints against you this month, for assault and battery.' 'From who? Hoods, dusters, mugs – a lot of nickel rats.'" HANDS-ON POLICE WORK BY THE MEN OF THE 16TH PRECINCT, FROM THE FILM *WHERE THE SIDEWALK ENDS*, 1950

Nighthawk

1. Taxi driver or cab
2. Late night person

See the jazz recording *Night Hawk Blues*, Coon-Sanders Original Night Hawk Orchestra, 1924. See also the painting *Night Hawks*, Edward Hopper, 1942

Nix

No, nothing, no thanks

No bats allowed

"No ugly people invited (girls)." DOCTOR HEPCAT DEMONSTRATES HIS WINNING WAY WITH A PARTY INVITATION. FROM THE BOOKLET *THE JIVES OF DOCTOR HEPCAT*, LAVADA DURST, 1953

No soap

No deal, nothing doing

Noggin

Brain

"'This dame,' I note, 'has got a noggin that works.'" FROM THE NOVEL *KILLERS DON'T CARE*, ROD CALLAHAN, 1950

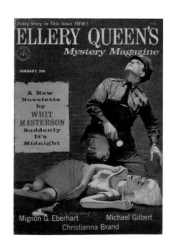

The nabbers on the scene of another homicide.

194

MONARCH BOOKS 35¢

A High Voltage Story Of Violence And Vice
Among Over-Privileged Teen-Agers

RUN TOUGH, RUN HARD

Carson Bingham

First Publication Anywhere

*So, the hell with Brett Sayers. Damn him to hell and gone. A no-goodnik from Creepville…
'violence and vice among over-privileged teenagers', 1961.*

Vince, there just ain't nobody like you when it comes to nosing a Tommy!

Why not let the gorilla snore on peacefully for the time being. It stuck out a mile he was not the kinduva guy to give much of a story. He just did not have enough above the eyes.

No-goodnik from Creepville

A despicable person, a waste of space

After the word Beatnik entered the language in the wake of the Russian Sputnik space mission, all kinds of slang words acquired similar endings

"So the hell with Brett Sayers. Damn him to hell and gone. A no-goodnik from Creepville." FROM THE NOVEL *RUN TOUGH, RUN HARD*, CARSON BINGHAM, 1961

Noodle it out

Think it through, come to a conclusion

Nose candy

Cocaine

ie: in *Dames Don't Care*, Peter Cheyney, 1937. However, in Dashiell Hammett's 1925 short story *Dead Yellow Women*, nose candy refers to heroin.

Nose paint

Alcohol

Nosing a Tommy

Handling a machine-gun

"Vince, there just ain't nobody like you when it comes to nosing a Tommy!" FROM THE NOVEL *'MAD DOG' COLL*, STEVE THURMAN, 1961

Not enough above the eyes

Unintelligent, hardly a main brain

"Why not let the gorilla snore on peacefully for the time being. It stuck out a mile he was not the kinduva guy to give me much of a story. He just did not have enough above the eyes." FROM THE NOVEL *NO DICE, SISTER!*, BART CARSON, N.D. (EARLY 1950s)

Not worth fifteen cents for parts

A loser, a nonentity, a worthless individual

"I don't get it, Ed. Billy-Billy isn't anybody. He's not worth fifteen cents for parts." FROM THE NOVEL *THE MERCENARIES*, DONALD E. WESTLAKE, 1960

Notch house

Brothel

Nothing shaking

No joy, nothing going on at all

"Why must she be / Such a doggone tease, / There's nothing shaking / But the leaves on the trees" FROM THE ROCK'N'ROLL RECORDING *NOTHING SHAKING (BUT THE LEAVES ON THE TREES)*, EDDIE FONTAINE, 1956

Now that you've laid me out, when you gonna bury me?

Have you finished criticizing me, or do I have to listen to more?

Now you're getting yourself some oxygen

Now you're talking, that's right

Nowhere

A failure, something worthless

eg: "Man, that lame Pat Boone platter they're spinning is strictly nowhere."

Nowhere drag

A real downer

Nuff sed

Need I say more, you can't argue with this

At the Lincoln Theatre, Baltimore in November 1920, The Four Jolly Jassers were billed as "a real Creole Jass Band from the Land of Jazz, New Orleans. Nuff Sed"

Numbers racket

Illegal lottery based on numbers printed in the financial or sports pages of newspapers

See the jazz recording *The Numbers Man*, Jack Sneed & his Sneezers, 1938

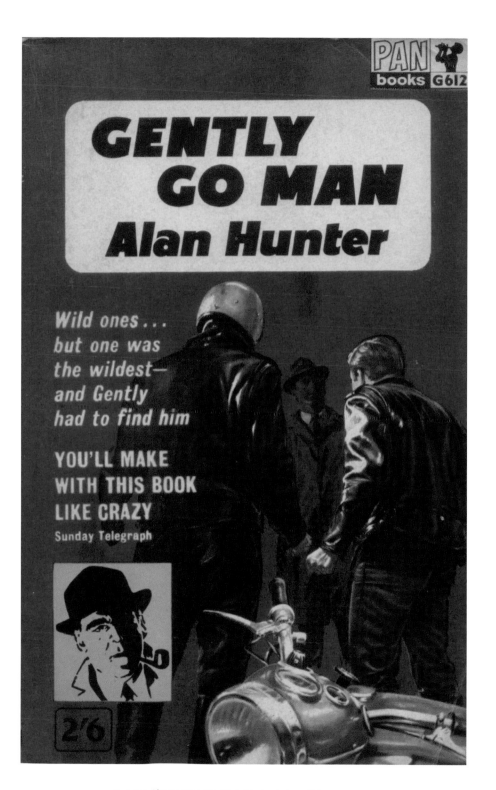

Squares. Always squares. It's a nowhere drag. It hangs me up.

O

Off

To steal

Off the cob

Something corny

Oil merchant

A flatterer

Old enough to vote

Vintage liquor or wine

"'The colonel's eyes brightened at the sight of the dust on the bottle. 'Fifteen years old?' 'Fifteen!' George Coffin's voice was indignant. 'Why this brandy was of voting age when Admiral Dewey sailed into Manila Bay.'" FROM THE NOVEL *THE SEARCH FOR MY GREAT-UNCLE'S HEAD*, JONATHAN LATIMER, 1937

On a roll

On a winning streak, lucky

On the beam

Intelligent, wise, alert

See the jazz recording *Theme On The Beam*, Lem Davis, 1946

"Well life is better / If you're on the beam, / And you dance to the rhythm / Of your wash machine..." FROM THE ROCKABILLY RECORDING *WASH MACHINE BOOGIE*, BILL BROWNING & THE ECHO VALLEY BOYS, 1956

"I had bought her a container of coffee on the way uptown, a sop to my concern about her. I wanted her on the beam." ie: I needed her to be thinking

straight. FROM THE NOVEL *DEATH IS CONFIDENTIAL*, LAWRENCE LARIAR, 1959

On the bop

Out looking for a gang fight

On the fly paper

Having your fingerprints on file

On the Jersey side

On the wrong side, in the wrong place

On the lam

On the run from the law

See the novelette *Death On The Lam* by G T Fleming-Roberts in the June 1939 issue of *Ten Detective Aces*

On the make

Ambitious, out for what you can get

See the 1951 novel *Girl On The Make*, Joan Sherman (author of *Pushover*) and *On The Make*, Roger James, c. 1965 "From hooker to mistress, lesbian lover to sex party hostess... she had only one desire – to reach the top at any price!"

On the skids

Down on your luck, a failure, tapped-out

"Don't lie! Lee was right on top as an actor, starring in Dead Shot, while you've been on the skids so long the grease is running hot. He was even making your ex-wife while all you could do was stand around and watch!" FROM

How to get on the beam, rhythmwise, 1948.

THE NOVEL *LAMENT FOR A LOUSY LOVER*, CARTER BROWN, 1960

On the sleeve

Habitually injecting drugs

"'I been on the sleeve since I got out of the army, Doc,' Frankie told him." FROM THE NOVEL *THE MAN WITH THE GOLDEN ARM*, NELSON ALGREN, 1949

On the take

Corrupt, accepting bribes

One bad stud

A hard guy, an evil dude

See the vocal group recording *One Bad Stud*, The Honey Bears, 1954

One-in-a-bar and live forever

"A bass player" FROM *DOWN BEAT'S YEARBOOK OF SWING*, 1939

One way ticket to Flipsville

Something mighty fine, really exciting

Onion ballad

A tearjerker, a sentimental song

Onion peeler

Switchblade knife

Only if you wanted to wear your face backwards for a while

Philip Marlowe tries to be reasonable, responding to a question with George Grosz's favourite tactic; a small yes and a big no. From the film version of *Farewell, My Lovely*, 1944, with Dick Powell as Marlowe

Oomph

Sex appeal

"Ferrell is a peculiar chap. He's married to a very attractive woman. What Lorraine Ferrell ever saw in Edgar is more than I know. She's a pippin, a swell looker, a smart, witty woman with lots of oomph." FROM THE NOVEL *THE CASE OF THE VAGABOND VIRGIN*, ERLE STANLEY GARDNER, 1948

Hollywood actress Ann Sheridan, who appeared in films such as *The Glass Key*, 1935, *Angels With Dirty Faces*, 1938, and *They Drive By Night* 1948, was billed as "The Oomph Girl"

Operator

1. Wheeler-dealer, one who knows their way around
2. Lover boy, stud, parlour snake

"'I think I met Jean once, in Joe's office.' Connie refilled his glass. 'That was Joe's canyon cutie. Then he had one in Hollywood and one in Studio City and down here in lowly Venice, he had Connie Garrity. Joe was quite an operator. Covered this town like a blanket.'" FROM THE NOVEL *RUN, KILLER, RUN*, WILLIAM CAMPBELL GAULT, 1955

See also the novel *The Swimming Pool Set*, Jason Morgan, 1964 "A novel that rips the roof off a resort rendezvous and its free-wheeling, free-loving 'operators'."

Orphan paper

Rubber cheques, funny money, counterfeit currency

The other half of a half-wit

Stupid

Out for kicks

Looking for a wild time, for entertainment

See the novel *Out For Kicks*, Wilene Shaw, 1959

I been on the sleeve since I got out of the army, Doc... Nelson Algren's 1949 jazz & junk masterpiece gets the big-screen treatment, 1955.

A DICTIONARY OF HIPSTER SLANG **129**

Out on the roof

A night on the tiles

"I was out on the roof last night and I've got a hangover like seven Swedes." FROM THE NOVEL *THE LADY IN THE LAKE*, RAYMOND CHANDLER, 1944

Out to the wide

Unconscious

Oversupply of mineral

Getting shot, being riddled with bullets

"'The last guy who bought her a drink they found him dead from an oversupply of mineral.' 'Mineral?' 'He had too much lead in his body.'" FROM THE NOVEL *RED GARDENIAS*, JONATHAN LATIMER, 1939

On a similar theme, see also the short story *Overdose of Lead* by Curtis Cluff in the November 1948 issue of *Black Mask*

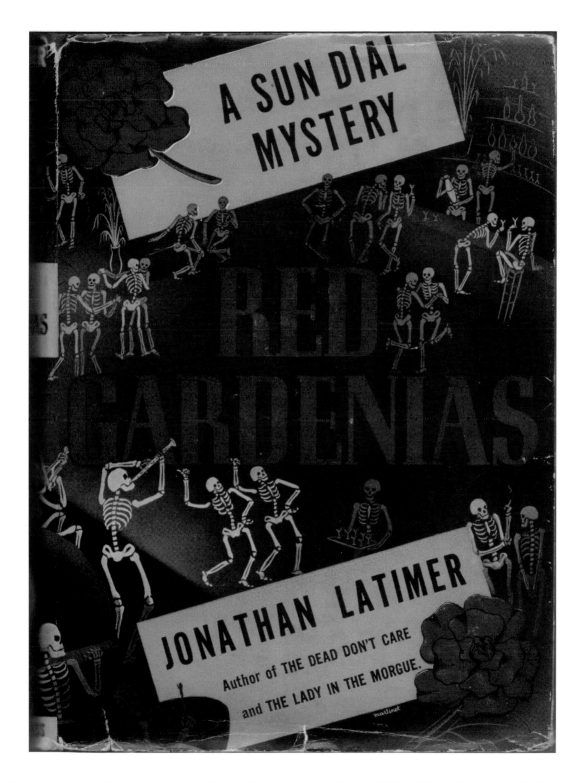

'The last guy who bought her a drink they found him dead from an oversupply of mineral.' 'Mineral?' 'He had too much lead in his body.'

Pp

P.D.Q.

Pretty damn quick

"In the Holland box at the post office there's an envelope with my scrawl. In that envelope there's a parcel-room check for the bundle we got yesterday. Now get that bundle and bring it here P.D.Q." PHILIP MARLOWE TELLING HIS SECRETARY HOW TO PICK UP THE BLACK BIRD, FROM THE FILM *THE MALTESE FALCON,* 1941

P.I.

Pimp

"It was about this time that Eddie Condon, Johnny Forton, Floyd O'Brien, and other hep kids were also hanging around to hear Joe and Louie. One night we saw a P.I. (one who lives and makes money from women) stabbed for making too much noise and annoying the girls at the table next to us." GEORGE WETTLING, QUOTED IN *THE ORAL HISTORY HEAR ME TALKIN' TO YA – THE STORY OF JAZZ BY THE MEN WHOMADE IT,* NAT SHAPIRO AND NAT HENTOFF, EDS., 1955

Pack, shack & stack

All your belongings – your clothes, your home, and your money

Pack your grip

Get your stuff together and go

Packing iron

Carrying a gun

Pad

1. Home, apartment, room

In 18th century English slang, your pad was your bed

"You gotta have a date with me before you fall in my pad, darling..." FROM THE NOVEL *IF HE HOLLERS LET HIM GO,* CHESTER HIMES, 1945

See also the novel *Pads Are For Passion,* Sheldon Lord (Lawrence Block), 1961 "Anita was a virgin – till the hipsters got hold of her!"

See also the rock'n'roll recording *The Pad,* Bobby Strigo & the Blue Notes, 1959

2. To tell, to inform

Pad down

Living arrangements, where you cop your flop

"I think he padded down with Benjy Kane. That's west on North Avenue near Pulaski." FROM THE NOVEL *SEARCH FOR A DEAD NYMPHO,* PAUL W. FAIRMAN, 1967

Pad money

Rent money, as quoted in the street-gang study *Apaches of New York,* A. H. Lewis, 1912

Painting the town

Going out and having a wild night

"A smile on my face / A song on my lips, / Pretending is all I do. / I'm painting the town red / To hide a heart that's blue." FROM THE JAZZ RECORDING *I'M PAINTING THE TOWN RED,* BILLIE HOLIDAY WITH TEDDY WILSON & HIS ORCHESTRA, 1935

"There ain't no use, hanging round, / While you paint up the town. / Crazy me, learnin' slow, / Baby you sure got your man feelin' low" FROM THE COUNTRY RECORDING *FEELIN' LOW,* ERNIE CHAFFIN, 1957

Chester Himes' 1945 debut novel included then-current jazz words like 'groovy' and 'pad' a full two decades before the hippies reckoned they invented them.

See also the self-confessed rockin' recording *Paint The Town Red* by Rocky And The Rocky Fellows (a pseudonym for singer Al Sweatt)

Palomino

Good looking woman

Palooka

A mug, a punter, an ordinary joe. A disparaging term for a man, deriving from a boxing expression for a third-rate fighter

Pan

Face

Hence the expression deadpan, showing as much change of expression as a corpse

Pancake

Dame, doll, tomato

Panel joint

Whorehouse where the rooms have sliding panels so that the clients can be robbed whilst otherwise engaged

"A panel joint is a fast shuffling clip. The girl brings the sucker in. A bedroom, see? They undress. She puts the sucker's pants over a chair for him. While they're in bed, a panel in the wall opens, and a guy reaches in and frisks the sucker's pants." FROM THE NOVEL *LITTLE MEN, BIG WORLD*, W.R. BURNETT, 1951

Panther piss

Bootleg liquor

Paper

1. Money
2. A cheque

Paper hanging

Passing forged cheques

Park the hot boiler

Hide the stolen car

Park yourself

Sit down

Parking pet

Girlfriend

Parlour snake

Lounge lizard, smooth talker, oily customer

"'Is that what the crowd does that keeps following you around tonight?' 'What crowd,' she asked innocently. 'The fifty per cent of the sophomore class that keeps following you around tonight?'' A lot of parlour snakes,' she said, ungratefully." FROM THE SHORT STORY *JOSEPHINE: A WOMAN WITH A PAST*, F. SCOTT FITZGERALD, 1930

Paws

Hands

Payola

Under-the-table payments, most famously from record companies to DJs in the late '50s in return for hyping certain slabs of wax

"The first night audience is people we hire to go there, or friends. They yak it up and he gets twenty encores. Then we slip the payola to the leg men of the big columnists – and a few columnists themselves. There are pictures and interviews. Payola to the disc jockeys... Believe me, John, if the property has any value at all, it can be sold – sold big and fast." RICHARD JESSUP'S 1958 MUSIC BUSINESS NOVEL *LOWDOWN* EXPLAINS HOW THE SYSTEM WORKS. FIFTY YEARS LATER, NOTHING'S CHANGED

See also the novel *Payola Woman*, Carson Bingham, 1960, and the comedy recording *The Old Payola Blues*, Stan Freeberg, 1957

Peach

Good looking

"A peach, a plum, a reg'lar steamer!" FROM *NIGHT CLUB MOLL*, NICK BARONI, 1930s

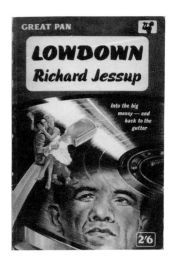

Slip the payola to the legmen – the dirty side of the music business, 1958.

See also the country recording *She's A Peach Of A Girl From Georgia*, Carl Bryant, 1960

Pearl diver

Someone who washes dishes

Pecks

Food

Pedal extremities

Feet

See the jazz recording *Your Feet's Too Big*, Fats Waller & his Rhythm, 1941

Peel the ears and get it

Listen closely

Peeper

Private detective

Peg out

Die

Pegs

1. Legs
2. Trousers

See the rockabilly recordings *Peg Pants*, Bill Beach, 1956, and *Pink Peg Slacks*, Eddie Cochran, 1956

Pen

Prison, penitentiary

Perforate

Shoot

Peter

A safe

Peterman

A safecracker

Picking iron out of your liver

Having gunshot wounds

The Public Enemy – having run out of pineapples, Jimmy Cagney uses a grapefruit.

"'Keep on riding me, they're gonna be picking iron out of your liver.' 'The cheaper the crook, the gaudier the patter, huh?'" **FROM THE FILM** *THE MALTESE FALCON*, 1941

Picking them up and putting them down

1. Running
2. Dancing

Piece

Gun, weapon

"I thinkin 'Watch out now. Watch out now all you Wolves. Here come one of the Priests customers. Stan back or get burned.' An my hand go all hollow you know feelin the coolness of the piece in it." **FROM THE NOVEL** *THE COOL WORLD*, WARREN MILLER, 1959

Piece of change

Some money

Pie chopper

Mouth

Pigeon

1. Sucker, mark, the victim of a con game
2. Dame, doll, chick

See the rock'n'roll recording *Cooing To The Wrong Pigeon*, Merrill E Moore, 1956

Pin

To observe, to notice

Pineapple

Hand grenade

"Johnny stopped a pineapple" ie: The dude's blown to pieces. **FROM THE NOVEL** *NIGHT CLUB MOLL*, NICK BARONI, 1930s

"Look at this dump, four pineapples tossed at us in two days..." **FROM THE FILM** *THE PUBLIC ENEMY*, 1933

Paul Cain wrote a story called *Pineapple* for the March 1936 issue of *Black Mask* magazine

Pinched

Arrested

Pine box parole

To die in prison

Pipe

Saxophone

Pitch a bitch

Complain

Plant you now, dig you later

Got to go now, see you later

See the rockabilly recording *Plant You Now, Dig You Later*, Bee Arnold with Amos Como's Tune Toppers, 1955

Planted

Buried

"If I need the stuff and don't have it, I'm dead. I'm not exaggerating. And if I get planted, you're sunk." FROM THE NOVEL DARLING, IT'S DEATH, RICHARD S. PRATHER, 1959

Plastered

Drunk, sluiced, oiled-up, loaded

See the jazz recording *Plastered In Paris*, Chauncey Morehouse & his Orchestra, 1938

Platters

Records, discs, waxings

"The platters that matter..." Defined as "A phonograph record" by *Down Beat's Yearbook of Swing,* 1939

Black Mask magazine published a story set in the record industry in May 1949 by Fergus Truslow entitled *Pardon My Poison Platters*

Play bedwarmer

Sleep with someone

Play the chill

Ignore someone

Play the duck

Avoid someone, go into hiding

Plumbers

Hit men, hired killers

"The big boys just give a couple of the plumbers your address and that's it. If the first set of plumbers don't fix the leak, they send another set." FROM THE NOVEL *LITTLE MEN, BIG WORLD*, W.R. BURNETT, 1951

Plumbing

A trumpet

Poke in the snout

A punch in the nose

Poker pan

A straight face, expressionless

Pokey

Prison

"The sheriff caught him out with Jezebel, / Threw poor Okie in the county jail..." FROM THE ROCKABILLY RECORDING *OKIE'S IN THE POKEY*, JIMMY PATTON, 1956

See also the jazz recording *Pokey Joe*, Bob Skyles & his Skyrockets, 1940

Polluted

Drunk

"'I've changed my mind.' 'About what?' 'About getting crocked.' 'You mean you're going to get crocked?' 'Absolutely pie-eyed. Polluted. I'm going to celebrate.'" FROM THE NOVEL *THIS IS MURDER*, ERLE STANLEY GARDNER, 1935

Pops

"A word of greeting between musicians." FROM *DOWN BEAT'S YEARBOOK OF SWING, 1939*

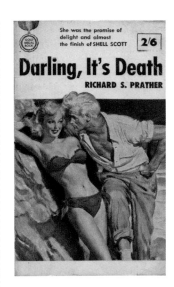

If I get planted, you're sunk.

Potatoes

Money, moolah, the folding green

"This house belongs to an old doll by the name of Miss Abigail Ardsley, and anybody who ever reads the newspapers will tell you that Miss Abigail Ardsley has so many potatoes that it is really painful to think of, especially to people who have no potatoes whatever. In fact, Miss Abigail Ardsley has practically all the potatoes in the world, except maybe a few left over for general circulation." FROM THE SHORT STORY *THE OLD DOLL'S HOUSE*, DAMON RUNYON, 1933, (FILMED IN 1934 AS *MIDNIGHT ALIBI*, AND THEN AGAIN IN 1941 AS A SHORT ENTITLED AT *THE STROKE OF TWELVE*)

Pouring on the coal

Stepping on the accelerator, driving fast

Pouring water on a drowning man

Cruel behaviour

"I saw her one day with a big old pan, / Pouring ice cold water on a drowning man." FROM THE ROCKABILLY RECORDING *EVIL EVE*, JOE D. GIBSON, 1957

Prayerbones

Knees

Preparing bait

Putting on makeup

Pressed stud

Well-dressed dude, a guy who's looking sharp

Pretzel

A French horn

Promote

1. Obtain, steal
2. Seduce

"That monkey's been trying to promote me for months." FROM THE NOVEL *RED GARDENIAS*, JONATHAN LATIMER, 1939

The late great Ronnie Dawson – one pressed stud.

3. To pimp

See the novel *The Promoter*, Orrie Hitt, 1957 "Vice was his business, and he loved his work!"

Prowl-car

Police vehicle

"He'd have called all the cops in all the counties, and there'd be even more prowl cars hunting me now." FROM THE NOVEL *ALWAYS LEAVE 'EM DYING*, RICHARD S. PRATHER, 1961

Pruning your peach-fuzz

Shaving your face

A phrase used by the rock'n'roll DJ The Mad Daddy, who later had a song named after him on the album *Songs The Lord Taught Us*, The Cramps, 1980

Pucker paint

Lipstick

See the rockabilly recording *Pucker Paint*, Danny Wolfe, 1958

Puff

"To ride, walk, or fly." FROM THE BOOKLET *THE JIVES OF DOCTOR HEPCAT*, LAVADA DURST, 1953

Puff down the stroll

Drive down the street

Pull a creep

Leave

Pull into the curb, Daddy-O, before your dreamboat becomes a battleship

This relationship is doing you no good, give it up

Pull up and squat

Have a seat, sit yourself down

"'Hi boys,' he said, and jerked a thumb to some chairs along the wall. 'Pull up

and squat.' FROM THE NOVEL *THE LENIENT BEAST*, FREDRIC BROWN, 1957

Pulling a Judas

Pulling the finger on someone, becoming an informer

Pulling the Dutch act

Committing suicide

"A girl pulled the Dutch act..." FROM THE NOVEL *VENGEANCE IS MINE*, MICKEY SPILLANE, 1951

Pump

Heart

"'What happened?' 'Got him right in the pump with this.' 'It's a Webley. English, isn't it?'" FROM THE FILM *THE MALTESE FALCON*, 1941

Pumped out

Shot and killed

"I see by the papers that Cherulli got pumped out." FROM THE NOVEL *GREEN ICE*, RAOUL WHITFIELD, 1930

Punk

1. Cheap crook, loser, mug

Philip Ketchum wrote a story for the January 1950 issue of *Black Mask* magazine called *One Sunk Punk*

2. Immature kid, upstart, whippersnapper

See the novel *The Punks*, Lee Richards, 1964 "SHE was the pretty new teacher; HE was the school's number-one 'lover boy'!"

Push-note

One dollar bill

Pushed

Killed, assassinated, knocked off

Puss

Face

"Ludco's rat-like puss twisted into a grin." FROM THE NOVEL *NIGHT CLUB MOLL*, NICK BARONI, 1930s

"My folks were tough. When I was born they took one look at this puss of mine and told me to get lost." FROM THE FILM *THE HITCH HIKER*, 1953

Put an egg on your shoe and beat it

Go away, get lost

Put on

To tease, to deceive

Put on the feedbag

To eat

"Say, Daddy-O, do you know where a cat can have a ball and put on a fine feedbag?" FROM THE JAZZ RECORDING *TWO BLOCKS DOWN, TURN TO THE LEFT*, CAB CALLOWAY & HIS ORCHESTRA, 1930s

Put on the wolf act

Act like a ladies man, run after women, make like a lounge lizard

"Arthur Cushing was going to marry me. That is, he said he was. I guess he said the same thing to others. I thought he was playing around, so I made arrangements with Nora Fleming to call me the next time he was getting ready to put on the wolf act." FROM THE NOVEL *THE CASE OF THE ANGRY MOURNER*, ERLE STANLEY GARDNER, 1958

Put some alcohol in the radiator

Have a drink to warm yourself up

"It's a cold night. Let's put some alcohol in the radiator." FROM THE NOVEL *SAVAGE STREETS*, WILLIAM MCGIVERN, 1959

Put that in writing and I'll paste it in my scrapbook

I don't believe you

"'I like you, Johnny O'Clock.' 'Put that in writing and I'll paste it in my scrapbook.' 'I mean it...'" FROM THE FILM *JOHNNY O'CLOCK*, 1947

A girl pulled the Dutch act.

TV's Private Eyeful puts the bite on someone.

Put the bite on someone

1. Blackmail, extort money

"Helena put the blackmail bite on our war hero for five thousand smackers. He paid off on New Year's Eve, but the murderer wound up with the dough." FROM THE NOVEL *A GUN FOR HONEY*, G.G. FICKLING, 1958

2. Borrow money

Put the polish on the furniture

Sort yourself out, reach the optimum level

"One little shot of bourbon to put the polish on the furniture." FROM THE NOVEL *YOUR DEAL MY LOVELY*, PETER CHEYNEY, 1941

Put to bed with a shovel

1. Buried
2. Totally drunk

Put your needle away

Stop bugging me, get off my back

Put your teeth on parade

Smile, flash some ivory

"The smile went lame until Janis introduced us. 'Neal, I want you to meet Enrique Trigo. This is Mr. Cotten.' He put the teeth on parade again. 'Pleased to meet you, Cotten.'" FROM THE NOVEL *SLEEP NO MORE*, SAM S TAYLOR, 1951

Putdown

Derogatory comment or criticism

Putting it down

Speaking, expressing an opinion

"I'm telling you what's bein' put down, You better pick up on it..." FROM THE R&B JUMP JIVE RECORDING *BEWARE, BROTHER, BEWARE*, LOUIS JORDAN & THE TYMPANY FIVE, 1946

"I'm putting it down, but you ain't picking it up." FROM THE FILM *HIGH SCHOOL CONFIDENTIAL*, 1958

Putting on the dog

Pretending to be better than you are, putting on airs

"'These three birds came in on the Memphis train. Said they was with the T.V.A., but I'd bet dollars to doughnuts they wasn't.' 'What makes you think so?' 'I don't know. They never looked right somehow.' 'Well, that's the world for you,' Sybil said philosophically. 'People always putting on the dog, trying to act like they're you-know-what on a stick.'" FROM THE NOVEL *VIOLENT SATURDAY*, W. L. HEATH, 1955

Putting on the style

Dressing suavely, going upmarket, having pretensions

"You were mine for just a while / Now you're putting on the style / And you've never once looked back / At your home across the tracks." FROM THE COUNTRY RECORDING *PICK ME UP ON YOUR WAY DOWN*, CHARLIE WALKER, 1958

Putting up paper for yourself

Bragging, singing your own praises

The reference is to running around town sticking up posters with your own face on them

Q

Q

San Quentin prison

"She would be very nice to come home to after a stretch in Q." FROM THE NOVEL OF THE SCREENPLAY OF *OCEAN'S ELEVEN*, GEORGE CLAYTON JOHNSON AND JACK GOLDEN RUSSELL, 1960

Q.T.

1. Secret

eg: "Strictly hush hush, and on the Q.T." ie: On the quiet, just between you and me

"You understand this is to be strictly on the Q.T.?" FROM THE NOVEL *THE GLASS KEY*, DASHIELL HAMMETT, 1931

"You thought your little romance / Was on the strict Q.T., / So if you want your freedom P.D.Q., / Divorce me C.O.D" FROM THE COUNTRY RECORDING *DIVORCE ME C.O.D.*, MERLE TRAVIS, 1946

2. "Cutie" – a slang term for a prostitute
3. "Cutie" – term of affection

See the rock'n'roll recording *Q-T-Cute*, Dart Ward & the Cut-Ups, 1958

Quail

Woman, girl

"'I say professor, you've hunted in all parts of the country. What kind of quail is that there, over there by the tree?' 'That is very unusual, Doctor. That kind of game is not typical in this section.' 'What would you say it was, Professor – a red-billed roadrunner?' 'No, no, no, Doctor, why I could say with perfect confidence that it's a black-topped cinch....'" GLEN MILLER'S BAND GET FRISKY, FROM THE FILM *ORCHESTRA WIVES*, 1942

One of the books written on Death Row by San Quentin's famous inmate, Caryl Chessman, who went to the gas chamber in the year of its publication, 1960.

Rr

Rack 'em back

Pull up the covers and go to sleep

Racket

Criminal enterprise, scam, business

See the novel *All In The Racket*, William E Weeks, 1930

Ragtop

Convertible car

Railroaded

Framed, fitted up on false evidence

Raise sand

Make a fuss, create a stir

"You're always raising sand baby, / And you're always doggin' me, / I believe to my soul, / You was stealin' back to your used-to-be." FROM THE BLUES RECORDING *TWO-TIMIN' WOMAN*, CASEY BILL WELDON, 1936

Rap

Criminal charge

Rap sheet

Criminal record

Blackie Audett, a bank robber who worked with Dillinger, Baby Face Nelson and Capone, published an autobiography in 1955 called *Rap Sheet*

Rat fink

A louse, a lowdown dog

"I got the word for you / Because that's what you is, / You is a rat fink,/ You is a rat fink..." FROM THE ROCK'N'ROLL RECORDING *RAT PFINK A BOO BOO THEME*, RON HAYDOCK & THE BOPPERS, 1966

Rat someone out

Betray, sell someone down the river, inform on them

Rattle your skeleton

Show off your figure, exhibit your charms

Rattler

Streetcar

Raw deal

Unfair break, tough shake of the dice

"Well I done had my last raw deal, / Baby I'm through with you..." FROM THE ROCKABILLY RECORDING *RAW DEAL*, JUNIOR THOMPSON & THE METEORS, 1956

Read 'em and weep

What do you think of that, I've won, I've beaten you

Ready

Hep, alert, knocking, aware of the scene

Real gone

1. Far out, wild, uninhibited, totally sent

"Hold it fellas, / That don't move me, / Let's get real, real gone for a change..." THE HILLBILLY CAT PUTS A 50,000 VOLTS UP THE BLUES AND WINDS UP WITH ROCKA-BILLY FROM *MILK-COW BLUES BOOGIE* ELVIS PRESLEY, 1955

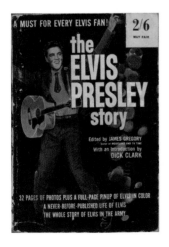

Let's get real, real gone for a change.

See also *Real, Real Gone*, John Lee Hooker, 1953

2. Insane

"You're a schizo, and real gone." SHELL SCOTT RECEIVES SOME PSYCHIATRIC ADVICE, FROM THE NOVEL *ALWAYS LEAVE 'EM DYING*, RICHARD S. PRATHER, 1961

Real wild child

Hip, gone, a righteous groover

"Well I'm just out of school / Like I'm real, real cool, / I've got to jump, got to jive, / Got the message I'm alive, / I'm a wild, I'm a wild one, / Ooh yeah I'm a wild one. / I'm gonna keep a shakin' / I'm gonna keep-a movin' baby / Don't you cramp my style / I'm a real wild child." FROM THE ROCK'N'ROLL RECORDING *REAL WILD CHILD*, JERRY LEE LEWIS, 1958 (ORIGINALLY BY AUSTRALIAN ROCKER JOHNNY O'KEEFE, AND LATER A SIZEABLE HIT FOR MR. JAMES OSTERBERG.)

Red hot and ready to moan

Fired up, all set for a wild night

Red onion

Low drinking joint

Louis Armstrong's first recording outfit when he left King Oliver's Band in 1924 was called The Red Onion Jazz Babies

Reefer

Weed, grass, dope

"'Man, what's the matter with that cat there?' / 'Must be full o' reefers.' / 'Full o' reefers?' / 'Yeah man.' / 'You mean that cat's high?' / 'Sailin'...'" FROM THE JAZZ RECORDING *REEFER MAN*, CAB CALLOWAY, 1932

Harlan Lattimore & his Connie's Inn Orchestra also recorded this tune in 1932, with *Chant of the Weed* on the flipside.

See also the novels *Reefer Girl* (a.k.a. *Young Sinners*) Jane Manning, 1952 "Girls of the Slums in a Mad Search for Teen-Age Thrills' and *Reefer Club*, Luke Roberts, n.d., (1950s) "The girl was the slave of marijuana – yet was she wholly bad?"

Reel in your tongue, you're getting your shirt wet

Stop leering at me

"Miss Harrington waved the cigarette at him. 'Hi Dad,' she says. 'Reel in your tongue. You're getting your shirt wet.'" FROM THE NOVEL *THE DIAMOND BIKINI*, CHARLES WILLIAMS, 1956

Reet

Right, ok

See the jazz recording *Are You All Reet?* Cab Calloway & his Orchestra, 1941

Refrigerator

Prison

Repo man

Debt collector, someone who will come round and repossess your car, your home etc

Rest the weight

Sit down, take it easy

"Rest the weight, Bob, you must be tired of toting it around all day..." FROM THE NOVEL *IF HE HOLLERS LET HIM GO*, CHESTER HIMES, 1945

Rewire job

Medical attention

"They gotta doc here. They're gonna rewire Crazy." FROM THE FILM *THE WILD ONE*, 1954

Rhino

Money

Late night raid on a jazz joint, 1951 – and you thought 50s London was just cups of tea and *Dixon of Dock Green*...

Gene Vincent sings *Spaceship To Mars* in the film *It's Trad, Dad*, a celluloid treat which was released in the US under the title *Ring-a-Ding Rhythm*.

"Give me my rhino instead of lip and I'll pull my freight." (ie: Give me my money instead of just talking and I'll be gone.) FROM THE SHORT STORY *THE BIG KNOCKOVER*, DASHIELL HAMMETT, 1927

Rib

Girlfriend (short for Adam's rib)

Ricky-tick

Corny music, or anything clichéd

Riding academy

Whorehouse

Riding for a fall

In for trouble

Riding herd

Being in charge

Riding rubber

Travelling by car

Riding the blinds

Hopping a freight, hitching a ride on a train

See *I'm Ridin' the Blinds on a West Bound Train*, Frank Marvin, 1930

Riding the ozone

Travelling on the elevated railway in New York

"Izzy Myers had told the two men to 'ride the ozone' uptown. One did not have to be deeply versed in the vernacular to understand what he had meant. Skinny and Maloch were to go up to Eightieth Street on the elevated." FROM THE NOVEL *THE BIG SHOT*, FRANK L PACKARD, 1929

Right guy

Trustworthy

"I came here with a straight proposition, take it or leave it, one right guy to another." FROM THE FILM *THE BIG SLEEP*, 1940

Right now, Jack, the panic is on

Times are hard, things are tough all over

Righteous

Cool, hip, in the groove and generally suave as all hell

Righteous bush

Marijuana

From the autobiography *Really The Blues*, Mezz Mezzrow and Bernard Wolfe, 1946

Ring-a-Ding

Solid-sent, knocked out, A-1, a gasser

See the novels *Ring-a-Ding-Ding*, Frank Kane, 1963, *Ring-a-Ding Lover*, Seth Ariman, 1962 and *The Ring-a-Ding UFOs*, Bob Tralins, 1967

The 1962 UK music film *It's Trad, Dad*, in which Gene Vincent sings *Spaceship To Mars*, was renamed *Ring-a-Ding Rhythm* for its US release

Ripe for the lilies

Dead

Roach

Marijuana cigarette, joint, reefer

Roach bender

Marijuana smoker

Roach killers

Shoes

Roadhouse

Lowdown roadside bar, outside city limits, often with a sleazy reputation

"They went further out on the highway to Buster's Roadhouse where chorus girls wore small panties. There were rooms to rent by the hour in the attached motel behind." FROM THE NOVEL *GO, MAN, GO!,* EDWARD DE ROO, 1959

See the novel *The Road House Murders*, Robert Portner Koehler, 1946, and also the novel *Roadhouse Harem*, Stanley Curson, c. 1963 *"Wild pagan orgies were a regular thing at the hostelry. Even murder couldn't spoil the party!"*

See the jazz recording *Roadhouse Blues*, George Williams, 1926 (the flip was called *Bootlegging Daddy*)

Rock and roll

Sex (often later thinly disguised as a term for dancing)

See the blues recording *My Man Rocks Me (With One Steady Roll)*, Trixie Smith, 1922

"If you wanna satisfy my soul, Come on and rock me with a steady roll." FROM THE BLUES RECORDING *YOU'VE GOT TO SAVE THAT THING,* ORA ALEXANDER, 1931

"Want you to roll me baby, / Like a baker rolls his dough, / Reel and rock and roll me, / Baby all night long." FROM THE BLUES RECORDING *ROLLIN' MAMA BLUES,* RUBY GLAZE & HOT SHOT WILLIE (BLIND WILLIE MCTELL), 1931

"Gonna hold my baby as tight as I can, Tonight she'll know I'm a mighty man..." FROM THE R&B RECORDING *GOOD ROCKING TONIGHT,* ROY BROWN, 1946

See also (among many others) the recordings *Rock, Jenny, Rock*, The Georgia Strutters, 1926; *Rocking And Rolling*, Robinson's Knights of Rest, 1930; *Rock and Roll*, The Boswell Sisters, 1934; *Rock It In Rhythm*, Tampa Red, 1938; See also *Rockin' Rollin' Mama*, Buddy Jones, 1939; *Rock And Rollin' Daddy*, Merline Johnson, 1939; *I Want To Rock,*

Cab Calloway & his Orchestra, 1942; *We're Gonna Rock, We're Gonna Roll*, Wild Bill Moore, 1947

See also the novel *Rock'n Roll Gal*, Ernie Weatherall, 1957 "The sizzling world of real gone guys – and dolls on dope!"

Rock crusher

Accordian

Rocket in your pocket

Erection

"Let's go someplace / Where we can rock a bit / I got a rocket in my pocket / And the fuse is lit." FROM THE ROCKABILLY RECORDING *I GOT A ROCKET IN MY POCKET,* JIMMY LOGSDON (AKA JIMMY LLOYD), 1958

Rocks in your head

Stupidity

Rod

1. Gun

"Turn around...then shed your rod. Drop it on the floor." FROM THE NOVEL *THE FAST BUCK,* JAMES HADLEY CHASE, 1952

2. Gunman

"Two of the hottest rods in town combing the joints looking for you and you don't even get bothered enough to stop eating." FROM THE NOVEL *KISS ME, DEADLY,* MICKEY SPILLANE, 1953

3. Car, short for Hot Rod

Rod merchant

Gunman

Rodded

Armed, carrying a gun

Roll

Bread stash, heap of green, the contents of your wallet

Rock'n'Roll hits London cinemas, August 1956.

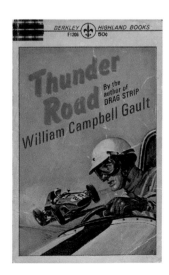

Every car with the hood off is a hot-rod to the papers. Chrome plating doesn't make a rod, or steel-packed mufflers, or a driver with goggles – from the Daddy-O of hot-rod books, 1952.

Roll it down the alley and see if it makes a strike

Try it for size, give it a go

Roll them bones

Roll the dice

"We're gonna pick 'em up an' shake 'em up / 'An let 'em roll, / All night long we're gonna roll them bones..." **FROM THE ROCKABILLY RECORDING** *PICK 'EM UP 'AN SHAKE 'EM UP,* **CECIL McCULLOCH & THE BORDER BOYS, 1956**

Roll with the punches

Go along with things, accept the inevitable

Rooked

Cheated

Roost

Dwelling place, abode

There was a jazz venue in New York in the 1940s called the Royal Roost – also known as the Metropolitan Bopera House

Roping and branding

Landing a husband

"He's very eligible and goes out with a lot of the girls around but none of them has been able to rope and brand him yet." **FROM THE NOVEL** *THAT NIGHT IT RAINED,* **HILLARY WAUGH, 1961**

Roscoe

Handgun, firearm

"He propositions me we should heist the Jitney Jungle and I axes him where we can get a couple of rods, and he says we oney need one, Homer, and I got that, and he pull a roscoe off his hip." **FROM THE SHORT STORY COLLECTION** *THE NEON WILDERNESS,* **NELSON ALGREN, 1947**

In the works of Damon Runyon, guns are generally called a John Roscoe or a Betsy

Rough-house

A fight or disturbance

Roundheels

Party girl, the original good time who's been had by all – deriving from a supposed natural ability to regularly fall over backwards

"'Little Miss Roundheels,' Madge Anderson said coldly, 'did a lot of things secretly, but none of them, my darling, was getting married. She specialised in gentlemen who were otherwise committed, didn't she, boys?'" **FROM THE NOVEL** *MURDER'S LITTLE HELPER,* **GEORGE BAGBY, 1963**

Rubdown

A beating

Rub-joint

A cheap dancehall where dancing partners can be hired

Rubbed out

Killed

"'Five thousand bucks for rubbing out a horse.' 'Ok, Pops, how do I get it?'" **FROM THE FILM THE KILLING, 1956**

Rubber

Automotive transportation

"You still on rubber?" – ie: Do you still have a car? **FROM THE NOVEL** *IF HE HOLLERS, LET HIM GO,* **CHESTER HIMES, 1945**

Rubbernecker

Tourist, out-of-towner gawking at the sights or anyone who stares

"'I saw you giving Peter March the gladeye.' She said, 'You were rubbering at Carmel, too...'" **FROM THE NOVEL** *RED GARDENIAS,* **JONATHAN LATIMER, 1939**

Hard-boiled roscoe-slingers, London-style, 1935.

Rube

A sucker, a hayseed, an easy mark

Rug

1 Hair

"I've got to pick up on a barber because my rug needs a good dusting." ie: I need a haircut **FROM THE BOOKLET** *THE JIVES OF DOCTOR HEPCAT*, LAVADA DURST, 1953

2. Dancefloor – as in 'cutting some rug'

Rumble

1. Fight, especially a gang fight

See the novels *The Big Rumble*, Wenzell Brown, 1955 "Teen-Age Gangs in the Harlem Jungle" and *Rumble At The Housing Project*, Edward de Roo, 1960 "Old Terror in New Buildings"

See the definitive instrumental recording *Rumble*, Link Wray, 1958

See also the 1956 exploitation film *Rumble on the Docks* – "The most savage teenage terror of them all – the teenage gangs on the waterfront."

2. A rumour, information

"I'd like to know if it shows up. You're in a position where you should catch the rumble, maybe, and if you do, let me know fast." **FROM THE NOVEL** *DARLING, IT'S DEATH*, RICHARD S. PRATHER, 1959

Run your mouth

Talk a lot

See the jazz recording *You Run Your Mouth, I'll Run My Business*, Louis Armstrong, 1933

Running a temperature

Slightly drunk, vaguely awash but still floating

Running around

Being unfaithful, painting the town

Runs on a spoonful of gas and a nod from a traffic cop

That car's a low-maintenance jalopy, doesn't eat petrol, goes like a dream

"I gave her a little imported English runabout she fancied, regular bug of a car, ran on a spoonful of gas and a nod from a traffic cop." **FROM THE NOVEL** *DRESSED-UP TO KILL*, E G COUSINS, 1961

Rupture head

Idiot, someone who's lost it completely

Rock'n'roll wildman Esquerita – rug clearly not in need of dusting.

S s

Sack

Bed

Sacked out

Asleep

Sacktime

Bedtime

Sailin'

High on drugs

Same old same old

Habitual, the daily grind

San Quentin quail

Underage girl, the kind that can land you in prison

Dale Clark wrote a story called *San Quentin Quail* for the October 1941 issue of *Black Mask* magazine

Sap

1. Fool, fall guy

eg: "Stop playing me for a sap."

2. Cosh

Satchel mouth

A wide mouth – longtime nickname for Louis 'Satchmo' Armstrong (although he was originally known in New Orleans as Dippermouth)

See also the jazz recording *Satchel Mouth Baby*, The Four Jumps Of Jive, 1946

Saturday night special

Home made or cheap handgun

Sauce

Alcohol, booze

Saucehound

Drunkard

Saucing a little on the much side

Getting drunk

Savvy

1. Knowledge, intelligence

"Jim Thompson was pure American writing at its best... He had more pistolero savvy than all the so-called great American writers." HARLAN ELLISON WITH SOME WORDS OF ADVICE FOR COLLEGE LECTURERS

2. Do you understand me?

Sawbox

A cello

Sawbuck

Ten dollars

See the jazz recording *(I Found a) Sawbuck*, Johnny Crawford & his Orchestra, 1949

Scarf

1. To eat
2. Food

Scat

1. Go away, get lost

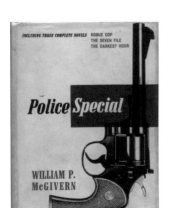

A Police Special, not a cheap Saturday Night Special, decorating this 1962 William P McGivern collection.

"'Shoo,' she said. 'Bon voyage. Scat. Scram. Goodbye. Yes?'" FROM THE NOVEL *THE ICEPICK IN OLLIE BIRK*, EUNICE SUDAK, 1966

2. Whiskey
3. Jazz singing using sounds instead of words

A scat singer is defined by *Down Beat's Yearbook of Swing, 1939*, as a "vocalist who sings rhythmically, but without using accepted English words."

Louis Armstrong is credited with starting this trend when he recorded *Heebie Jeebies* in Chicago with his Hot Five on February 26, 1926

"The records were very successful, and Heebie Jeebies was what today would be called a hit record. That was the record where Louis forgot the words and started scattin'. We had all we could do to keep from laughing. Of course, Louis said he forgot the words, but I don't know if he intended it that way or not. It made the record, though." HOT FIVE TROMBONE PLAYER KID ORY RECALLS THE *HEEBIE JEEBIES* SESSION, QUOTED IN *THE ORAL HISTORY HEAR ME TALKIN' TO YA – THE STORY OF JAZZ BY THE MEN WHO MADE IT*, NAT SHAPIRO AND NAT HENTOFF, EDS., 1955

"Louis (Armstrong) first got me freed up from straight lyrics to try scatting... I don't know how it got started, really, the scat singing. I think one night in the Cotton Club I just forgot the words to a song and started to scat to keep the song going. It was 1931." CAB CALLOWAY, FROM HIS AUTOBIOGRAPHY OF *MINNIE THE MOOCHER AND ME*, 1976.

Cab recorded a jazz tune called *Scat Song* in 1932

A fine example of scat being used in a song title would be *Wham (Re-Bop-Boom-Bam)* by Doctor Sausage & his Five Pork Chops, which was made available to a suitably appreciative public back in 1940

Jazz singer Scatman Crothers, in the latter part of his career, provided one of the voices for the film *The Aristocats*, before meeting a horrible end as a character in Stanley Kubrick's *The Shining*

Scatter gun

A sawn-off shotgun

Schmo from Kokomo

An idiot, a square

Scoff

Food

Scram

Leave in a hurry, blow the joint

Scran

Food

The scramble egg treatment

Sex show

"Ah yes, this joint I am familiar with. They do the scramble egg treatment on the floor to the delight of all onlookers" FROM THE NOVEL *DIG A DEAD DOLL*, G.G. FICKLING 1960

Scratch

1. Kill someone
2. Money
3. To write

Scratched from the big race

To die

Scream sheet

Newspaper

Screaming mimis

Bad reaction to drugs, or withdrawal symptoms

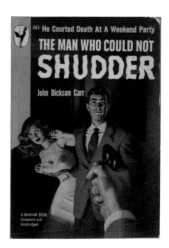

The cover stars of this 1949 John Dickson Carr novel, clearly in danger of being scratched from the big race.

Ah yes, this joint I am familiar with. They do the scramble egg treatment on the floor to the delight of all onlookers.

See the novel *The Screaming Mimi*, by Fredric Brown, 1956. Also filmed under the same title, 1958

See also the rockabilly recording *My Screamin' Screamin' Mimi*, Ray Campi, 1958, and the rock'n'roll recording *Screamin' Mimi Jeanie*, Mickey Hawks & the Night Raiders, 1960

Screw it on

Open up the throttle, cut loose

Screw up

Make a mistake

Screwed, blued and tattooed

A wild night out

See you in church

Hipster farewell

Selling a bill of goods

Swindling someone, lying, conning

"When we come around by the platform again I saw Socks and Rocky talking earnestly to Vic Lovell and Mary Hawley, Couple No. 71. 'Looks like Socks is selling her a bill of goods,' Gloria said. 'That Hawley horse couldn't get in out of the rain.'" FROM THE NOVEL *THEY SHOOT HORSES, DON'T THEY?*, HORACE MCCOY, 1935

Send

1. To thrill, enrapture and generally fry the wig

Down Beat's Yearbook of Swing, 1939, rather narrowly defines it as, "To arouse the emotions with Swing music."

See the jazz recording *She Sends Me*, Frankie 'Half Pint' Jaxon, 1937

2. To smoke marijuana

Seven come eleven

A dice player's expression calling for good luck

See the jazz recording *Seven Come Eleven*, Benny Goodman Sextet, 1939, and the rockabilly recording *Sebbin Come Elebbin*, Jimmy Heap, 1955

Seven veils look

Inscrutable, mysterious

"'How the hell did you find that out?' I demanded. He gave me the seven veils look. 'I get around,' he said." FROM THE AUTOBIOGRAPHY *WE CALLED IT MUSIC*, EDDIE CONDON WITH THOMAS SUGRUE, 1948

Sew up your mouth

Shut up

Sex appeal

Falsies

Sex pot

Friendly gal, unabashed, stacked, alluring

See the frankly aquatic novel *Sea Going Sex Pot*, Joe Martin, 1962 "On land she fit the debutante label, but 3 ml. out she was a Sea Going Sex Pot."

Shack up

1. Live with, cohabit

"Nothing could be finer than to shack up with a minor..." DEAN MARTIN, ONSTAGE AT *THE SANDS*, LAS VEGAS, FEBRUARY 1964

2. To live somewhere

"Just so happens I know where he's shacked up." FROM THE FILM *PICKUP ON SOUTH STREET*, 1953

Shag

1. *"A form of dance inspired by Swing music..."* FROM *DOWN BEAT'S YEARBOOK OF SWING*, 1939

See also the rock'n'roll recording *The Shag (Is Totally Cool)*, Billy Graves, 1958

Ultra-suave Eddie Condon giving the punters that seven veils look, 1948.

Documentary proof that they sure knew how to Shag back in 1937.

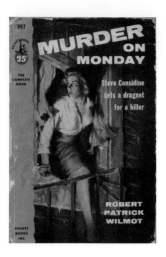

Mrs Delancy is shagging a woman who was sitting next to Deirdre...

2. To tail or follow someone

"Mrs Delancy is shagging a woman who was sitting next to Deirdre..." FROM THE NOVEL *MURDER ON MONDAY*, ROBERT PATRICK WILMOT, 1952

Shake a leg

Get moving

Shake a tail feather

A dance which involves waving your hind quarters around in what some guardians of youthful morals would take to be a shameless and lascivious fashion

See the vocal group recording *Shake A Tail Feather*, The Five Du-Tones, 1963

Shake, rattle & roll

Having a wild time, originally specifically sexual

A show called *Shake, Rattle & Roll* ran at the Lafayette Theatre in Harlem in 1927 "with a Cast of Fifty Noted Colored Entertainers"

See also the jazz recording *Shake, Rattle & Roll*, Charlie Barnet & his Orchestra, 1940

Shake that thing

Dance

"When I say git it, I want you to shake that thing..." FROM THE *LOUIE LOUIE* OF BOOGIE-WOOGIE RECORDINGS, *PINE TOP'S BOOGIE WOOGIE*, PINE TOP SMITH, 1928

Shake the lead out of your shorts

Get moving, hurry up

Shake till the meat comes off the bones

Dance yourself ragged, strut your stuff

Shake your business up and pour it

Say what's on your mind

Shake your feet

Dance

"Well the old jukebox was blowin' out the beat, The cats and the gators were shakin' their feet..." FROM THE ROCKABILLY RECORDING *THREE ALLEY CATS*, ROY HALL, 1956

Shaking two nickels together

Broke, down on your luck

"I've been shaking two nickels together for a month, trying to get them to mate." FROM THE NOVEL *THE BIG SLEEP*, RAYMOND CHANDLER, 1939

Shakedown

1. Swindle, confidence trick, robbery, extortion

"But it'd serve that pokey right if somebody slapped him silly. He's been shaking down the greenhorns in here fourteen years." FROM THE NOVEL *THE MAN WITH THE GOLDEN ARM*, NELSON ALGREN, 1949

See also the novels *Shakedown Hotel*, Ernest Jason Fredericks, 1958, and *Shakedown Dame*, Dorothy Herzog, n.d. (1940s)

George Bruce wrote a short story called *The Shake-Down* in the April 1932 issue of *Black Aces*

See the jazz recording *Honey Don't You Shake Me Down*, The New Orleans Jazz band, 1924

2. Police search

Shamus

Private detective

Sharp as a tack

1. Well-dressed, stylish

See the rock'n'roll recordings *Sharpest Guy In Town*, Big Moe & The Panics, c.1957 and *Sharpest Little Girl*, The Benders, 1965

2. Intelligent, clued-up in the wig department

See the jazz recording *Sharp As A Tack*, Harry James & his Orchestra, 1941

Sharp enough to shave

Well dressed, stylish

She's my witch

She's my girlfriend

"Artie swung to confront Rick. 'You better blow,' he said stiffly. He jerked a thumb at Pat. 'This is my witch.' 'Was, you mean,' Pat said loudly. 'I told you nobody orders me around.'" FROM THE SHORT STORY *A HOOD IS BORN*, RICHARD DEMING,1959

"Got hair as black as night, Got a skirt that's ooh, so tight, Tellin' you I've got an itch, She's my witch." FROM THE ROCK'N'ROLL RECORDING *SHE'S MY WITCH*, KIP TYLER & THE FLIPS, 1959

Sheep-dip

Bullshit, horse feathers, a load of old flannel

"I didn't have to read beyond the headlines to know the police were still sitting on the Lamont story. Well, they couldn't freeze up on the press much longer. Tomorrow Homicide would probably release it with the customary sheep-dip about important arrests expected momentarily." FROM THE NOVEL *SLEEP NO MORE*, SAM S TAYLOR, 1951

Sheik

Boyfriend

Shill

Someone in league with a card sharp who helps to swindle other players by pretending to be an innocent participant in the game

"She's a shill for a gambler and she's got her hooks into a rich man's pup." FROM THE SHORT STORY *TROUBLE IS MY BUSINESS*, RAYMOND CHANDLER, PUBLISHED IN *DIME DECTECTIVE* MAGAZINE, AUGUST 1939

2. Police baton

Shimmy

Shaking, suggestive dance, supposedly originated by the performer Little Egypt at the 1893 Chicago World's Fair

See the jazz recording *I Wish I Could Shimmy Like My Sister Kate*, The Cotton Pickers, 1922

Shiv

Small knife for stabbing people, sometimes home-made

"'Let's see the shiv,' he said. 'The what?' 'The pig-sticker, the switchblade, the knife, for Christ's sake. Don't you understand English?'" FROM THE NOVEL *SAVAGE NIGHT*, JIM THOMPSON, 1953

Shoo-in

A dead cert, bound to win

Shoot the sherbert to me, Herbert

Give me a shot of booze

Also Slip the juice to me Bruce, and Pour a gallon in me, Alan

Shoot the works

Spill the beans, tell all

Ann Sheridan appeared in a film in 1934 called *Shoot The Works* and Brett Halliday also published a Mike Shayne crime novel in 1957 using this phrase as the title.

See also the novel *Shoot The Works*, Richard Ellington, 1948

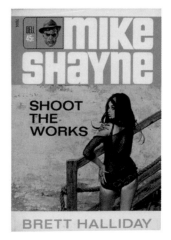

Yet another street slang expression finds itself used as the title for a pulp crime novel.

Leigh Brackett's 1957 novel *The Tiger Among Us*, filmed as *13 West Street*.

Shoot your cookies

Vomit

"You better go lay down somewhere, buddy. If I'm any judge of colour, you're goin' to shoot your cookies." FROM THE SHORT STORY *FINGER MAN*, RAYMOND CHANDLER, 1934

Shooting a line

Lying, telling a fanciful story

Shooting party

Drug binge

Shootin' the dream-dust

Mainlining drugs

"I show him the drunks and the hop-heads, and I tell him that's what happens to guys who go on the booze or start shootin' the dream-dust." FROM THE NOVEL *THE TIGER AMONG US*, LEIGH BRACKETT, 1957

Short

An automobile

"Your fly chick is looking most frantic and your short is all gassed up and ready to roll." FROM THE BOOKLET *THE JIVES OF DOCTOR HEPCAT*, LAVADA DURST, 1953

Short con

Short term confidence trick

Shot all to hell

Worn out, broken, destroyed

Shot-rodder

Someone who's lost it, a crazy guy, a mess

Shove in your clutch

Get moving, get on with it

Shovel city

To like something ie: To dig it

Shoving the queer

Passing counterfeit money

"He seems to have a finger in every pie. One pie isn't big enough for him. He seems to be out after all the plums — making and shoving the 'queer'; bootlegging on a large scale; a crap circuit; and a general following of stick-up men and steerers." FROM THE NOVEL *THE BIG SHOT*, FRANK L PACKARD, 1929

Showcasing

Showing off, bragging

Shower down

Empty your pockets

Shroud-tailor

Undertaker

Shuck & jive

Mess around, waste time

Shucker

Stripper, burlesque dancer

Shuffle

Fist-fight

Shutterbug

Photographer

Sidekick

Follower, pal, flunky

Sideman

Musician in a band, but not the leader of the band

Sides

Records, tunes, recordings

Sing

Confess, spill the beans

"'I wouldn't tell you the time if I owned a watch factory,' the man growled at him. 'That's what makes horse racing – a difference of opinion. Me, I think you're going to sing like a sluge-struck canary-' He studied the contemptuous expression on the other man's face. 'Or I'm going to leave you as toothless as the day you were born.'" FROM THE NOVEL *ESPRIT DE CORPSE*, FRANK KANE, 1965

Sinhound

A priest

Sissy gun

Small calibre weapon

Sister

Dame, doll, etc

"She's a first-class four flushin' double dealin' twicin' sister of Satan who would take a sleepin' man for the gold stoppin' in his right-hand eye tooth" FROM THE NOVEL *DAMES DON'T CARE*, PETER CHEYNEY, 1937

Sit in the old rocking chair up at Sing Sing

Be electrocuted, take the hot squat

Six-gun payoff

Death, getting shot

"You saw a nice way to drop it in my lap and promised the two witnesses a six-gun payoff unless they saw it your way." FROM THE NOVEL *VENGEANCE IS MINE*, MICKEY SPILLANE, 1951

Sixty minute man

Lover with staying power

"Looky here girls I'm telling you now, they call me Lovin' Dan, I rock 'em, roll 'em all night long, I'm a sixty minute man…" FROM THE VOCAL GROUP RECORDING *SIXTY MINUTE MAN*, BILLY WARD & THE DOMINOES, 1950

Sizzler

The electric chair

Skating on dope

Getting high on drugs

"'She's liable to run out of the supply of the stuff she keeps in her room.' 'You mean she skates on dope?' Clarice nodded. 'She keeps so much in her room and I keep the rest in case she goes berserk.'" FROM THE NOVEL *DAMES IS MY UNDOING*, MCCALL HORGAN, N.D. (EARLY 1950s)

Ski jumps

Breasts

"Janice was a dish for a collector. Everything was in its right place and generously rationed. Thick redwood hair, parted on one side, tumbled laterally to her shoulders. She was wearing a black crew sweater pulled tight, a black and red plaid sports skirt, and low shoes. Her only jewellery was a slave bracelet of heavy gold links. As she stood there the rhythms of her body seemed in constant motion. I wondered if those two delightful ski jumps in black wool were real." FROM THE NOVEL *SLEEP NO MORE*, SAM S TAYLOR, 1951

Ski ride

Cocaine binge

Skin beater

Drummer

Skin show

Striptease performance

Skinny

Information, hot news

Skins

A kit of drums

She's a first-class four-flushin' double-dealin' twicin' sister of Satan…

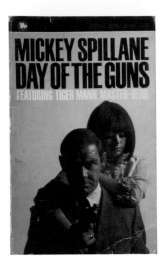

Mickey Spillane's new hero Tiger Mann – always ready for a romantic assignation at a local slop chute.

Skull orchard

Cemetery

Skull work

Thinking

Sky-pilot

Preacher

Slammer

Prison

Slap happy

Keen, possibly over-enthusiastic

"He's a slap-happy bird with a gun." FROM THE FILM *THE DEVIL THUMBS A RIDE*, 1947

Slaughter in the pan

Beefsteak

Slave

A job, employment

Slay me now, I don't want to go another further

I'm having a really good time

Slinky piece of homework

Good looking woman

"She's a slinky piece of homework with auburn hair and green eyes. She's wearing a low cut dress of shimmering black which clings seductively to her ripe curves. Me, I get a thrill just looking at her." FROM THE NOVEL *KILLERS DON'T CARE*, ROD CALLAHAN, 1950

Slip him the boodle

Give him the money

Slip him the dose

Shoot him

Slipped disc party

A house hop with the wildest waxings

"'You goin' to Norma's, Eliz? It's a slipped disc party.' 'Will do, Mildew.' I said, 'I don't want to be an old square, but what's a slipped disc party?' 'Discs are platters, you know, records, and slipped means, well, you're out of this world, slipped over the edge.'" FROM THE NOVEL *DRIVE EAST ON 66*, RICHARD WORMSER, 1962

Slop

Food

Slop chute

Restaurant, hash house, eating joint

"'Feel like getting dressed and going out?' 'Where?' 'Who knows? Maybe some slop chute. I feel like talking to a broad.'" TIGER MANN MAKES A ROMANTIC PHONE CALL, FROM THE NOVEL *DAY OF THE GUNS*, MICKEY SPILLANE, 1964

Sloppy drunk

Soused, smashed, juiced to the gills

See the jazz recording *Sloppy Drunk Woman*, Blue Chip Norridge Mayhams & his Blue Boys, 1936, and the rockabilly recording *Sloppy Drunk*, Mac Banks, 1956

"Down in New Orleans where everything's fine, All them catfish drinkin' that wine, Drinkin' that mess is pure delight, Get sloppy drunk and start fightin' all night..." FROM THE R&B RECORDING *DRINKIN' WINE SPO-DEE-O-DEE*, STICK MCGHEE, 1949

Slow, lowdown gut-strut

Down-and-dirty blues or jazz dance, custom-made for bodily contact

Slower than molasses in January

Not very bright, not quick on the uptake

Slug

1. A bullet

"'Shut up, you squealer!' Baird exclaimed. 'We're both in this! You try and walk out on me and I'll put a slug into you!'" FROM THE NOVEL *THE FAST BUCK*, JAMES HADLEY CHASE, 1952

2. A punch

"'Orlik?' he sniffed, checking it against his memory. 'Not the big shot? Last time I read the name, he slugged a guy in a city club. Right?'" FROM THE NOVEL *DEATH IS CONFIDENTIAL*, LAWRENCE LARIAR, 1959

3. A dollar

"Last week a kid got a respectable job, running errands for a whore-house at fifteen a week. Showed what things are. Two years ago that same kid was knocking out forty slugs working twice a week, rest of the time free for whoring." FROM THE NOVEL *BRAIN GUY*, BENJAMIN APPEL, 1934

4. A shot of booze

"She gets a few slugs under her girdle and she thinks it's Christmas." FROM THE NOVEL *RED GARDENIAS*, JONATHAN LATIMER, 1939

Slush pump

A trombone

A smack in the face with a steam shovel

A punch in the mouth

Small change

1. An insignificant guy

"'Get her out,' Raglan exploded angrily. 'Flop her in a hotel or something but get her out!' The fire came up in Lela's eyes. 'Listen, small-change, Who do you think you are, Friar Tuck? I'm with Chick.'" FROM THE NOVEL *ROAD BLOCK*, HILLARY WAUGH, 1960

2. A short guy

Small potatoes

Unimportant

"She was a damn good burlesque stripper. She had what it takes and she gave what she had, but she's small potatoes. She got hers and now she's out of it. As of tonight I'm taking over." FROM THE NOVEL *TOP OF THE HEAP*, A A FAIR (ERLE STANLEY GARDNER), 1952

Smart up in the top storey

Intelligent

Smeller

Nose

Smooching party

Kissing

Snatch

Kidnapping

"'But Bryan, they said they would – kill poor little John if we did anything like that.' 'Nonsense! They wouldn't dare.' 'But Mr Lee says they might, if it is a gang of foreigners.' 'What does he know about kidnapping cases?' 'He knows a lot. He's been telling me about how they do these things in America. The snatch-racket, he calls it.'" FROM THE NOVEL *GUN BUSINESS*, GRIERSON DICKSON, 1935

Sneaky Pete

Cheap wine

See the rockabilly recording *Sneaky Pete*, Sonny Fisher, 1955

Sniffing Arizona perfume

Going to the gas chamber

Snort

A drink

"Come on over to Plunkett's and we'll have a snort on it." FROM THE NOVEL *BLOW UP A STORM*, GARSON KANIN 1959

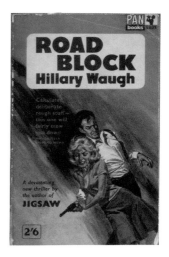

Listen, small-change, who do you think you are, Friar Tuck?

My mother sells snow to the snow-birds / My father makes barbershop gin / My sister sells jazz for a living / And that's why the money rolls in – Teenage hoods on the loose in The Young Savages, *1960.*

Snow

Cocaine

Snow job

A misleading story, a pack of lies designed to divert attention from the real situation

See the rock'n'roll recording *Snow Job*, Chip Fisher, 1960

Snowbird

Cokehead

"My mother sells snow to the snowbirds, My father makes barbershop gin, My sister sells jazz for a living, And that's why the money rolls in." JAIL SONG FROM THE FILM *THE YOUNG SAVAGES*, 1960

The April 1928 issue of *Black Mask* carried a story by Erle Stanley Gardner called *Snow Bird*

So long Pal, be pure

Hipster farewell

So mean you won't even spend a weekend

Stingy, a tightwad

So round, so firm, so fully packed

Good looking

See the country recording *So Round, So Firm, So Fully Packed*, Merle Travis, 1947

Soak your face

Get drunk

Sob sister

Sad, crying, miserable

Sob story

Hard-luck tale, depressing story

Sock

1. Close dancing

"'... would you mind, you're dancing too close.' Lover grinned. 'Don't like to sock it in, huh?' 'Why get ourselves all excited?' Mary said, looking at him coolly now. 'It's too hot to raise a temperature.'" FROM THE NOVEL *TOMBOY*, HAL ELLSON, 1952

2. Great, really good, outstanding

Sock hop

Teenage dance party

"Sock hop / At the high school gym / Sock hop / You can count me in" FROM THE ROCKABILLY RECORDING *SOCK HOP*, CHARLIE GORE, 1956

A sock on the button

A punch in the face

Sodom by the Sea

Coney Island

Soft money

Easy money

Solid

Good, in order, righteous

See the jazz recordings *Solid, Jack, Solid* Ollie Shepard, 1938; also *You're Solid With Me*, Lovin' Sam with the Burns Campbell Orchestra, 1938

"She never ever wants to go to sleep, / She says that everything's solid all-reet..." FROM THE JAZZ RECORDING *WHO PUT THE BENZEDRINE IN MRS. MURPHY'S OVALTINE?*, HARRY "THE HIPSTER" GIBSON, 1946

Solid, Jack, I'll dig you in your den gradually

The proper reply when invited to someone's house for a visit, according to Cab Calloway's Swingformation Bureau

Solid sender

A real knockout

Down Beat's Yearbook of Swing, 1939, defines a sender as "1. A musician capable of playing good hot solos, and 2. A performance that pleases Swing fans."

"Oh my Linda, She's a solid sender, You know you'd better surrender." FROM THE ROCK'N'ROLL RECORDING *SLIPPIN' & SLIDIN'*, LITTLE RICHARD, 1956

Roy Milton had an R&B group from 1946 to 1956 called the Solid Senders

"Boy, that man's a solid sender, when he gets riding on that go-toy the cats really start cryin'." FROM THE FILM *ORCHESTRA WIVES*, 1942

Some dollars to walk and wake up with

Spending money, working capital

Somebody ought to sew buttons on his face

He shouldn't talk so much, he should button his lip

"'I didn't say anything about a jade necklace.' 'No, but Lieutenant Randall did.' 'Somebody ought to sew buttons on his face.' 'He knew my father. I promised not to tell.'" FROM THE NOVEL *FAREWELL, MY LOVELY*, RAYMOND CHANDLER, 1940

Songbird

Female vocalist

At Harlem's Lafayette Theatre in July 1919 the Five Dixie Girls were being advertised as "A Quintette of Classy Songbirds"

Sound

To listen

"Talk up, man, I don't sound you at all..." FROM THE FILM *HIGH SCHOOL CONFIDENTIAL*, 1958

Sounds

Music

Soup

1. High-performance hotrod fuel, a special mixture
2. Swearing

"Kicking him off the team for that little burst of soup, it wasn't fair. What did the coach have against him?" FROM THE NOVEL *SCANDAL HIGH*, HERBERT O. PRUETT, 1960

3. Explosives

"The two Cs got him. For that many pieces of paper he could take his chances with a gallon of soup." ie: For that much money he'd risk being blown up. FROM THE NOVEL *KISS ME, DEADLY*, MICKEY SPILLANE, 1953

Sourpuss

Bad tempered, ugly

South of the slot

The wrong side of the tracks, the poor part of town, from humble beginnings

Southpaw

Left handed

See the boogie-woogie recording *Southpaw Serenade*, Will Bradley & his Orchestra with Freddie Slack on piano, 1942

South view

Damned good looking. An interesting viewpoint

"I am tellin' you that the south view of this dame from the east when she is walkin' north would make a blind man turn to hard liquor." FROM THE NOVEL *YOUR DEAL, MY LOVELY*, PETER CHEYNEY 1941

Soused

Drunk

Kick him off the team for that little burst of soup?

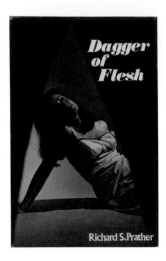

'Look, Ann, honey' I said, 'This ain't no party. See? Just a pleasant chat, and I need some info. Spill'.

The guy finished with the spike and handed it to me, and I looked it and blew my brains out, and then I passed the spike to somebody else... from the novel Second Ending (aka The Big Fix), 1952.

"Poppa's gone to town. He'll get himself soused and shoot his mouth off." FROM THE FILM *THEY LIVE BY NIGHT*, 1948

Sousepot

Drunkard

Spare me the hot air

Shut up, I'm not interested

Spigot bigot

Prohibitionist, anti-alcohol campaigner

Spill

Out with it, tell me the news

"'Look, Ann, honey,' I said, 'This ain't no party. See? Just a pleasant chat, and I need some info. Spill.'" FROM THE NOVEL *DAGGER OF FLESH*, RICHARD S. PRATHER, 1956

Spill your guts

Confess, tell all, become an informer

"Little Joe waggled the bottle admonishingly at his companion. 'You hadn't ought to have done that,' he said, 'Just when he was going to spill his guts.'" FROM THE NOVEL *HEADED FOR A HEARSE*, JONATHAN LATIMER, 1935

Spike

Needle, syringe

Spinach

Dollar bills

Splinter your toupee

Go crazy, flip your wig

Split, no-tomorrow style

Leave in a great hurry

Splitting the freight on a crash-pad

Sharing the rent for an apartment

Sporting house

Brothel

Squeaking shoe leather

Walking around

Squealer

An informer, a dime-dropper, one who rats out his pals

See the novel *The Squealer*, Edgar Wallace, 1928

Squall & ball & climb the wall

Have a wild time

This was the catch-phrase of "Smilin'" Eddie Hill, a 1940s country performer and DJ on WMC radio in Memphis

Square a beef

Sort out a problem or a grievance

"You couldn't square a beef with a stupe." ie: You can't settle an argument with an idiot. FROM THE NOVEL *THE GRIFTERS*, JIM THOMPSON, 1963

Square from Delaware

Unenlightened person

See the jazz recordings *(You're A) Square From Delaware*, Fats Waller & his Rhythm, 1940; *It's Square But It Rocks*, Count Basie & his Orchestra, 1941; *Serenade to a Square*, Sonny Stitt & The Be Bop Boys, 1946

See also the rock'n'roll recording *Square From Nowhere*, Loretta Thompson, 1959

"'It's hard to get the right sort of help these days.' 'I have the same trouble. The squares want security, and the hipsters want a chance to push people around at fifty dollars a day.'" FROM THE NOVEL *THE GALTON CASE*, ROSS MACDONALD, 1959

Square meal on a round plate

Food

Squawkers

Parents

"Must be a lot of our squawkers could give a finger." ie: A lot of our parents could lend a hand. FROM THE FILM *SHAKE, RATTLE & ROCK,*1957

Squeaker

A violinist

Squeal

Confess

Squealer

Informer

Squeeze the heater

Fire a gun

Squirting metal

Firing a gun

Stabbing heels

High heels

Stacked

Well built, a good figure

"She was stacked. She was pretty. She was just about everything you could want in a woman." FROM THE NOVEL *SAVAGE NIGHT*, JIM THOMPSON, 1953

See also the novel *Men On Her Mind,* Matt Harding, 1962 "Well-stacked, well-heeled Charlotte Mears offered Al Lenhart the money he needed – if he agreed to her very special plans!"

Stacked up

A car crash

"'What happened?' 'I stacked it up,' Brad said slowly, looking her right in the eye. She blinked under his hard level stare. 'You,' she said with a gasp. 'You stacked it up? You mean you had an accident?'" FROM THE NOVEL *RUN TOUGH, RUN HARD*, CARSON BINGHAM, 1961

Stag

A single male

Stag party

Gathering of solo studs featuring lewd entertainment designed to heat the zipper

See the short story *Stag Party* by Charles G Booth in the November 1933 issue of *Black Mask*. See also the novel *Stag Starlet*, Paul V Russo, 1961

Stagger-juice

Alcohol

"This dame is plumb full of stagger-juice." FROM THE NOVEL *DAMES DON'T CARE*, PETER CHEYNEY, 1937

Stallion

Boyfriend, stud

"She's been tied in knots with so many stallions, no detective on earth could pick the right goon out of that mob in the restaurant." FROM THE NOVEL *DEATH IS CONFIDENTIAL*, LAWRENCE LARIAR, 1959

Stand by while I pad your skull

Listen carefully

Stand-up guy

Reliable, helpful, good in a tight spot

"We'll probably never see each other again after we split up the money and break up tonight, but in my book you'll always be a stand-up guy." FROM THE FILM *THE KILLING*, 1956

Paul Muni in *Scarface*, a past master at squirting metal.

Jimmy cuts loose with some static, *Rebel Without A Cause*, 1955.

Ruby Keeler: *'Stick with us, kid, you'll come in on the tide'*.

Static

Complaints

"A little less static out of you." STATION COP TO JAMES DEAN. FROM THE FILM *REBEL WITHOUT A CAUSE*, 1955

Stay cool, hang loose, admit nothing

Recommended behaviour when dealing with the forces of law and order

Steady as rain

Going steady, having a regular partner

Step-ins

Underwear

Step off

1. To die

"Come back and see me, Tom. I don't want to – to step off alone." FROM THE NOVEL *RUN, KILLER, RUN*, WILLIAM CAMPBELL GAULT, 1955

2. Be executed, killed by the State

Step off was 18th century English slang for being hung, literally to step off the gallows or the cart that was supporting you

Step on a snake or get bitten

Make a decision, it's your choice

Steppin'

Dancing

"You wake me every night at twelve o'clock, You say we're goin' steppin' You put on your shoes, I got the midnight blues" FROM THE ROCK'N'ROLL RECORDING *MIDNIGHT BLUES*, WES VOIGHT & THE TOWN THREE, 1958

Steppin' on the gas

Literally, to drive fast, but also just to cut loose and get wild

See the jazz recording *Steppin' on the Gas*, Jimmy O'Bryant's Famous Original Washboard Band, 1925

Stewed to the gills

Drunk

The Edison company put out a wax cylinder in 1913 with a comedy sketch called *Funny Doings At Sleepy Hollow*, in which one of the characters utters the line "I'm a little stewed, yer see..."

Stick

Reefer, joint

See the jazz recording *Burnin' Sticks*, Toots Mondello & his Orchestra, 1939

"'One more question,' Gently said, 'then we'll stop being a nuisance to you. What sort of cigarettes did your son smoke?' Mrs Lister looked puzzled. 'Guards, I think.' 'Did he ever talk of sticks?' Gently asked. 'No,' she said. 'What are sticks?' 'Reefers,' Gently said. Still Mrs Lister looked puzzled. 'Cigarettes,' he explained, 'with a percentage of marijuana added.' 'Oh,' she said. She flushed slightly. 'That's dope, isn't it?'" FROM THE NOVEL *GENTLY GO MAN*, ALAN HUNTER, 1961

2. Bar

eg: "Behind the stick", where a barman stands

Stick with me, you'll come in on the tide

I'll look after you

"Stick with us kid, you'll come in on the tide." THE CHORUS GIRLS LEND RUBY KEELER A HAND, FROM THE FILM *42ND STREET*, 1933

Stiff

Corpse, victim, our late friend

See the novel *The Frightened Stiff*, Kelley Roos, 1942 (filmed in 1943 as *A Night To Remember*)

See also the short story *A Stiff in Time Saves Nine* by Frederick C Davis in the May 1944 issue of *Dime Detective*

Stiff one

A drink with a high alcohol content

Stinking

1. Completely drunk
2. Loaded with money

Stir

Prison

Stone

Complete, full

Stone college

Prison

Stoned

1. Drunk

"I would say, roughly, that Dean Martin has been stoned more often than the United States embassies..." FRANK SINATRA ONSTAGE AT *THE SANDS*, LAS VEGAS, 1966

2. On drugs, particularly marijuana

Stool pigeon

Informer

See the novel *Stool Pigeon*, Louis Malley, 1953

There was a one-off pulp magazine published in 1931 entitled *Confessions of a Stool Pigeon by One of Them*

See also the December 12, 1936 issue of *Detective Fiction Weekly* for the novelette *Stool Pigeon* by Frederick C Painton

Storage

Jail

"Ah, maybe we better put this nut in storage." FROM THE NOVEL *ALWAYS LEAVE 'EM DYING*, RICHARD S. PRATHER, 1961

Stow it

Shut up

Stow the hot talk

Shut up

Straight dope

The truth, reliable information

"Had The Man given me the straight dope? He might have..." FROM THE NOVEL *SAVAGE NIGHT*, JIM THOMPSON, 1953

Straight down to hell in a low-top car

Reckless, self-destructive, doomed

"What did I know about his life, his friends? He bust up from me long ago and went on his own road, straight down to hell in a low-top car." FROM THE NOVEL *THE BARBAROUS COAST*, ROSS MAC-DONALD, 1956

Straight from the cookhouse

Inside information, a hot tip

Straight from the fridge

Cool

"Great dad, great, straight from the fridge." FROM THE FILM *BEAT GIRL*, 1960

Straight, no chaser

The undiluted truth, the real thing, reliable information

Art Taylor put out a jazz track in 1959 called *Straight, No Chaser*

Adam Faith serenades a group of real gone gassers in *Beat Girl*.

Great, dad, great, straight from the fridge – Adam Faith and his 'jiving, stripping scum' give London teens a taste of jive talk, 1960.

Back in 1927 Louis Armstrong sang about *Struttin' With Some Barbecue*. The hep crowd dug what he meant, but the squares hadn't a clue.

Straighten up and fly right

Behave properly, do the decent thing, sort yourself out

"'All right!' Schaeffer's voice was savage. He was the cop again. 'Do what you want. But for God's sake, Pop, come out of it. Straighten up and fly right.'" FROM THE NOVEL *VIOLENT NIGHT*, WHIT HARRISON, 1952

"Straighten up baby, / Why don't you fly right sometimes, / That will ease my temperature / And cool my worried mind." FROM THE BLUES RECORDING *STRAIGHTEN UP BABY*, JAMES COTTON, 1954

Stretch

Prison sentence

Strictly for the birds

1. Useless, a pack of lies
2. It's not for me, I'm not interested

"'How do you like being a deputy G-Man, Janson?' 'It's crazy, man,' I told him. 'Real crazy. Strictly for the birds.'" ie: I don't like it. FROM THE NOVEL *CHICAGO CHICK*, HANK JANSON, 1962

Strictly union

Corny music, unadventurous

Stroll

The street

Strolling date

Out-of-town gig, tour schedule requiring travel

Struggle

Dance

"Hey, how 'bout you? You wanna struggle?" FROM THE FILM *THE WILD ONE*, 1954

Struggle-buggy

Automobile

See the jazz recording *Struggle Buggy*, King Oliver & his Orchestra, 1930

Strut yo' stuff

Dance, perform or otherwise show what you're made of

A theatre production called *Strut Yo' Stuff*, billed as "A Stupendous Musical Satire", was running in New York in December 1920

See also the blues recording *Get Yourself A Monkey Man, And Make Him Strut His Stuff*, Butterbeans & Susie, 1924

Struttin'

Dancing

See the blues recordings *I'm A Doggone Struttin' Fool*, Noble Sissle, 1921, and *Learn To Do The Strut*, Don Parker & his Orchestra, 1923

Stud

Guy, hepcat, dude

"I'm set to drift when Elmo pops up with two other studs. Elmo's the President of the mob, the boss cat. He's not too big, but a rough stud when the chips are down." FROM THE SHORT STORY *THE RITES OF DEATH*, HAL ELLSON, 1956

Stud dog

Sexually demanding, a bit of a caveman

"She had tried to tell Sylvia that Willie-Joe was a stud dog." FROM THE NOVEL *SCANDAL HIGH*, HERBERT O. PRUETT, 1960

Stuff with the dead ones' pictures

Paper money

From the autobiography *Really The Blues*, Mezz Mezzrow and Bernard Wolfe, 1946

Suck the bottle

Drink, get drunk

"Four bottles... And you sucked up three of 'em. I had to practically clip you to get a swallow. You said your leg hurt 'an you wanted a drink." FROM THE NOVEL *FAST ONE*, PAUL CAIN, 1933

Sucker

A rube, a mark, one who's ripe for the taking

See the novel *The Sucker*, Orrie Hitt, 1957 "Slade had his women figured from every angle – except one!"

See also the novel *Con Girl*, anonymous, 1962 "She could hook any sucker using her luscious body as bait."

Sucker bait

Inducement, advertising, a come-on – any kind of bait to lure the suckers

See the novel *Sucker Bait*, Robert O Saber, 1955

See also the novel *Passionate Lovie*, Dolores Dee, 1958 "Lovie flaunted her charms. 'Sucker bait' was what she called it – her key to the future."

Sucker for the ponies

Racetrack enthusiast, flinging their money at anything with four legs

"Capone never carried less than $50,000 in cash, scattering $25 tips to hat check girls and $100 gratuities to waiters. He was known around the gambling spots as 'a sucker for the ponies'." FROM THE BOOK *THE UNTOUCHABLES*, ELLIOT NESS & OSCAR FRALEY, 1957

Sucker list

Client base, mailing list

Suds

Beer

"'I was just thinking,' he said, 'how a nice beer would go right now. A nice, ice-cold suds with about an inch of cuff on it." FROM THE NOVEL *VIOLENT SATURDAY*, W.L. HEATH, 1955

Suitcase

A kit of drums

Suited down

Well dressed, sharp

Suppose we get together and split a herring

Would you like to go out with me one night?

Swagger joint

An impressive layout, decorated with no expense spared

"The attorney's office was no more than a few blocks away. It was a swagger joint, and I was shown into its owner's private sanctum without delay." FROM THE NOVEL *NO DICE, SISTER!*, BART CARSON, N.D. (EARLY 1950s)

Swapping chews

Kissing

Sweating out the rest of it

Serving a life sentence in the slammer

Sweet meat on the hoof

Attractive, good looking

"Cowboy say 'I believe it Man. She got the stuff.' 'Nothin' but bones,' Rod say. 'Sweet meat on the hoof,' Cowboy say, an he lick his lips. Everybody laugh." FROM THE NOVEL *THE COOL WORLD*, WARREN MILLER, 1959

Sweet swingin' sphere

The world

"I'm gonna put a cat on you that's the sweetest, gonest, wailingest cat that

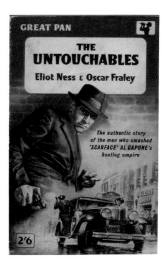

Capone never carried less than $50,000 in cash, scattering $25 tips to hat check girls and $100 gratuities to waiters. He was known around the gambling spots as 'a sucker for the ponies'.

You too can swing, brother, for just four shillings and seven pence, 1939.

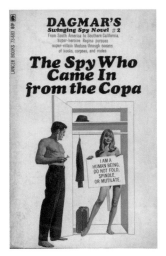

By the mid-1960s, the jazz term 'swinging' was being rather more loosely defined…

Do you wanna jump, children? – some real gone swingers, 1939.

ever stomped on this sweet swingin' sphere…" FROM THE SPOKEN WORD RECORDING *THE NAZZ*, LORD BUCKLEY, 1951

A swell piece

Good looking woman

Swelling up like a poisoned pup

Pleased with yourself, conceited, proud

Swing

1. Term for jazz music that became popular from the very end of the 1920s

Down Beat's Yearbook of Swing, 1939, defines the word as "The latest name for hot jazz music; more freely used as a term applied to all popular jazz"

See the jazz recording *Swing, You Cats*, Louis Armstrong & his Orchestra, 1933

2. Mode of behaviour

"'I don't know,' Frankie sympathized, 'It's just that some cats swing like that, I guess.'" FROM THE NOVEL *THE MAN WITH THE GOLDEN ARM*, NELSON ALGREN, 1949

3. Allegiance

eg: "Which gang do you swing with?"

4. To be sexually adventurous

See the novel *Swing Low Sweet Sinner*, Jason Hytes, c. 1963 "Swinging low was her specialty, and she swung in both directions – with men and women."

Swinger

One who swings (see entry no 4 above)

"He had also left, in the bathroom cabinet, a toothbrush and a tube of

toothpaste, a three-dollar razor, a jar of hair grease, and a spray can of a spicy scent called Swingeroo." FROM THE NOVEL *THE GOODBYE LOOK*, ROSS MACDONALD, 1969

Swing shift

Evening work

For a very loose interpretation of the term, see the novel *Swing Shift*, Grant Corgan, 1964 "It was a sleepy little town by day… but a glittering jewel of corruption by night!"

Switch-hitter

Someone who sleeps with both sexes

From the baseball term for a batter who works both right and left-handed

See the novel *The Switch-Hitters*, Carl Dodd, 1965 "Lesbians, Nymphos, Fags… and what have you… they used him for an erotic yo-yo till he didn't know which way was which!"

Swingin'

Cool, crazy, in the groove, the best

Switching channels

Changing your story

Swooner

Someone good looking

Sympathy

"Let me put it this way; I should be sincerely sorry to see my neighbour's children devoured by wolves." WALDO LYDECKER POSITIVELY OOZING SYMPATHY. FROM THE FILM *LAURA*, 1944

T†

T.C.B.

Taking care of business – the personal motto of Elvis Presley

See also the R&B recording *Taking Care of Business*, Titus Turner, 1959

Tab-lifter

Nightclub customer

'T'aint no crack but a solid fact

It's the truth

From the autobiography *Really The Blues*, Mezz Mezzrow and Bernard Wolfe, 1946

Take a bite of air

Get lost

Take a raincheck

Pass up an opportunity

Take a run-out powder

Leave in a hurry

"He had too much to lose. Molly would peel him skinless if he ever decided to take a powder." FROM THE NOVEL *RUN TOUGH, RUN HARD*, CARSON BINGHAM, 1961

See also the short story *The Corpse Takes a Powder* by Emile C Tepperman in the May 1942 issue of *Ten Detective Aces*

Take it on the lam

Run from the law

Take off your stomping shoes

Stop looking for trouble, calm down, I don't want a fight

Take some hot groceries

Eat a meal

Take some ice

Cool it, calm down

"'Take some ice, Sid,' Deeming said. 'And stop behaving like a cornball.'" FROM THE NOVEL *GENTLY GO MAN*, ALAN HUNTER, 1961

Taken for a ride

Killed, rubbed out, scratched from the big race

"Who did it? ... How did it happen? ... Took him for a ride, eh?" FROM THE NOVEL *THE BIG SHOT*, FRANK L PACKARD, 1929

Taken off the payroll

Killed, assassinated

Takes the paint off your deck

It's rough booze, strictly low class

Talking in dribbles

Speaking rubbish, making no sense

Talking that talk

Speaking in jive-talk, using hipster slang

See the vocal group recording *Talk That Talk*, The Du Droppers, 1955

LOUIS ARMSTRONG'S LIFE THREATENED

Chicago Gangsters "Spot" Him

AS reported in last month's issue, Louis Armstrong is at present playing in a club called "My Cellar," in Chicago.

Apparently he has attracted the attention of the gangsters, those odd phenomena of Chicagoan home life, who followed him round and threatened to put him " on the spot " unless he paid for " protection."

His manager, John Collins, reported the matter to the police, who furnished Louis with an escort to see him safely home in the small hours of the morning.

Collins is reported to have said that the more the hoodlums scare his principal, the better becomes Louis' playing.

" He gets those shivery shaky, tremolo effects that the customers like," he said. Oh, yeah ?

There has been a rumour current in the West-end recently that Louis was to appear at the Café de Paris as a solo act.

Owing to his recording contracts in America, and other reasons, this is now definitely off.

In Capone's Chicago, most musicians worked in joints run by the mob. This June 1931 report shows that even Satchmo ran the risk of being taken for a ride.

A cardboard Joan Crawford offers a literal interpretation of the title of her 1927 film, *Taxi Dancer*.

Talking trash

Verbal abuse

Talking turkey

Straight talking, honesty

Tall

Drunk

"'I think you are a splendid woman,' he said. 'I'm high, wide and handsome,' she said. 'I'm tall.' 'Tall?' 'High. Tight. Crocked. Drunk.'" FROM THE NOVEL *RED GARDENIAS*, JONATHAN LATIMER, 1939

Tamp on down the stroll

Walk down the street

Tank town

Small town, out in the sticks, the opposite of a big city like New York or Chicago

"What's a fast guy like you doing at a tank-town teacher's college?" FROM THE NOVEL *SAVAGE NIGHT*, JIM TOMPSON, 1953

Tanked

Drunk

Tap the bottle

Drink

Tapped

Arrested

Tapping a jug

Robbing a bank

"He blasted a couple of fuzz while he was tapping a jug." ie: He shot a couple of policemen when robbing a bank." FROM THE NOVEL *MURDER ON MONDAY*, ROBERT PATRICK WILMOT, 1952

Tapsville

Broke

Taxi dancer

Paid dancing partner at a dance-hall, not the most respectable of professions

"'I can tell you where she works.' 'Where?' 'At the Clark-Erie ballroom. She's a hostess there.' 'A taxi-dancer?' 'I reckon that's what you calls 'em...'" FROM THE NOVEL *THE LADY IN THE MORGUE*, JONATHAN LATIMER, 1936

"Listen: it's a safe bet Baird's just knocked off one of Rico's taxi-dancers." FROM THE NOVEL *THE FAST BUCK*, JAMES HADLEY CHASE, 1952

See also the short story *Taxi Dance Murder* by Cornell Woolrich in the September 1937 issue of *Ten Detective Aces*

For a further example of the less-than-spotless reputation of dance-halls, see the entirely un-sensationalist *From Dance Hall To White Slavery*, John Dillon, 1912. Yes children, dancing is evil, you read it here first... "Thrilling stories of actual experiences of girls who were lured from innocence into lives of degradation by men and women engaged in a regularly organized white slave traffic. Showing the evils of the dance hall with the usual saloon or bar attachment and the easy steps by which young girls are led to their downfall. Based upon the investigations and reports made by a committee of prominent women appointed by the Mayor of Chicago, to help fight the evils of public dance halls and the work of white slave traders."

Tea

Weed, marijuana

"I didn't know what was happening to me, and I suddenly realized it was only the tea that we were smoking; Dean had bought some in New York. It made

me think that everything was about to arrive – the moment when you know all and everything is decided forever." SAL PARADISE GRAZES ON SOME GRASS. FROM THE NOVEL ON THE ROAD, JACK KEROUAC, 1957

Tea hound

A marijuana smoker

Tear it down, soup it up, and strip it for speed

Sort it out, adapt things to suit your own requirements

Teenage fluff

Young girl

From the novel *If He Hollers Let Him Go*, Chester Himes, 1945

Teeth and tongue will get you hung

You talk too much

Tell it like it is

Straight talking, telling the truth

Tell that to a mule and he'll kick your head off

That's a lie, I don't believe you

Ten toes up

Having sex, earning a living on your back

See the novel *Ten Toes Up*, Anthony Scott, 1951 "A Novel About Sisters In Sin"

Terpsichorical

Dancing

"Hey baby, how's about you and me getting terpsichorical? Let's go downstairs and fly." OLIVER REED INVITES A CHARMING YOUNG LADY TO DANCE, FROM THE FILM BEAT GIRL, 1960

That ain't second base

Watch where you're going

"Man, lookout where you're steppin' / That ain't second base" FROM THE BOOGIE-WOOGIE RECORDING DOWN THE ROAD A PIECE, RAY MCKINLEY 1942

That chick is locked up in this direction, so just cut out while your conk is all in one portion

"How you can tell someone to stop annoying the young lady you are escorting." FROM PROFESSOR CAB CALLOWAY'S SWINGFORMATION BUREAU

That don't move me

I'm not impressed

See the rockabilly recording *That Don't Move Me*, Carl Perkins, 1956

That gives me a large charge

I'm excited, I'm impressed

That thing

Sex organs

"My friend picked a new girl / In a little dance-hall / He used to be a high-stepper / But now he can't walk at all / Somebody's been using that thing / Somebody's been using that thing / Just as sure as you're born / Somebody's been using that thing." FROM THE BLUES RECORDING SOMEBODY'S BEEN USING THAT THING, THE HOKUM BOYS, 1929

The phrase became something of an obsession with blues songwriters of the Twenties and Thirties, ie: *Shake That Thing*, Ethel Waters, 1925; *I'm Wild About That Thing*, Bessie Smith, 1928; *Let Me Pat That Thing*, The Hokum Boys, 1929; *Bury That Thing*, Roosevelt Sykes, 1929; *It's A Pretty Little Thing*, Tampa Red, 1930; *She's Dangerous With That*

'That ain't second base' – Sticksman Ray McKinley getting ready to beat the traps.

The finance company must have repossessed her broom.

Thing, Lonnie Johnson, 1931; and, on an educational note, *What's The Name Of That Thing?*, The Chatman Brothers, 1936

That vibrates me

I'm impressed, I really like it

That'll learn ya, durn ya

That'll teach you

See the hillbilly boogie recording *That'll Learn Ya, Durn Ya*, The Maddox Brothers & Rose, 1950

That's a bringer, that's a hanger

That's a bringdown, that's a hangup, that's depressing

See the jazz recording *That's A Bringer, That's A Hanger*, Slim Gaillard & his Flat Foot Floogie Boys, 1939

That's a gas

1. That's great, that's really good
2. That's a laugh, what rubbish

"Afraid of you? That's a gas! He could stamp you out like an ant. You're nothing to him." FROM THE NOVEL *TWO TIMING TART*, JOHN DAVIDSON, 1961

That's a panic and a half

That's really amusing

That's a pipe

That's easy – a lead pipe cinch

That's the kind of stuff that killed vaudeville

That ain't funny

That's the way the mop flops

That's life

See the rockabilly recording *That's The Way The Mop Flops*, Jimmy Wayne & The Scarlet Combo, 1961

The finance company must have repossessed her broom

She's a bitch

"Charming old biddy," she said, as if she were speaking out of the side of her mouth. "The finance company must have repossessed her broom." FROM THE NOVEL *THE LONG SATURDAY NIGHT*, CHARLES WILLIAMS, 1962

The heat's on

There's trouble, the law are after us

"'Things are very rocky. The heat's on. I hope to hell nobody was watching this place.' He went around the room, closing the Venetian blinds. Then he flopped into a big chair near to the entrance to the kitchen, and regarded Tom gravely. Tom was still sitting on the davenport, leaning forward, the tension still with him. 'Is the heat temporary or permanent? Just for the newspapers maybe?' Jud shrugged wearily. 'Who knows?'" FROM THE NOVEL *RUN, KILLER, RUN*, WILLIAM CAMPBELL GAULT, 1955

The words don't go with the music

I don't believe you

Them's the breaks, kid

That's life

There'll be a harp in your hand

You'll be dead

"Turn around, now, and we start walking. Slow and easy! Put a smile on your kisser. We're going to take a ride, together. Make it good, now! You let that smile slip, or try to tip anybody, next thing you know there'll be a harp in

your hand - " FROM THE NOVEL 'MAD DOG'
COLL, STEVE THURMAN, 1961

They don't run trains there anymore

Far out

They threw babies out of the balcony

That performance went down a storm

They'll pat you with a spade

You're likely to get yourself killed

*"I got lead in this here rod and my fin-
ger's itching. One crack out of any of
you and they'll pat you with a spade."*
RICO TALKS TOUGH, FROM THE NOVEL *LITTLE
CAESAR*, W.R. BURNETT, 1929

Thin man

Non-existent person on the payroll,
whose wages find their way into the
pockets of the boss

Thinking room

Signs of intelligence in the face

*"Her eyes were wide set and there was
thinking room between them."* FROM
THE SHORT STORY *TROUBLE IS MY BUSINESS*,
RAYMOND CHANDLER, 1939

Thinner than the gold on a weekend wedding ring

Extremely thin

Third degree

Heavy duty interrogation, often involving fists, clubs and other subtle
methods of persuasion

Third degree pulchritude

Sex appeal, attractiveness, bait for
the wolves

*"'She's a friend of yours I suppose?'
'No, I'm a detective.' Her face bright-*
ened. 'Well, I saw her go into the Dew-
drop Inn, that's the second place down
from here. It's about time somebody
cleaned out that den of iniquity. Are
you after her for some crime?' 'Third
degree pulchritude.' She chewed on
this like a camel, then shut the door
in my face."* FROM THE NOVEL *THE BARBA-
ROUS COAST*, ROSS MACDONALD, 1956

This bird's gonna pull his freight

I'm leaving, I'm outta here

Thou shalt not bug thy neighbour

The hip commandment

ie: Be cool, don't annoy people

Threads

Clothes

Threaded down

Well dressed, sharply turned out

Three-dollar bill

Fake, unconvincing, counterfeit

*"Directly across from me was a man
who gave his name as Sidney Selma,
a complete phony, three-dollar bill type
of individual who obviously assayed
fourteen carat brass."* FROM THE NOVEL
SOME WOMEN WON'T WAIT, A A FAIR (ERLE
STANLEY GARDNER), 1953

Three sheets to the wind

Drunk

Three singles or a large shakedown

Three single rooms or a suite?

Three time loser

Prisoner serving a life sentence after
three convictions

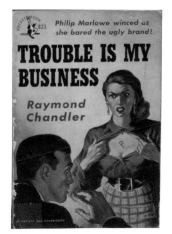

*Her eyes were wide set and there
was thinking room between them.*

Brando (and thumbs) in *The Wild One.*

Thrill up on the hill

Dance or party

"There's a thrill up on the hill, let's go, let's go, let's go." FROM THE R&B RECORD-ING *LET'S GO, LET'S GO, LET'S GO*, HANK BAL-LARD, 1960

Throttle jockey

Hot-rodder

Throw that dirt in your face

Being buried

"A guy's got a right to expect his family to show up when the time comes to throw dirt in his face." FROM THE NOVEL *HALO IN BLOOD*, HOWARD BROWNE, 1946

"I'll hire a black Cadillac / To drive you to your grave / I'm gonna be there baby / Throw that dirt in your face / I'll wear a black mink coat / A diamond ring on my hand / Before they put you underground / I'll have myself another man..." FROM THE ROCK'N'ROLL RECORD-ING *BLACK CADILLAC*, JOYCE GREEN, 1960

Throwing lead

Shooting, firing guns

"Why, you bone-headed gazooma, you ain't even got a mind of your own. Okay, so nobody knows him. That's fine. Maybe tomorrow, the day after, some other finger-man'll be up here throwin' lead around. And to think I pay you guys dough. Get the stiff dumped in the river. And for Christ's sake put weights on the feet." PROBLEMS WITH THE HIRED HELP, FROM THE NOVEL *HOT DAMES ON COLD SLABS*, MICHAEL STORME, 1950

Thrush

Female singer

Thumb

Hipster handshake

"Hey Pops, thumb me will ya Daddy-O?" FROM THE FILM *THE WILD ONE*, 1954

Ticker

Time bomb

"... somebody got past the protection on the Joanna and left another ticker. It damn near blew her in two; they beached, finally got into dry dock." FROM THE NOVEL *FAST ONE*, PAUL CAIN, 1933

Tie one on

Get drunk

Tight as a vault with a busted timelock

Closed, impenetrable

Tighten someone's wig

Introduce them to marijuana

Tighteye

Sleep

Tight-wad

Stingy, a cheapskate, morbidly incapable of unchaining their wallet

"I gave a dollop of dough to the Memorial Hospital so they couldn't call me a tight-wad." FROM THE NOVEL *DRESSED-UP TO KILL*, E G COUSINS, 1961

Tijuana bible

Pornographic magazine

Till-tapper

Thief, store burglar

Time box

Jail

Tin ears strictly around the block

Unsophisticated people

From the film *High School Confidential*, 1958

Tip-top daddy

Suave, in the groove, a righteous dude

Tip your hole card

Give the game away, reveal your intentions

Tip your mitt

See Tip your hole card

Toeology

Tapdancing

eg: "An upstate guy wigs you with some most burnt toeology." ie: A hip dude impresses you with the skill of his tapdancing.

Togged to the bricks

Dressed up, sharply turned out, suave

Tomato

Good looking woman

"Here was I in my own apartment with three beautiful tomatoes and all I could think of was getting rid of them. Life can be really cruel sometimes." FROM THE SHORT STORY *THE LIVE ONES*, RCHARD S. PRATHER, 1956

"She's a real sad tomato, / She's a busted valentine..." LAUREN BACALL'S SONG FROM THE FILM *THE BIG SLEEP*, 1946

"Give a lift to a tomato you expect her to be nice, don't you?" FROM THE FILM *DETOUR*, 1945

Tomcatting around

Chasing dames, playing the wolf

"'Did I hear a seduction!' Bertha exclaimed. 'I heard a whole damn medley of seductions. I realise now why they talk about the young man of today tomcatting around. When they say that, they don't mean a guy's prowling around, so much as that he's getting out in some public place and yowling about it.'" FROM THE NOVEL *OWLS DON'T BLINK*, A A FAIR (ERLE STANLEY GARDNER), 1942

See also the rockabilly recording *Tom Catin' Around*, Jimmy Selph, 1956

Tomorrow is a drag

I'm bored

"We cough blood on this earth / Now there's a race for space / We can cough blood on the moon soon / Tomorrow is dragsville cats / Tomorrow is a kingsize drag / Tool a fast short/ Swing with a gassy chick / Turn on to a thousand joys / Smile on what happened / Or check what's gonna happen / You'll miss what's happening / Turn your eyes inside and / Dig the vacuum / Tomorrow drags..." FROM THE BEAT POEM *TOMORROW IS A DRAG*, PHILLIPA FALLON, IN THE FILM *HIGH SCHOOL CONFIDENTIAL*, 1958

Tonsil paint

Alcohol

Too lovely to feed to the hogs

Very attractive, good looking

Tool

1. Weapon
2. To drive an automobile

Toots

1. Term of affection

eg: "Best take a shot, toots." ie: Have a drink, honey.

Sometimes the word is spelt Tutz as in "How're you gettin' along with tutz?" From the novel *Red Gardenias*, Jonathan Latimer, 1939

Jane Mansfield in *The Girl Can't Help It*: too lovely to feed to the hogs.

2. Patronising or threatening term of address

"'Watch your step, Toots,' he said evenly. 'I shan't tell you again.'" **FROM THE NOVEL** *THE FAST BUCK*, JAMES HADLEY CHASE, 1952

Top eliminator

The fastest hotrod, or hotrod driver. A total shutdown artist

Top storey

Head, brain

Top stud

The leader, the head honcho, the boss

Too much

The best, really good, a total knock-out

See the vocal group recording *Much Too Much*, The Hollywood Flames, 1959

Torch song

Slow-burning dramatic ballad

See the novel *Torch Singer*, William Arnold, 1951 "There Was Invitation In Her Voice – Passion In Her Eyes."

Torn up

Wasted, upset, ragged, unsettled, maybe impressed

Torpedo

Gunman, hitman

Torso-tosser

Hootchie-coochie dancer, strip artist

Tough

The most, the best, outstanding

Tough enough to swap punches with a power shovel

Hard, resilient, not exactly a pushover

Tramp on it

Hurry up, get moving, go faster

"Tramp on it, friend, make speed." **FROM THE NOVEL** *THE LITTLE SISTER*, RAYMOND CHANDLER, 1949

Trash

Gossip, chatter, loose talk

Trifling

Unfaithful, a flirt

"Who's been playin' around with you, / A real cool cat with eyes of blue? / Trifling baby are you being true, / Who's been fooling around with you?" **FROM THE ROCKABILLY RECORDING** *RED CADILLAC AND A BLACK MUSTACHE*, WARREN SMITH, 1957

Trigger-man

Assassin, hit-man

"He'd killed several men. Nobody knew how many except George, and he probably couldn't count that high. He'd been a trigger-man for a couple of the top men of the US crime syndicate, and was noted for his efficiency and stupidity." **FROM THE NOVEL** *DARLING, IT'S DEATH*, RICHARD S. PRATHER, 1953

Trottery

Dancehall

Troubled with the shorts

Broke, poverty-stricken

From the autobiography *Really The Blues*, Mezz Mezzrow and Bernard Wolfe, 1946

Trucking

1. Fucking

SAX APPEAL

Oyez! Oyez! Oyeah! Calling your attention to what the well-dressed gent was wearing in 1911.

Exhibit "A": Gents' very natty side-buttoned patent boots. Very fetching to the ladies. Note also with interest the stance: perfect taking off point for a spot of Truckin'.

Going Up! Smart ankle-length dress pants. Cut on cunning lines of economy round the knees. Get a load of the crease. That is the Power of the Press you hear so much about.

Very snappy jacket, belted at waist, with entrancing flare therefrom. High buttoned, with delicate lapels. Collar "en suite": great moral support to the ears. I remember my pa always reminded me of an earwig looking over a gate in one of these.

The entire ensemble completed by elegant straw.

Ladies' costume has me floored.

The Austel Four was one of the first saxophone acts to appear in this country. Came over from New York in 1911 where they played the Orpheum Circuit. Opened at Kilburn Empire, September, 1911, and booked by De Vere Agency for Gulliver Circuit. Played "You're My Baby," "Snooky-ookums," "You Made Me Love You," "Get Out and Get Under," "Broken Doll," etc. Jack Austel, who played baritone sax and owned the Quartette is now part of the famous acrobatic act, Austel and Arthur, who have worked all the big tours.

The Austel Four were a swell act, and were amongst the earliest saxophone pioneers.

Perfect taking off point for a spot of Truckin' – a 1937 jazz publication reveals what the hot saxophone player was bearing back in 1911.

See the blues recordings *Let's Get Drunk And Truck*, The Harlem Hamfats, 1936; *Caught My Gal Truckin'*, Tampa Red, 1936; and the country recording *Can't Nobody Truck Like Me*, Cliff Bruner's Texas Wanderers, 1937

2. Dancing

A dance made popular at the Cotton Club in Harlem in the early 1930s

"'Aw, come on, Camelia,' called Miss Day, moving her torso slowly from side to side. 'I'd like to do a little truckin'." FROM THE NOVEL *THE DEAD DON'T CARE*, JONATHAN LATIMER, 1937

3. Walking

"Truck on down and dig me, Jack..." FROM THE R&B JUMP JIVE RECORDING *FIVE GUYS NAMED MOE*, LOUIS JORDAN & THE TYMPANY FIVE, 1942

Trump

Money

"There was a lot of trump at Delavan; I have seldom seen so many clean people." FROM THE AUTOBIOGRAPHY *WE CALLED IT MUSIC*, EDDIE CONDON WITH THOMAS SUGRUE, 1948

Trust

"I trusted Amy about as far as I could have pushed the tractor and trailer with two broken legs." FROM THE NOVEL *THE LADY IS A LUSH*, ORRIE HITT, 1960

For another heart warming example of faith in one's fellow man, there's also the character in James A Howard's 1960 novel *Murder in Mind* who shackles his fellow robber to an iron pipe when leaving the room, rather than take the risk that he'll run off with the loot: "You can look at all that lovely money until we get back, Carey. That should keep you from feeling hurt that I don't trust you any farther than I could throw a bull buffalo by the balls."

Tuckered out

Worn out, exhausted

Tucson blanket

A newspaper, the usual item of hobo bedding, also known as a California blanket

Turn on the phonograph

Confess to the police

Turn the duke

Short change someone

Turning your damper down

Sexually satisfied

For the finest double-entendre blues song of them all, see *My Handy Man*, Ethel Waters, 1928, which includes the following: "Don't care if you believe it or not, / He sure is good to have around, / Why, when my burners get too hot, / He's there to turn my damper down. / For everything he's got a scheme, / You oughta see the solder he uses on my machine, / My man, is such a handy man. / He flaps my flapjacks, / Cleans off the table, / Feeds the horses / In my stable, / My man, is such a handy man. / Sometimes he's up long before dawn, / Trimming the rough edges off my lawn, / My man, is such a handy man."

See also the country recording *I Think I'll Turn Your Damper Down*, Jimmie Davis, 1937

"With a blonde-headed woman / you need to get around, / but a black haired girl / will turn your damper down." FROM THE ROCKABILLY RECORDING *FORTY NINE WOMEN*, JERRY IRBY & THE TEXAS RANCHERS, 1956

1950s London master-criminal College Harry – not about to turn on the phonograph any time soon...

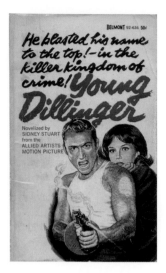

Nick Adams sends a fond message with his typewriter in *Young Dillinger*, 1965.

Twicin'

1. Cheating on your partner, sleeping with two people at once
2. Double crossing

Twist

Woman, dame, doll

"The twist might die...there was a prowl car not more than ten yards away. I had to hit her." YET ANOTHER JAMES HADLEY CHASE CHARACTER COMES OVER ALL CHIVALROUS AND SENSITIVE. FROM THE NOVEL *THE FAST BUCK*, 1952

Two-bit porch climber

Low-class house burglar

Two hands full of piano

A damn good player, hot stuff at whippin' that ivory

"He had the beat to steady down a little combination, just like a good drummer. He really kept two hands full of piano." FROM THE NOVEL *BLUES FOR THE PRINCE*, BART SPICER, 1950

Typewriter

Machine gun

U

Ufftay

Tough

Ultimate yelp

Superlative, the best

"She is the last word, the ultimate yelp." FROM THE NOVEL *YOUR DEAL MY LOVELY*, PETER CHEYNEY, 1941

Uncork your supper

Have a drink

Under glass

In prison

Underpinning

Legs

Undertaker's friend

Gun, firearm

Unglued

Worked up, losing it, flipping your wig

Elvis kisses his co-star, then asks: *"How's your headache?"*, to which she replies, *"I'm coming all unglued."* FROM THE FILM *JAILHOUSE ROCK*, 1957

Unhook your ears, Dad

Listen closely

From the film *Shake, Rattle & Rock*, 1957

Unwound

Losing it, falling to pieces, cracking up

Up jumped the devil

An unexpected piece of bad fortune

"Then up jumped the devil, like the crapshooters say when seven pops up

wrong." FROM THE AUTOBIOGRAPHY *RAP SHEET*, BLACKIE AUDETT, 1955

Up north

In jail

"Pimping will get you a couple of years up north." FROM THE NOVEL *THE DROWNING POOL*, ROSS MACDONALD, 1950

Upping some real crazy riffs

Playing cool music

Upholstery

Figure, curves, build, etc

"'Where is he?' she panted. 'Where's that two-timing, four-flushing bum of mine? If he's with that oversexed, pneumatic piece of well-worn upholstery that dares to call herself an actress, I'll cut his heart out – and hers!'" FROM THE NOVEL *LAMENT FOR A LOUSY LOVER*, CARTER BROWN, 1960

Uptight

1. Worried, tense
2. In trouble

Used-to-be

Ex-lover

See the blues recording *I'm Going Back to my "Used to Be"*, Bessie Smith & Clara Smith, 1924

"You say you're through with me, / You're settin' me free, / You're just out with your used-to-be, / I can't hardly stand it, you troublin' me, / I can't hardly stand it, it just can't be. / Well you don't know babe I love you so / You got me all tore up, all tore up..." FROM THE ROCKABILLY RECORDING *I CAN'T HARDLY STAND IT*, CHARLIE FEATHERS, 1956

Pulp author Carter Brown: he's been there, so you don't have to.

Where is he? Where's that two-timing, four-flushing bum of mine? If he's with that oversexed, pneumatic piece of well-worn upholstery that dares to call herself an actress, I'll cut his heart out – and hers!

V v

Vag

Vagrant, hobo, bum

"Look at you, all banged-up like a barrel-house vag..." THE POLICE CAPTAIN TAKES A DIM VIEW OF THE BATTERED APPEARANCE OF ONE OF HIS DETECTIVES. FROM THE FILM *WHERE THE SIDEWALK ENDS*, 1950

Vamoose

Run away, leave in a hurry, get lost

See the rock'n'roll recording *Vim Vam Vamoose*, Bob Temple with The Dave Martin Orchestra, 1956

Varicose alley

Stripclub runway

Ventilator

Mouth

"Cope, who was smaller than I, had a ventilator large enough for eight people." FROM THE AUTOBIOGRAPHY *WE CALLED IT MUSIC*, EDDIE CONDON WITH THOMAS SUGRUE, 1948

Vines

Suits, jackets, hipster threads

Babs Gonzales tells the story in his 1967 autobiography (*I, Paid My Dues, Good Times...No Bread, A Story Of Jazz*) of how Charlie Parker apologised for stealing some of his suits: "Babs, baby, I know I downed your threads, so here's the tickets." ie: I stole your clothes, and here are the pawnshop tickets

Viper

Marijuana smoker

See the jazz recordings *The Viper's Drag*, Cab Calloway & his Orchestra, 1930; *Song of the Vipers*, Louis Armstrong & his Orchestra, 1934; *Sendin' The Vipers*, Mezz Mezzrow Orchestra, 1934

Vomit on the table

Speak up, let's hear what you've got to say

"Come on, fess up. Vomit on the table..." FROM THE NOVEL *GO, MAN, GO!*, EDWARD DE ROO, 1959

Voodoo boilers

A kit of drums

Fats Waller preparing to motivate some pedal extremities with the *Viper Drag*.

WHACKED . . . FINISHED . . . CORPSED !

Gene Krupa, with perspiration running down his face, his hair awry, and with a look of utter exhaustion . . . as he always is after a bout of his strenuous drumistics.

King of the skins Gene Krupa after a hard night belting the voodoo boilers, 1939.

Wail

Cut loose, let off steam, have a wild time

"Now, if you're gonna stay cool, you've got to wail, you've got to put something down, you've got to make some jive. Do you know what I'm saying?" MAR-LON BRANDO TELLS IT LIKE IT IS. FROM THE FILM *THE WILD ONE*, 1954

Waffle iron

The electric chair

Walking papers

Release from jail

Walking spanish

Being frogmarched out of somewhere

Wanna oil your ankles?

Would you care to dance?

Want a real rear?

Do you want something that'll really get you high?

"'Want a real rear?' she inquired. 'Laudanum?' 'Yeah. A dash with the next whisky.'" FROM THE NOVEL *RED GAR-DENIAS*, JONATHAN LATIMER, 1939

Want a weed?

Would you like a cigarette?

Warble

Sing

"They do tell me lots of dames make the grade if they can warble a few notes

and if they can show a shapely pair o' gams." FROM THE NOVEL *HOT DAMES ON COLD SLABS*, MICHAEL STORME, 1950

Phonograph Monthly Review from New York ran a Miscellaneous War-blers column in its dance music re-views section in the early 1930s

Watch my smoke

I'm outta here, I'm gone

See the rockabilly recording *Watch My Smoke*, Vince Anthony & The Blue Notes, 1958

Ways like a mowing machine

Agricultural metaphor for good sex-ual technique

"She's long, she's tall, / She's a hand-some queen, / She's got ways like a mowing machine." FROM THE COUNTRY RECORDING *SHE'S A HUM DUM DINGER*, BUDDY JONES, 1941

Compare this to the blues recording *I've Got Ford Movements In My Hips*, Cleo Gibson & Her Hot Three, 1929

Wax a disc

To make a recording

Wear the green

Have some paper money

Wearing a concrete footmuff

Taking a swim in the river with your feet encased in concrete, courtesy of the Mafia

A dancing dame waxing a deadly disc on the cover of this 1962 Ellery Queen novel.

the high window

RAYMOND CHANDLER

AUTHOR OF "THE BIG SLEEP"

Detective Marlowe in a shocking, thrilling murder mystery

Talk like that to me, and you are liable to be wearing lead buttons on your vest.

Wearing lead buttons on your vest

Getting shot

"'Talk like that to me,' Morny said 'and you are liable to be wearing lead buttons on your vest.'" FROM THE NOVEL *THE HIGH WINDOW*, RAYMOND CHANDLER, 1943

Weedhead

Cannabis smoker

See the blues recording *Weedhead Woman*, Champion Jack Dupree, 1941

Week at the knees

Unsuccessful courtship

eg: "Man, I spent a week at the knees once, never got any further."

Weiner

Penis

In Nelson Algren's 1941 novel *Never Come Morning*, the prostitute Tooki asks a prospective client "Ain't you gonna play Hide The Weenie, Hon? C'mon, Slim, let's slam it around a little."

"Some said it takes hot water / Baby can't you see, / But your heat baby / Is plenty warm enough for me, / Baby please warm my weiner..." FROM THE BLUES RECORDING *PLEASE WARM MY WEINER*, BO CARTER (BO CHATMAN), 1936

Wet your tonsils

Drink

What do you shake them for?

How do you earn a living, what's your occupation?

What do you think of the stackup?

How does the situation appear to you?

What know, man?

Hipster form of greeting

From the autobiography *I, Paid My Dues*, Babs Gonzales, 1967

What's all the shooting about?

What's up? Why the fuss?

From the film *Don't Knock The Rock*, 1956

What are you going to do for friends when your brain gives out?

You're a moron

What's cookin'? Nothin' but the spaghetti and it ain't ready

Nothing's happening, I don't have any news

What's on the agenda, Brenda?

What's happening? How are you doing?

What's the belch, friend?

What's happening, what's the news?

From the novel *Halo In Blood*, Howard Browne, 1946

What's the good word?

What's happening, what's the news?

Used by Dashiell Hammett in the novel *The Glass Key*, 1931

What's the pitch?

What's the story, what's happening?

What's tickin', chicken?

What's happening, how are you?

C'mon Slim, let's slam it around a little.

Wheel a spiel

Make a speech, talk big

When I have to ride a horse I'll dress like you

Your clothes are a joke

ie: There's so many clashing colours you look like a jockey.

When they made you, they scraped off the mould

You're a louse, you're the lowest of the low

Where do you hang your hat?

Where are you from, where are you staying?

While I'm eating meat

While I'm alive

From the autobiography *We Called it Music*, Eddie Condon with Thomas Sugrue, 1948

Whippin' that ivory

Playing the piano

Sam Goold released a piano solo in 1923 called *Whipping The Keys*

A whiskey sour to all the beer in Brooklyn

A dead cert, a sure thing

Whisper

Rumour, news

Whistle bait

A good-looking woman, someone worth whistling at

"Her name was Rhoda Stern. She didn't have to tell us that she wasn't whistle bait, if she ever had been." FROM THE NOVEL *THE LENIENT BEAST*, FREDRIC BROWN, 1957

The Lenient Beast - no sign of whistle bait.

See also the rockabilly recordings *Whistle Bait*, Don Johnston, 1957 and *Whistle Bait*, Larry Collins, 1958

Whistling through the graveyard

Bluffing, putting up a front

"Phil Duncan slid two blue chips into the centre of the table. 'Two blues say you're whistling through the graveyard.'" FROM THE NOVEL *THIS IS MURDER*, ERLE STANLEY GARDNER, 1935

White mule

Low-class bootleg liquor

"I couldn't place the hoarse voice but he quickly identified himself. 'This is 'Mule' Davis.' I pictured him immediately. A pudgy, bald-headed man, Davis was a small-time bootlegger who received his nickname because of the bad hooch, or 'White Mule', that he sold." FROM THE BOOK *THE UNTOUCHABLES*, ELLIOT NESS & OSCAR FRALEY, 1957

Who broke your doll?

Why are you crying?

"'What's the pitch, bitch?' I demanded. 'Who broke your doll?'" MATT HELM COMES OVER ALL SENSITIVE AND CONCERNED, FROM THE NOVEL *MURDERER'S ROW*, DONALD HAMILTON, 1961

Who's been kissin' your puss?

Where'd you get the black eye? Who beat you up?

"The kids had a swell time kidding Spat, rubbing it in. Some fighter he was, the hell he was. You bunk inta door, huh Spat? Hey, Spat, who's been kissin' your puss?" FROM THE NOVEL *BRAIN GUY*, BENJAMIN APPEL, 1934

Wholesale banking business

Bank robbery

Whoopee

Mostly this was a euphemism for sex, although it was also taken more generally to mean having a good time, whooping it up

"Most always when a man leaves his wife, there's no excuse in the world for him. She may have been making whoop-whoop- whoopee with the whole ten commandments, but if he shows his disapproval to the extent of walking out on her, he will thereafter be a stranger to all his friends." FROM THE SHORT STORY *EX PARTE*, RING LARDNER, 1920S

"Lonnie Johnson goes in for the fantastically macabre in his blues She's Making Whoopee in Hell Tonight and Death Valley is Half Way to My Home." FROM THE MAGAZINE *PHONOGRAPH MONTHLY REVIEW*, NEW YORK, APRIL 1930

"I was out last night, / At the cabaret, / Came in this morning / 'Bout the break of day / Been makin' whoopee..." FROM THE BLUES RECORDING *TIGHT WHOOPEE*, MOZELLE ALDERSON, 1930

See the jazz song *Makin' Whoopee*, written by Walter Donaldson, 1928, for the Broadway show *Whoopee!*

Whoopee mama

Girl, flapper, party animal

Why buy a cow when you can get milk through a fence?

What's the point of getting married when the dames are just throwing themselves at you?

Elvis used this expression in a 1956 interview, and it showed up the previous year in a slightly different form in William Campbell Gault's novel *Run, Killer, Run*: "'I should have married,' Nannie said. 'But who'd buy a cow, the milk I had?'"

Why did you do me this way?

How could you treat me like that?

Wide-open town

Wild, lawless, packed with late-night entertainment

"Aw, come on, man. Have a couple of drinks and you'll feel better. This is a wide-open town." FROM THE NOVEL *THE DROWNING POOL*, ROSS MACDONALD, 1950

Wig

1. Head or hair

See the jazz recording *Gassin' the Wig*, Roy Porter, 1948

2. Mind

"I've often wondered about the condition of the wigs of the busy radio censors if they ever learned the truth about the significance of such recorded titles as The Skronch, T.T. on Toast, Warm Valley, and others." NED E WILLIAMS RECALLS SOME NEAR-THE-KNUCKLE SONG TITLES FROM HIS DAYS WITH DUKE ELLINGTON'S COTTON CLUB ORCHESTRA, QUOTED IN *THE ORAL HISTORY HEAR ME TALKIN' TO YA – THE STORY OF JAZZ BY THE MEN WHO MADE IT*, NAT SHAPIRO AND NAT HENTOFF, EDS., 1955

Wig chop

A haircut

Wig out

Go crazy, have a wild time, enjoy

Wig tightener

Something, or someone, very impressive

Wiggle

Dance, strut your stuff

"She's got a wiggle / Make a dead man awake, / She don't rock / She

Have a couple of drinks and you'll feel better, this is a wide-open town.

just stands there and shakes." **FROM THE ROCKABILLY RECORDING** *MY BABY DON'T ROCK,* **LUKE MCDANIEL, 1957**

Windy

Scared, apprehensive

Wine Spo-Dee-O-Dee

An obscene U.S. army drinking song

The lyrics were cleaned up slightly by Stick McGhee for his 1949 R&B recording entitled *Drinking Wine Spo-Dee-O-Dee.* The original lyric went "Drinking wine, motherfucker, drinking wine..."

By the time Jack Kerouac got around to including the term in *On The Road* (1957), it had somehow become just another name for a drink: "Dean and I had ended up with a coloured guy called Walter who ordered drinks at the bar and had them lined up and said 'Wine-spodiodi!' which was a shot of port wine, a shot of whisky, and a shot of port wine. 'Nice sweet jacket for all that bad whisky!' he yelled."

Wino time

A short jail sentence

Wiper

Assassin, hitman, rub-out artist

Wise guy

1. Mobbed up, a made man, a member of the Mafia

Damon Runyon published a story called *Three Wise Guys* in 1933, and it became the title of one of his story collections in 1946. He knew a thing or two about wise guys – he was friends with mafia kingpins such as Arnold Rothstein and Al Capone, and owned an estate on Biscayne Bay in Florida near to Scarface Al's place

What do you mean by busting in here like a walrus and gumming up our wedding? Damon Runyon knew a thing or two about wise guys – he was friend with mafia kingpins like Arnold Rothstein and Al Capone.

2. Smart aleck

"'A wise guy!' Bert commented, slapping me across the face..." **FROM THE JACOBEAN REVENGE TRAGEDY** *TWO TIMING TART,* **JOHN DAVIDSON, 1961**

Wise up

1. Get smart
2. To educate or inform someone

With the buttons off

Run-down, tatty

"That spring Bessie Smith also came to town; we went to hear her at the Paradise, a battered joint with the buttons off at 35th and Calumet." **FROM THE AUTOBIOGRAPHY** *WE CALLED IT MUSIC,* **EDDIE CONDON WITH THOMAS SUGRUE, 1948**

Wolf

A fast guy with the ladies, a stud, a lecher, a tomcat on the prowl

See the hillbilly recordings *Baby He's a Wolf,* Werly Fairburn, 1954, and *Stop Whistlin' Wolf,* Maddox Brothers & Rose, 1957, and the rockabilly recording *Wolf, Wolf,* Al Barkle, 1959

Wolf-pack

A bunch of guys with an eye for the dolls

See the novel *The Shame of Jenny,* John Carver, 1963 "The suburban wolf-pack had country-club manners... and motel morals"

Wolf trap

A gal the guys can't resist

See the novel *Wolf Trap Blonde,* Luther Gordon, 1949

Woo number

Girlfriend or boyfriend

Wooden kimono

Coffin

See the short story *Parade of the Wooden Kimonos* by Emile C Tepperman in the February 1941 issue of *Ten Detective Aces*

Woodpile

Xylophone

Woodshed

"A place for a private rehearsal, often used as a verb, meaning to practise in private." FROM *DOWN BEAT'S YEARBOOK OF SWING*, 1939

"It was here that the term 'woodshedding' originated. When one of the gang wanted to rehearse his part, he would go off into the woods and practice until he made it. If anyone would biff a few too many, Nesbitt would send him off to the woods for a private rehearsal. Sometimes, more than half the band would be woodshedding." CUBA AUSTIN RECALLS HIS DAYS WITH THE IMMORTAL MCKINNEY'S COTTON PICKERS AT MANITOU BEACH, MICHIGAN, IN 1924, QUOTED IN *THE ORAL HISTORY HEAR ME TALKIN' TO YA – THE STORY OF JAZZ BY THE MEN WHO MADE IT*, NAT SHAPIRO AND NAT HENTOFF, EDS., 1955

Wordsville

A library

"Look out, or we'll be thrown out of Wordsville." FROM THE NOVEL *RUN TOUGH, RUN HARD*, CARSON BINGHAM, 1961

Working for the Woolworths

Doing a low-paid job, ie for nickels & dimes

Working horizontally

Taking the mattress route to success

See the novel *Horizontal Secretary*, Amy Harris, 1964 "She did her best work after five."

Working your groundsmashers overtime

1. Walking or running fast
2. Dancing in an impressive fashion

Wouldst like to con a glimmer early with me this black?

Would you like to go to a movie with me this evening?

From Professor Cab Calloway's Swingformation Bureau

Wound up like an eight-day clock

Uptight, tense, stressed out

Wrecking crew

Police interrogation operatives

"Take this baby down the cellar and let the wrecking crew work on him before you lock him up." FROM THE NOVEL *RED HARVEST*, DASHIELL HAMMETT, 1929

The Wrecking Crew was the title of a novel from 1960 which was part of Donald Hamilton's Matt Helm series, the film versions of which starred Dean Martin, and it was also the collective name for the regular musicians who played on Phil Spector's Wall of Sound recordings in the early Sixties

A wrong gee

A bad sort, an untrustworthy guy

Wrong side of the tracks

The bad part of town, lowdown, poverty row

She has her old beatnik costume on – the tight black pants, the bulky black sweater – and her hair was brushed and her lipstick was bright and straight – Hamilton's novel is from 1960, when beatniks were big. By the time Dean starred in the film, the sixties were almost over, and the hippies had landed.

Jonathan Latimer – the man with the x-ray eyes.

X-ray eyes

"Either we got x-ray eyes, or those babies are dancing in their underwear." THE LURE OF THE TAXI-DANCEHALL BECOMES APPARENT TO A FIRST-TIME CUSTOMER. FROM THE NOVEL *THE LADY IN THE MORGUE*, JONATHAN LATIMER, 1936

Yak

Talk, run your mouth

"If there's anything I can't stand, it's a cheap jerk who yakkity-yaks all the time. Kick him in the teeth if he keeps talking, Pete." **FROM THE NOVEL** *THE DEADLY LOVER*, **ROBERT O. SABER**, 1951

"I was so stunned I let him keep on yakking." **FROM THE NOVEL** *ALWAYS LEAVE 'EM DYING*, **RICHARD S. PRATHER**, 1961

Yammer

Talk

"He felt nausea whirl in him again, and the sun seemed unbearable. 'Murdered - ? Joe Hubbard murd-' She pushed him roughly. 'Get in the car. Don't stand there, yammering like an idiot for heaven's sake.'" **FROM THE NOVEL** *RUN, KILLER, RUN*, **WILLIAM CAMPBELL GAULT**, 1955

Sometime written as Yama, as in the R&B recording *Yama Yama Pretty Mama*, Richard Berry, 1955

Yap

1. Talk
2. Mouth

eg: "Shut your yap."

Yard

One hundred dollars. After 1930 it often meant one thousand dollars

Yas Yas Yas

Ass, backside

"I used to play slow but now I play it fast, Just to see the women shake their yas, yas, yas..." **FROM THE BLUES RECORDING** *SHACK BULLY STOMP*, **PEETIE WHEATSTRAW**, 1938

See also the blues recordings *The Duck's Yas Yas Yas*, James Stump Johnson & Alex Hill, 1929 and *Yas Yas Yas Number 1*, Jimmy Strange, The Yas Yas Man, 1936

Blues singer Merline Johnson, who recorded many songs (including *Don't You Make Me High*, 1938, and *You're A Pain In The Neck To Me*, 1939) was generally billed on the labels as "The Yas Yas Girl"

Yaks

Laughs, fun

"We had a lotta yaks, huh Johnny?" **FROM THE FILM** *THE WILD ONE*, 1954

Yegg

1. Criminal, originally this was a specific term for a safe-cracker, but came to have a more general use

"The big man was a yegg. San Francisco was on fire for him." ie: He was a criminal, and he was the object of a city-wide manhunt. **FROM THE SHORT STORY** *FLY PAPER*, **DASHIELL HAMMETT**, 1929

"The dame shrugged her bare shoulders. 'You know it all, mac. Sure my old man was a gangster, a tough yegg...'" **FROM THE NOVEL** *THE CORRUPT ONES*, **J.C. BARTON**, C.1950

See also the short story *Yellow Yeggs* by Sidney Herschel Small in the April 23 1932 issue of *Detective Fiction Weekly*, and also the novel *The*

The great Peetie Wheatstraw, who called himself the Devil's Son-in-law and the High Sherrif From Hell.

Scrambled Yeggs, Richard S. Prather, 1958

2. A beggar

Yen?

Do you need some drugs?

"'Yen?''Uh huh. I was about to cook up a couple of loads when you busted in with all this heavy drama.' Cullen jerked his head towards the stair. 'Eileen is upstairs.' Kells said: 'I thought the last cure took.' 'Sure. It took.' Cullen smiled sleepily. 'Like the other nine. I'm down to two pipes every other day.'" FROM THE NOVEL *FAST ONE*, PAUL CAIN, 1933

You ain't just whistling Dixie

That's right, I agree with you, you're speaking the truth

You are a triple scream and a big yell

I really like you

You burn me up

1. You excite me
2. You make me angry

See the jazz recording *Cold Mamas Burn Me Up*, Bailey's Lucky Seven, 1924

You can bet your bottom dollar

It's the truth, it's a certainty

You can cook him up brown

You can get your own back, you can have your revenge

"If you want to get back at him, here's your chance. You can cook him up brown." FROM THE NOVEL *VIOLENT NIGHT*, WHIT HARRISON, 1952

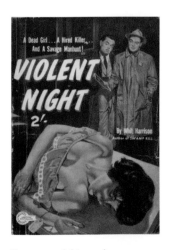

You can cook him up brown.

You can sing two choruses of that

You can say that again

You can take that to the bank and cash it

It's the truth, I mean it, this is reliable information

You could sell hell to a bishop

You're very persuasive, you've got the gift of the gab

You flip me

You're the most, I'm solid-sent

See the rockabilly recording *You Flip Me*, Jack Owens, 1958

You fracture me

You make me laugh

"'You fracture me, Elmer,' she said. 'To look at you, a person would think you just came in with a car-load of cattle.'" FROM THE NOVEL *LITTLE MEN, BIG WORLD*, W.R. BURNETT, 1951

You give me hot pants

I find you very attractive

You got any happy money on you?

It'll cost you

"'You got any happy money on you?' 'Happy money?' 'Yeah. Money that's gonna make me happy, what else?' 'How much?' 'Fifty dollars.'" FROM THE FILM *PICKUP ON SOUTH STREET*, 1953

You jet me

You're the most, I'm really impressed

"You positively jet me! Gone, gone, gone! Jet, jet, jet!" STOICAL UNDERSTATEMENT FROM THE NOVEL *GO, MAN GO!*, EDWARD DE ROO, 1959

You paralyse me

You make me laugh, you surprise me, you knock me out

You put the hurt on me

You done me wrong, I'm hung up and brung down

See the rock'n'roll recording *You Put The Hurt On Me*, Tam Duffill, 1962

You said a mouthful

That's the truth, that's it exactly

You send me

I'm gone, you flip me out, I'm impressed

See the ballad *You Send Me*, Sam Cooke, 1957

"Every time she loves me/ She sends my mellow soul." FROM THE BOOGIE-WOOGIE RECORDING *ROLL 'EM PETE*, PETE JOHNSON & JOE TURNER, 1938

You send me to the end

You *really* send me

You slay me

1. I'm amused
2. I'm impressed

For a somewhat more literal meaning, see the short story *You Slay Me, Baby* by Frederick C Davis in the July 1942 issue of *Dime Detective*

You upset me

I dig you, you knock me out

"You upset me baby, / You upset me baby, / Like bein' hit by a fallin' tree / Woman what you do to me. / Thirty-six in the bust, / Twenty-eight in the waist, / Forty-four in the hips / She's got a-real crazy legs, / You upset me baby" FROM THE ROCKABILLY RECORDING *YOU UPSET ME BABY*, RED SMITH, 1954

You snap the whip, I'll make the trip

I'll do what you say, I'm all yours

You'd better get your flaps down or you'll take off

Don't get so excited, calm down

From the first film version of *Farewell, My Lovely*, 1944

You'll find my name on the tail of my shirt

Traditional response to police questioning, especially by tramps and drifters

"Told them my name was on the tail of my shirt, / I'm a Tennessee hustler, I don't have to work..." FROM THE COUNTRY RECORDING *T FOR TEXAS (BLUE YODEL NO. 1)*, JIMMIE RODGERS, 1927

Your brain's a little dusty

You're rather stupid, you're not thinking straight

Your roof is leaking

You're not all there, you're a little crazy

Your teeth are swimming

You're plastered, you're full up with booze

"You're drunk, Al. Your teeth are swimming." FROM THE NOVEL *WHAT MAKES SAMMY RUN?*, BUDD SCHULBERG, 1941

You're a panic

You crack me up, you're really funny

You're batting a thousand

That's right, you've got it

You're killing me with your sad pan

Why the long face, you look depressed

You're my habit, rabbit

I dig you the most

You're drunk, Al. Your teeth are swimming.

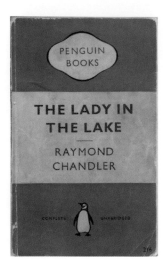

You've got a hell of a crust.

You're not comin' through at all

You're making no sense, explain yourself

You're not just saying it

That's right, I agree with you

You're stepping on your motor to hear your cut-out roar

You're bragging, you're all talk

You're talking on a dead phone

I'm not interested, save your breath

You're the swinging end

You're the best

You've got a crust

You've got a nerve

"You've got a hell of a crust assuming I'll go down there and take a getaway stake to somebody I know the police are looking for." FROM THE NOVEL *THE LADY IN THE LAKE*, RAYMOND CHANDLER, 1944

"'To hell with you,' she blazed. 'You got a crust, tearing my clothes like that.'" FROM THE NOVEL *HOMICIDE LOST*, WILLIAM VANCE, 1956

You've got a date with the fireless cooker

They're going to send you to the electric chair

You've got my nose wide open

You've got me all worked up

"'You'd better take it easy from now.' 'That's what I intend to do, only trouble is m'nose opens up and I can't tell what I'm doing.'" FROM THE NOVEL *ON THE ROAD*, JACK KEROUAC, 1957

See the R&B recording *When It Rains It Really Pours*, Billy The Kid Emerson, 1955

Also the vocal group recording *She's Got His Nose Wide Open*, Ike Perry And The Lyrics, 1960

You've had your chance and folded

You wasted the opportunity, you blew it

Zip gun

Home made pistol, Saturday Night Special

"With the technical ingenuity characteristic of American youngsters, these lads think nothing of converting a toy cap pistol into a single-shot arm which will fire cartridges, nails or pins. Many fashion their weapons in trade school or high school shops, assembling them at home. Such jobs – consisting of wooden handle taped to metal tube, with a filed key to serve as firing-pin and rubber bands doing duty to spring the trigger – form the famous 'zip' or 'zipper' guns. They take .22 calibre ammunition." FROM THE BOOK *JAILBAIT*, WILLIAM BERNARD, 1949

See also the novel *Zip-Gun Angels*, Albert L Quandt, 1952 "A Powerful Story of Teen-Age Girls Who Fight Recklessly for Life and Love!"

Zip your lip

Keep quiet

Zoot suit

Draped and sculpted Hep Cat suit, long in the body, narrow at the waist, as worn by His Royal Hepness, Cab Calloway, onstage at Harlem's Cotton Club

Very popular with the Chicano gangs in Los Angeles during the early stages of World War Two, memorably described by James Ellroy in *The Black Dahlia* as "Reet-pleat, drape-shape, stuff-cuff, Argentinian-duck-tailed Mexican gangsters." This type of clothing was condemned by government officials as a waste of cloth and counter-productive to the war effort. A particularly brutal series of gang rumbles which broke out in 1943 were known in the press as the Zoot Suit Wars

"He was tall, lithe and was wearing a finger-tip cream gabardine with pillows under the shoulders. The double-breasted was as snug as a cellophane wrapper. Black hair glistened with pomade and bunched at the neckline. A thin black moustache pointed to a quarter of three. Conceit was stamped all over his darkly handsome mug, and he was about twenty-eight. I liked him – the way I liked a cold in the head." FROM THE NOVEL *SLEEP NO MORE*, SAM S TAYLOR, 1951

"The young hoodlums wore long coats, pegged pants and drooping keychains. They were about eighteen. They looked out at the world coldly and arrogantly. A tough place, chum! But we're tougher." FROM THE NOVEL *LITTLE MEN, BIG WORLD*, W.R. BURNETT, 1951

See the jazz recording *A Zoot Suit (For My Sunday Gal)*, Bob Crosby & his Orchestra, 1942

A 1978 crime novel set during the wartime Zoot Suit wars.

Later, gators…

Max Décharné – Photo by Katja Klier

About the author

Max Décharné was born in England, and can still speak English when his business demands it. During the past eighteen years he has flung six books and numerous records at the public – firstly as a member of Gallon Drunk, then since 1995 as the singer with The Flaming Stars – spreading peace, goodwill and partial deafness among the youth of the world. He treasures his copies of Sexomatic Pilot and Dig That Crazy Grave, and lives in hope that the world will pay closer attention to the theories of the anonymous British newspaper writer in 1919 who claimed to have discovered the origins of jazz, and put it all down to 'grotesque and indecent movements invented by drunken cowboys in the Argentine'.

Albums by The Flaming Stars

Songs From The Bar Room Floor, Vinyl Japan, June 1996

Bring Me The Rest Of Alfredo Garcia (Singles 1995-1996), Vinyl Japan, March 1997

Sell Your Soul To The Flaming Stars, Vinyl Japan, October 1997

Pathway, Vinyl Japan, May 1999

The Six John Peel Sessions, Vinyl Japan, June 2000

Tijuana Bible, Nippon Columbia (Japan only), July 2000

A Walk On The Wired Side, Vinyl Japan, February 2001

Ginmill Perfume, Alternative Tentacles (US & Canada only), October 2001

Sunset & Void, Vinyl Japan & Alternative Tentacles, September 2002

Named and Shamed, Vinyl Japan & Alternative Tentacles, October 2004

London After Midnight (Singles, Rarities & Bar Room Floor-Fillers), Big Beat, 2006

Born Under A Bad Neon Sign, Big Beat, 2006

www.myspace.com/theflamingstars